TRADE UNIONS
IN THE VICTORIAN AGE

VICTORIAN SOCIAL CONSCIENCE

A series of facsimile reprints of selected articles from
*The Edinburgh Review, The Westminster Review, The Quarterly
Review, Blackwood's Magazine* and *Fraser's Magazine*
1802–1870

THE SERIES INCLUDES:

Poverty 4 vols.
Urban Problems 2 vols.
The Working Classes 4 vols.
Prostitution
Emigration
Population Problems 2 vols.
Trade Unions 4 vols.
Working Conditions
Public Health 2 vols.

TRADE UNIONS IN THE VICTORIAN AGE

Debates on the issue

from 19th century critical journals

With an introduction

by

G. W. Crompton

VOLUME I

1823–1834

1973

GREGG INTERNATIONAL PUBLISHERS LIMITED

ISBN 0 576 53271 1

Republished in 1973 by Gregg International Publishers
Limited, Westmead, Farnborough, Hants, England

Printed in Germany

CONTENTS

CONTENTS

INTRODUCTION

This collection of documents from five separate magazines, and spanning a half century which saw massive changes in industry, government, and society, shows much consistency of theme and attitude, both over time, and from source to source. Unsurprisingly, there was much awareness that social issues, such as those posed by the rise of trade unionism, were more important questions for government than ever in the past, and could not always be comfortably accommodated within the framework of traditional political debate. There was a widespread, and disturbed, realisation that combinations of workmen had enormous potential for conflict and destruction, and that they might reflect, and further stimulate, an independent working class consciousness on fundamental questions of social organisation.

As a rule the greatest clarity and consistency was displayed by the *Edinburgh Review*, which by virtue of its contributors, and the amount of space and attention devoted to economic topics, was generally regarded as the most influential and authoritative publication.[1] The *Edinburgh* was a major vehicle for the advocacy and popularisation of the system of economic and political analysis known as 'Political Economy', of which the principal element bearing on issues of wages and combinations was the doctrine of the wages fund. In the 1820s 'Political Economy', if an orthodoxy at all, was still of fairly recent origins as such. By the end of this period, it had been well and truly consolidated, in a widely popularised form, despite challenges from the *avant garde* of economic theory.[2]

An *Edinburgh* writer was asserting the wages fund theory as confidently as ever in the late sixties: 'there is no dispute among economists as to the law which regulates the payment for labour. It is determined by the proportion between the circulating capital which forms the "wages fund" and the number of labourers seeking employment'.[3] By then the additional certainty had been acquired that in a 'nation ... governed as it now is by Political Economy',[4] no body of men could hope to be permitted to contravene the laws of Political Economy. Support for the view that Political Economy and the wages fund either were, or ought to be, dominant in the nation's affairs was forthcoming from the *Quarterly Review*.[5] *Fraser's* expressed a parallel thought that there could 'be no doubt that when a wrong principle of Political Economy is allowed, endorsed, and acted on, very serious consequences are certain to ensue';[6] and even *Blackwood's* employed the term 'Political Economy', without its former pejorative overtones, and reproved trade union leaders for their 'ignorance of economical laws'.[7] It was left to the *Westminster* to sound a note of trenchant dissent in an article reviewing W. T. Thornton's recent assault on orthodoxy.[8]

The implication of the wage fund theory was that only an increase in capital, or a relative decrease in population, and hence labour supply, could benefit workers in the long run. The wage fund was fixed in size at any one time. Anything which threatened profits and capital accumulation could only have the effect of diminishing the wage fund, and therefore the amount available for distribution to the workers in wages. Deriving directly from these propositions were some of the most absolute statements in all the following articles – e.g. 'the chief laws of Political Economy, however darkly they may lead to their result, are as unchangeable as those of nature, and it would be as possible to make the quicksilver in the thermometer expand beyond the temperature of its atmosphere as to fix wages at any other rate than that at which would fix themselves, if undisturbed either by trade unions or acts of parliament'.[9] It could also follow quite directly, for a commentator in a confident vein that 'the only test of what is fair and reasonable in an industrial dispute is the actual result'.[10] But the logically associated judgement, that on the merits of an industrial dispute, the opinion of the masters was in no way superior to that of their employees,[11] was to meet indignant repudiation in a later issue of *Blackwood's*.[12]

But a general framework of belief in the inability of combinations to influence wages could often accommodate strong views as to the harmful economic effects of their current activities. Despite constant danger of self contradiction, much could be achieved by the operation of a simple distinction between the short and the long term so as to maintain both positions. The most fundamental charge, expressed in its customary violent imagery, came in *Blackwood's* characterisation of unions as institutions which 'lay the axe to the root of the national resources.'[13] Rather more specifically, trade unions are variously accused of weakening British industry in relation to foreign competition, in both the domestic market and overseas, of ruining individual firms, of driving manufacturers out of the district, or even the country, of raising prices at the expense of consumers,[14] and, inadvertently, promoting the use of machinery in place of human labour.

The damage caused to exporters was keenly felt by *Blackwood's*, where a patriotic strain was pronounced: 'these masters [i.e. in export industries] will never be suffered to obtain fair and necessary profits: they will at the best, be kept in such a state, that any unfavourable turn in the market will plunge them into bankruptcy.'[15] Whereas, in contrast, it was thought that those producing for the domestic market might be able to raise their prices, or struggle on by raising more capital.[16] An article in the *Edinburgh* provides an example of a calico-printing firm in Scotland which was forced out of business in 1835, the year following an expensive strike, throwing some two thousand out of work. It also gives an estimate of £489,000 as the alleged extra cost of coal to consumers in the Glasgow area over a period of time (18 months) in 1836 and 1837 as a result of a six months' strike, which had followed a year in which output had been greatly reduced by restrictive practices such as an unusually short working week.[17]

The possibility that union obstruction might accelerate mechanisation, and thus displace labour with 'inconvenient rapidity', was noted, with some satisfaction, as among the 'alleviating circumstances' which had mitigated the ill-effects of trade union expansion. A list of examples from the recent pamphlet on the 'Character, Object and Effects of Trades Unions' by the factory inspector Tufnell was cited in support of the suggestion that machinery might sometimes be introduced, not so much to supply an increased demand for the product, as to circumvent an 'unnatural deficiency in the supply of labour' induced by combinations.[18] Meanwhile an attempt to demonstrate the futility of machine-breaking had already hinted at the possibility that someone might stand to lose from over-rapid mechanisation: 'machinery then, like the rain of heaven, is a present blessing to all concerned, provided it comes down by drops, and not by tons together.'[19]

What was common to all these objectionable union practices was the ability of combinations in some degree to interfere with the free supply and circulation of labour, and to develop various limited forms of job control. To be able to do this was essential for the partial success which some of the stronger combinations of skilled workers were to achieve during this period, mainly in local labour markets. Typical of the methods involved were restricting entry to the trade by limiting the proportion of apprentices or boys to adult workmen, keeping unemployed members off the labour market with benefit payments, and obtaining priority for them in re-employment, and, wherever possible, imposing union rates of pay and norms of output on the employer. The belief in the right to work which sustained such actions was not of course compatible with the main tenets of political economy.

It was often taken for granted, however, that all such interference with the workings of the labour market could achieve no more than a purely temporary success. It was a common argument that even successful wage demands or strikes would be self-defeating because of their effect in depressing demand, and hence employment, or because a conspicuously higher rate of pay in one trade or factory would automatically attract additional, and eventually excessive labour, whose arrival would either force wages down again, or oblige those in employment to support the newcomers out of their own funds.[20] On this point, though, there was sensible enough criticism from a *Blackwood's* writer of unrealistic assumptions about the complete interchangeability of labour among different trades.[21]

All too often a grossly exaggerated impression was given of the actual progress of union endeavours to establish control over hiring and firing, whether of workmen or supervisors,[22] and overstatement of the degree of unilateral regulation of working practices which organised workers currently had it in their power to impose. But it is clear enough that many of these basic trade union principles and objectives gave powerful offence almost regardless of the exact degree to which they were actually implemented. Foremost among them was the levelling tendency implicit in the demand that all men doing the same job should be paid at the same rate irrespective of variations in their individual ability or willingness to exert themselves.

Precisely the same objection applied to the demand that men should be engaged on the principle of rotation, rather than individual selection and discrimination by the employer.[23,24] Piece work payment was of course a means by which one of these difficulties could be partly overcome by the employer. Accordingly union resistance to piece work called forth the blistering comment 'to prohibit piece work is to extinguish every ardent and progressive faculty in men'.[25] Trying to check the enthusiasm and the speed of the workman who was inclined to get on too fast was also a common and much-resented union principle. The fact that 'to be zealous for the master is esteemed as treason to the mate' summed up for one writer much that was mischievous and misguided in the aims and values of trade unions.[26]

A much-recurring assumption was that the number of inferior or mediocre performers among the labour force always exceeded that of the abler and more talented, and that a major part of the appeal of unionism was grounded in the interest of this sluggish majority in the devaluation of human endeavour. On this point, disapproval rose to some of its most pompous heights: 'We have a sense of the fitness of things which is outraged by the domination of inferior over superior.'[27] The inferior faculties attributed to the majority applied as much to their mental as to their physical activities, at least in the absence of sufficient learning. The conviction that 'the workingmen, though often unduly flattered on the score of their intelligence, are after all but imperfectly educated, and political economy certainly does not come by the light of nature,'[28] could lead to a condescending pessimism about union behaviour, and perhaps support for restrictive legislation. On the other hand there was always the hope that experience, of the costs and failures of union aggression, would ultimately produce a better understanding among the workers.

But effective combination required that the dull majority should be organised typically by 'a few active scheming men' who 'enlist the multitude of inferior workmen, and organise them for mischief under promises of an equality of wages.'[29] It was a commonplace dream that the whole menace of unionism might be ended if it were possible to upstage the schemers and agitators, and appeal directly to the honest and sober elements among the membership. Prominence was accordingly given to cases like that of John Tester, a leader of the Bradford clothiers' strike of 1829, and subsequently a defector from the union cause who supplied material to the press and to writers hostile to unionism. His changed attitude was that strikes and combinations could achieve nothing for the workers, and his account of his experiences put heavy emphasis on the petty corruption of union officers, on the amounts claimed in bogus expenses and spent on such items as drink.[30] A later reference to a strike in the Midlands indicates that solids were not neglected either, with its vivid description of committee men 'fattening on salmon and green peas'.[31] Union committees often used public houses as meeting places or strike headquarters (in fact the secretary was quite often a publican), and were obviously vulnerable to the repeated accusation that a substantial part of their members' dues was ultimately squandered on drink for the officials. During an extended strike, when union members would naturally experience severe hardship, the divisive potential of this line of attack was obviously enhanced.

A drink-related variant of this stricture was the proposition that sudden and probably temporary increases in wages, such as might be induced by strikes or restrictive practices, would prove of little benefit, because they would lead to dissipation, involving both heavy drinking and other kinds of immorality. On the other hand, the encouraging prospect was held out that steady wage increases thoroughly earned by 'order, industry, and blameless conduct'[32] would have a more permanent and beneficial effect.

The relationship between leaders and led, and the internal structure of trade unions, could provoke changes both of tyranny and excessive democracy, even simultaneously. The two were linked in an early article in *Blackwood's* which characterised combinations as the 'worst of democracies'[33] – not perhaps a surprising reaction from a journal which had bitterly opposed the modest extension of the parliamentary franchise involved in the Reform Act of 1832. But similar conceptions were both widespread and persistent. 'Universal suffrage' and 'despotic power' were phrases found in close proximity in an *Edinburgh* article a few years later.[34] And later still, the point was made, with a brief comparative glance abroad, that whilst the English workman might have escaped from the guilds, protective systems and political espionage from which his counterparts in various continental countries were still suffering, he remained subject to the tyranny, secrecy and irresponsible power of trade unions.[35] The same article expands on this even more forcibly in the context of its justification of the use of 'the document' by the employers in the then current London building strike. The tactic of imposing 'the document' meant that the master builders intended to restrict employment in future to those applicants willing to sign a statement declaring themselves free to make their own labour bargains – i.e. that they were not members of a trade union, and would not join one. It was a weapon which had probably become more popular with employers during the fifties, and had been used with considerable success by engineering firms after the lock-out of 1852. In the London building strike 'the document' eventually had to be withdrawn, but not before it had drawn from one writer the judgement that misguided workmen were failing to see that it was a thousand times less injurious to their absolute freedom and independence than the trade union articles by which they were voluntarily bound.[36]

When the more direct democracy of the local unions was in some cases modified by the development of nation-wide organisation, the tendency was often for militancy to be restrained, as the national officers sought to exercise tighter and more cautious control over strike funds. But this was not necessarily the aspect which caught the attention of contemporary commentators. It was rather the discretionary powers of the centre over the branches, the centralisation of funds etc., which simply gave a further dimension to the old charge of tyranny. An examination of the rules of the Amalgamated Society of Engineers suggested a highly improper degree of central control, with a nine-man council in London empowered to decide such questions as the rate on which a member should be allowed to accept work. This prompted comparisons with American negro slaves being let out on hire.[37]

Trade union action, being essentially collective rather than individual in nature, was always liable to fall foul of commonly accepted notions such as that of the ultimate harmony of separate individual interests. Occasionally it was recognised explicitly that only a combination of workmen including either all, or a powerful majority of a firm's employees, would be able to exert any serious pressure on an employer over wages – and that otherwise workers were simply dependent for leverage on competition for labour among employers.[38] But the core of the question for most observers was the undoubted fact that effective combination required rules, and methods of enforcement, which must periodically limit the freedom of individuals or minorities among the membership, and sometimes compelled reluctant acquiescence. The extreme case of course was the individual who suffered personally as a result of his decision to defy union discipline. Such individuals could normally depend on much distant sympathy from critics concerned to expose the oppressive aspects of combination.[39]

But, much more broadly, the mere requirement to pay regular subscriptions to the union was often interpreted as an objectionable constraint on the individual. It was suggested that unions might exact contributions of up to one third, or even half, of members' earnings, and also to enforce large entry payments from apprentices. Perhaps the most outraged concern is expressed on behalf of strikers obliged to support themselves on tiny payments from the union after they had withdrawn their labour. For example, we are told that striking spinners in Glasgow in 1837 received eighteen pence ($7\frac{1}{2}$p) a week from the union, as against their normal earnings of thirty to thirty-five shillings a week. It was such hardships inflicted on their own members which earned the unions some of the most extravagant condemnations, in which their tyranny was compared with that of Czars and Sultans.[40]

In this way combinations could be presented as a virtually independent and malign third force, interposing themselves between masters and men, and damaging the interests of both, by reducing the trading profits of the former, and reducing the latter to semi-starvation by preventing them from working. This approach also produced attempts at global computations of the costs of strikes, in which losses to employers, consumers and workmen are all lumped together.[41] Of course this interpretation involves the rejection of the straightforward view that such privations were endured voluntarily, if reluctantly, by the workers concerned, in the belief that only by striking could they improve, or preserve, their wages and living standards in the long run. Instead it is assumed that the psychological context and the disciplinary sanctions, legal and illegal, of collective action, were leading workers to persist in behaviour, which, if operating as individuals, they would have been able to recognise as foolish and self-destructive. A further consideration was that once led into a strike by the union, members might well feel obliged to see it out in the interests of the organisation and its accumulated benefit funds.

There is hardly room for doubt that in this period union subscriptions could amount to a serious burden on working class incomes. This was in fact a major reason why union membership was confined to a small minority of the labour force. This was why it was possible to state, with some accuracy, that 'we never . . . hear of combination or strikes among the ordinary or unskilled operatives'.[42] As a general rule only skilled workers with above-average bargaining potentialities could sustain the regular payments necessary for stable organisations able to provide a full range of friendly society benefits and to ride out problematic periods of depression and unemployment, or to survive the occasional expensive strike. Hence attempts to organise the less skilled, or those in less strategic bargaining positions, proved so often unsuccessful or ephemeral. Even established unions catering for a skilled membership were accused of financial unsoundness on the basis of an actuarial report presented to the Royal Commission of 1867–69.[43] It was of course easy to exaggerate the proportion of earnings normally consumed in union dues. A recent study of the background to the Sheffield 'outrages' suggests an average figure of 10 per cent to 15 per cent, although in an atypical case such as that of the saw grinders where a substantial proportion of the membership had to be kept 'on the box' (i.e. off the labour market) by means of fairly generous benefits, this proportion might rise to something rather more than 20 per cent.[44]

But, important though it was, it may be doubted whether financial exactions from the membership was the root of the 'tyranny' argument. What was the most offensive was the thought that voluntary organisations, and their purposes, rule and rituals, constituted a virtually private system of law and government within society, and, through the loyalty they commanded, legitimated values which were quite unsanctioned by employers, the state, and political economists. This was the context which gave meaning to charges of secrecy and irresponsibility. Of course the use of violence and physical intimidation provided a clear and simple basis for condemnation on those grounds alone, but discussion of union 'outrages' frequently recognised that such tactics owed much of their success to the fact that so many possible witnesses felt greater loyalty to their union than to the law of the land. One article on the trial of the leaders of the Glasgow spinners' strike of 1837 complained of the extreme difficulty of obtaining evidence because people in a position to testify felt morally bound by the oath they had taken to the union, in addition to any fear of possible violence against themselves.[45] In particular, this situation facilitated the defence of false alibi, which in the case of the defendant McLean, was alleged to have resulted in an unwarranted verdict of 'not proven' on the more serious charges against him. The upshot was, that although a series of extremely violent acts, including murder, fire-raising, and disfigurement by vitriol-throwing, was held to have been committed on the initiative, and in the interest of the union, it had not been possible to pin these crimes squarely on the organisation responsible.[46] And on the positive as well as the negative side, it was a matter of regret that unions could so often rely for the enforcement of their own rules on members' willingness to spy on each other.[47]

Many similar difficulties were apparent in the task of the sub-commissioners who investigated the Sheffield 'outrages'. It was quite clear that the practice of 'rattening' (removing the tools of workmen who offended against union norms, and fining them for replacement) was deeply entrenched in many of the Sheffield metal trades, and rested on a strong sense of its legitimacy among the union membership. Even the harsher sanctions of personal violence suffered by the victims of the most serious incidents (those guilty of recruiting excessive numbers of apprentices) could command wide support, or at least an attitude of ambiguity.[48] Significantly, relatively full information about the Sheffield events was unearthed by use of the highly unorthodox legal device of empowering the investigators to grant indemnity to any witnesses who were regarded as having made full and truthful statements which would normally have inculpated them. Despite its irregularity, this method was generally approved as an essential means of bringing the truth about trade union involvement in the 'outrages' into the full glare of national publicity[48] – no doubt in anticipation of an unfavourable impact on public opinion and on the main Royal Commission itself.

Initial reactions to the Sheffield incidents do, however, make clear some of the limitations of trade union solidarity, especially where physical force and illegality were involved. Actions which might be acceptable within the traditions of the local metal trades might look very different to union members elsewhere. One of the first moves made by the leaders of the London Trades Council was to call a public meeting at Exeter Hall in July 1867 in order to dissociate themselves from what had happened in Sheffield,[50] which, it was doubtless felt, stood to prejudice the prospects for legislative change in favour of the unions. In the event, the proceedings of the main commission in London, before which prominent union leaders carefully presented themselves in a far more creditable light, were to assume greater importance than those of the sub-commission devoted to the outrages. Furthermore the sub-commissioners themselves were to accept that even in Sheffield, violence had for some time been on the decline, and had been employed by only a minority of the local unions.

Closely related to the issues of both tyranny and violence, and forming another major moral count against the unions, was the question of the impact of combinations on workmen who were not themselves members. As usual, one of the sharpest formulations was to be found in the pages of the *Edinburgh*: 'the unions are antagonistic, not so much to the employer of labour as to the labourer outside the body – the multitude outside the pale are the poorest of their class'.[51] All attempts to control entry to a particular trade, whether of adults or apprentices, could be held to have the necessary effect of further exacerbating the problem of excessive labour supply in other occupations, and hence of keeping wages low. This criticism was pushed to its furthest limits when combinations were held responsible for the existence of current wage differentials among various trades. Different wage rates were cited, stressing the miserable rewards for hand-loom weaving and agricultural labour. From this it was deduced that 'there is clearly something interfering with the free circulation of labour, and which has prevented the high wages in one line from drawing to itself the superfluous hands from other branches of industry.'[52] The conclusion was that only trade union activity could account for these discrepancies – which was of course to ignore every non-labour factor contributing to the unevenness of industrial development, and every non-union source of rigidities and imperfections in the labour market.

This distinction between the interests of members and outsiders could, like so many possible divisions in the ranks of labour, be demonstrated with most plausibility during an extended strike. In these circumstances attempts by strike-bound employers to recruit fresh labour were likely to meet resistance by union pickets. '(K)nobs' or '(k)nobsticks' (strikebreakers or 'scabs' in more modern terminology), who might well have been found among the unemployed or in some exceptionally depressed or badly paid occupation, were sometimes driven away by force or the threat of force. Even if persuaded to leave voluntarily, they might well be induced by means regarded as disreputable, such as being plied with drink, or supplied with railway tickets to distant destinations.[53]

Even those commentators who explicitly accepted the justification of voluntary combination – for the purpose of improving the wages and hours of workmen who met to agree on such demands (roughly what was conceded by the act of 1825) – normally disapproved sharply of anything which smacked of coercion of others not directly involved. Picketting was thus regarded as unfair because of the intention to produce a 'fictitious scarcity' of labour, by driving away anyone else seeking employment. So instead of excluding non-members, trade unionists were urged to 'let freedom be the rule, except for those who prefer the yoke of voluntary self-restriction'.[54] The sphere of operations left to them would then be 'the legitimate action of the unions, whereby they simply enforce the law of the market', on a basis of fair competition between capitalist and worker.[55] A pointer to the implications of this position is given by the reference elsewhere to 'a combination to refuse work without coercion', followed by the rapid parenthetic afterthought, (if with human nature as it is there ever was or can be such an anomaly)'.[56] It seems that to insist on the moral distinction between combination which involved no element of coercion against anyone at all, and that which employed the customary protective strategies, with picketting and entry-restrictions, was to adopt the opinion that unions ought to conduct themselves on lines which would guarantee their ineffectiveness.

It was nonetheless a formidable line of attack on trade unions to assert that their group solidarity functioned only, or mainly, at the expense of

outsiders who were on the whole fellow workers even less fortunately situated
– even if one may doubt whether most attacks on 'monopolies of skilled
against unskilled labour'[57] were primarily motivated by sympathy for the
latter. Aspects of trade union practice which depended on fraternal co-
operation, or self-sacrifice, were less commonly noted, and even when they
were, sometimes excited contempt rather than admiration. The Amalgamated
Society of Engineers, Machinists and Smiths was ridiculed for having made a
donation to shoemakers who were on strike against the introduction of
machinery in their own trade – a strike contrary, therefore, to the interests,
narrowly conceived, of a section of the Engineers' own membership.[58]
The Engineers, by then one of the stronger unions financially, also made well-
known and substantial contributions to the funds of the London building
strike of 1859.[59] Altogether between 1853 and 1866, this union made 179
grants of assistance, ranging from £5 to over £3,000. There was in fact nothing
particularly unusual about trade unionists responding to appeals for assistance
when their own interests were not at stake in any direct sense.

In the context of the labour market of the middle decades of the nineteenth
century the concern of unionism with protecting the worker in his capacity
as a wage earner led inevitably to the protection of a specific job. Great
variations in the level of skill and training required for different jobs, and the
size of the available labour reserves made this an inescapable fact. Equally
the uneven development of different industries, regions, and production
techniques constrained trade unionism within a slow and untidy pattern
of growth, and virtually guaranteed that it would establish a secure foothold
in certain corners of the industrial structure long before other expanses
were regarded as remotely within reach of union organisation. The collapse
of various over-ambitious schemes to build a general union (of which Owen's
Grand National Consolidated Trades Union in 1833–34 was the most
spectacular example) were well-appreciated evidence of these difficulties and
limitations.

But the established craft unions of the fifties and sixties not only strengthened their own organisations and bargaining positions, but initiated several
moves of wider significance for the future of trade unionism. There were campaigns for the reduction of hours, over which some major disputes were to be
fought, notably in 1871. This had implications for the spreading of employment as well as for the working conditions of those most directly concerned.
There was the establishment of trades councils, local federations of unions in
different trades for common action. Perhaps, above all, there was the staking
of the claim, however arguably inaccurate or presumptuous, by the leaders
of the major unions and trades councils, to speak for the whole of labour on
questions of legislation affecting relations between employers and workers.
The origins of the Trades Union Congress,[60] initially an annual congress
of trade unions and trades councils, are to be found in the need for more
powerful mobilisation of union opinion in the late sixties, especially with a
view to securing urgently needed legislative changes.

Among the major results of these campaigns were the Trade Union Act of 1871 which provided legal status for unions as registered (friendly) societies, with protection for their funds; and the two Acts of 1875, one of which abolished the old law of master and servant, making employers and workmen equal parties to a civil contract, and the other ending separate criminal legislation against trade unions, apparently allowing peaceful picketting. Of course this progress was neither easy nor continuous: some of the most energetic struggles were stimulated by serious setbacks. The decision in the case of Hornby *v.* Close of 1867, in which a union was refused financial redress against a defaulting official, because of the extent to which unions acted in restraint of trade, was understandably regarded by many union members as equivalent to inciting petty thieves to do what the propertied classes were afraid to do themselves.[61] The *Edinburgh's* comment on this was almost embarrassed: 'we are free to own that we do not altogether like this indirect mode of punishing trades unions – nor are we quite satisfied to leave the discretion of deciding what is a "restraint of trade", which may chance to be a nice question of political economy, to the legal tribunals – but such is the law'.[62] And there were other severe blows, such as the Criminal Law Amendment Act, of 1871, which actually tightened up the law against picketting.

However, this concentrated series of legislative gains removed for the time being the main state-imposed obstacles to basic trade union practices – though the position was to shift again with the employers' and judges' counter-offensive of the nineties. Broadly it appears that the efforts of the established trade unions in these years greatly facilitated the spreading of trade union ideas, and indeed of membership – as evidenced by the rise of the 'new unionism' of semi-skilled workers and labourers, previously widely considered as unorganisable, which can be indentified in the seventies, and which became a major phenomenon in the late eighties. But long before such confirmation was available, the occasional bold commentator of the sixties was prepared to assert that 'all the advantages, whether material or moral, which the unionist gains for himself, he gains also for his non-unionist fellow-worker'. By reference to the spill-over effects of the higher social standards and better pay obtained by unionism, it was claimed as 'a system operating for the benefit of workmen as a class, and not merely for a few privileged individuals.'[63,64]

The improvements in the legal status of trade unions reflected also an awareness on the part of employers and legislators of the increased strength and resilience of union organisation which pointed to the desirability of coming to terms with them on a basis other than that of the 1825 act. The prudential case for concessions may have reinforced by the further extension of the franchise in 1867 which gave the vote to a high proportion of urban workers. And the shift in opinion was also helped by the success of union spokesmen and sympathisers in representing violence and intimidation of the Sheffield type as atypical, and stressing in contrast the sober virtues of unionism, such as the provision of insurance benefits for members.

This branch of a union's functions had normally met universal approval. Like the common practice of paying bounties to members who decided to emigrate, it seemed quite compatible with the requirements of political economy. But what caused qualification was the allegedly dangerous and incongruous linking of these insurance schemes with the union's other, anti-employer, activities. Separation of benefit and strike funds was recommended in the majority report of the Royal Commission of 1867–9. And it was claimed elsewhere that the benefits were designed as 'a bait to attract but still more forcibly as a tie to retain members in their allegiance.'[65]

This was sometimes part of a wider belief in the insincerity of trade unions in presenting a bland and amiable face to the public, and concealing the coercive reality of their behaviour. In fact union spokesmen were often frank enough about the job protection purposes of their organisations, and their lack of belief in the harmony of interests, even when they were concerned about the need for good public relations, as when giving evidence to the Royal Commission. Even so, specific union demands were often represented as cover-ups for less creditable intentions. The demand for limitation of hours, despite the handsome concession that the 'moral' or 'sanitary' grounds for this might be good, was deplored as merely a dishonest wage claim.[66] A similar criticism, echoing Tufnell's book under review, had been made in relation to the cotton spinners' support for the Ten Hours' Bill in the thirties.[67]

A cool tone of suspicion was evident in several comments indicating that the most publicised and spectacular deeds and aspirations of unions may not be the most dangerous ones. An article in the early thirties dismissed union advocacy of co-operative production, appropriation of profits etc. as merely symptoms of failure and disillusion, and argued that the more harmful combinations were generally the quietest. And in the late fifties, it was noted that 'our story today is not one of torture and murder. That phase of the struggle between employers, and employed seems to be over', but it was also recognised that union power had become more formidable, though less conspicuous.[68]

These may well be realistic assessments, in the sense that, irrespective of fluctuations in political consciousness, or in the incidence of physical violence, the basic bargaining strength of trade unions at workshop level was gradually increasing over the half century between the twenties and the seventies. This point has sometimes been blurred by the tendency to find major discontinuities around mid century in the development of the labour movement.[69] This periodisation normally stresses the large-scale, if brief and sporadic, involvement of workers in radical or revolutionary movements such as Owenism and Chartism in the years before 1850, and the contrasting appearance of sectionalism, caution and narrowed horizons in the best known figures in the trade unions over the next few decades. It has been forcefully argued that lack of revolutionary ambition did not imply a passive union acquiescence in capitalist economic ideas.[70] From the opposite angle it would not appear that the absence of a revolutionary threat induced any confidence among the propertied classes that organised workers had lost their consciousness of opposing class interests, or were being converted to the truths of political economy. This is not of course to deny that some union leaders, such as Robert Applegarth[71] of the carpenters, or Alexander MacDonald[72] of the miners showed a degree of subservience to the interests and attitudes of the employers which earned them much criticism both then and subsequently.

Inevitably, when articles were written for largely ad hoc purposes, arguments were sometimes employed, perhaps in the course of a specific polemic, which implicitly contradicted basic elements of the orthodox analysis of trade union functions, to which the author doubtless subscribed. An early *Edinburgh* writer advocating the abolition of the Combination Laws of 1799–1800[73] knocked the bottom out of many conventional criticisms of combination by workmen, pointing out that every single employer should be regarded as 'forming of himself, a perpetual and indivisible combination against his workmen'. The employer had the power to alter his rates of pay at any time, without having to combine in the formal sense, and could rely on all the 'secrecy, promptitude, vigour and decision of the single individual.'[74] Workmen were therefore being punished for meeting combination with combination. Furthermore, it was argued that in a struggle in which the employer invariably enjoyed great natural and acquired advantages, 'hitherto the law has run altogether in favour of the stronger side'.[75] This latter point was supported by apposite quotation from a judge in a case seven years earlier, who had said that any employer conceding a pay rise to workers on strike was to be regarded as an enemy of the country. And in the fifties *Blackwood's* was prepared to attack Lancashire textile employers for attempting to crush unions, and insisting on wage cuts despite suggestions by the operatives for the adoption of short-time working, and cutting back purchases of raw materials.[76] Much of the utility of this interpretation to *Blackwood's* lay in the fact that the Lancashire manufacturers included John Bright and other radical opponents of the Crimean War.

It was also inevitable that the subject of labour relations over half a century of industrialisation and urbanisation should have prompted many thoughts other than direct analysis of union behaviour. To a writer in *Blackwood's* consideration of the causes of disorder and distress in the forties, and the theme of the mutual ignorance of employer and employed produced the doleful reflection that 'all large manufacturing communities must necessarily present a peculiarly artificial state of society.'[77] However much disapproval of trade union coercion they shared, this perspective was far removed from the *Edinburgh's* normal assumption that if wages, and most other things, could be left to the fair competition of the market, then an economy of gradually rising wages had the capacity to attach the great mass of the people to the institutions under which they lived.[78]

Recent changes and conflicts in society also called forth theories of stages in the development of the relations of production. A review article in the *Westminster* suggested that an historical epoch of comprehensive subjection and corresponding protection had given way to an age of vassalage, with imperfect submission and partial protection, to be followed by the modern age of simple service and simple payment, on a contractual basis. According to this analysis, Britain was currently in transition between stages two and three, and conflict was generated by the fact that both capitalists and workers still entertained anachronistic expectations – of automatic deference and respect on the one side, and of paternal protection on the other.[79] Whereas this, and a later *Westminster* article, broadly accepted the desirability of progress towards more strictly contractual relationships subject to certain provisoes about the obligations of citizens and Christians, and about power being the measure of duty,[80] *Blackwood's* regarded the decline of the master-servant relationship as a matter for serious regret.[81]

The same publication "The Claims of Labour" which generated some of these thoughts was reviewed for the *Edinburgh* by John Stuart Mill,[82] who was eloquent in repudiating the paternalism which he detected in the advocacy of some of labour's ostensible friends (e.g. Young England): 'Obedience in return for protection is a bargain only made when protection can be had on no other terms. Men now make that bargain with society, not with an individual . . . obedience in return for wages is a different matter . . . goodwill and gratitude form no part of the conditions of such a contract'.[83] Mill's own prescription was that some form of co-ownership or profit-sharing offered the only way of narrowing the gap between 'those who toil' and 'those who live on the produce of former toil'.[84]

Advocacy of arbitration as a means of allieviating industrial conflict is encountered in the fifties. One discussion of recent major strikes in Lancashire put forward arbitration as a possible alternative to 'counter-combination' – the use of lock-outs and other aggressive anti-union tactics by employers acting in concert.[85] There had in fact been legislation to promote the resolution of disputes through conciliation and arbitration from the Combination Act of 1800 onwards. But it was exceptional for regular machinery to be devised and used in the period before 1870. Ideas more modern-sounding than either arbitration or co-ownership can be seen surfacing briefly in other articles. For example the concept of labour as human capital is stated by Thorold Rogers in a signed article in *Fraser's*.[86]

But, however interesting and suggestive are the varieties of mood and style, of positions on specific issues of legislation, of suggested remedies for future conflict, there is no doubt that the vast majority of contributors to this collection of articles have a great deal in common in their attitude towards trade unionism.[87] Even more than an economic orthodoxy, what they share is a clear class orientation to the conflict of interest between labour and capital. As often, the *Edinburgh* expressed the instincts of many others with greater clarity and acerbity (and said as much about itself as about its subject), when it observed that 'over a large portion of the union rules pure class selfishness appears to dominate.'[88] Union rules spoke this message precisely because it was the most basic aims and methods of trade unionism which were opposed by the people and the ideas which dominated in society. The same writer summed it up bluntly when he wrote: 'In fact the vicious principle that the workman owes a duty to his fellow workmen paramount to his obligation to his employer, underlies the whole system of the trades unions.'[89] The fact that he felt obliged to add three pages later 'We ourselves are conscious of no bias or prepossession in favour of the masters' cause' need not cause any confusion.

G. W. Crompton

Notes

[1] See F. W. Fetter, 'The Authorship of Economic Articles in the *Edinburgh Review* 1802–1847' *Journal of Political Economy* vol. LXI (1953) pp. 232–4.

[2] For examples elsewhere of the persistence of wage fund orthodoxy, see R. V. Clements 'British Trade Unions and Popular Political Economy 1850–1875' *Economic History Review*, 2nd series vol. XIV 1 (1961), pp. 95–6.

[3] *Edinburgh Review* vol. CXXVI (Oct. 1867) p. 446.

[4] Ibid p. 442.

[5] *Quarterly Review* vol. CXXIII (1867) pp. 356–7, 365.

[6] *Frazer's Magazine* vol. I (1870) p. 500.

[7] *Blackwood's Magazine* vol. CVII (June 1870) p. 749.

[8] Ibid p. 442.

[9] *Edinburgh Review* vol. LIX (1834) p. 349.

[10] *Edinburgh Review* vol. XXXIX (1824) p. 323.

[11] Ibid p. 323.

[12] *Blackwood's Magazine* vol. XXXV (May 1834), p. 847.

[13] *Blackwood's Magazine* vol. XXXV (March 1834) p. 331.

[14] *Frazer's Magazine* vol. I (1870) p. 507.

[15] *Blackwood's Magazine* vol. XVIII (Oct. 1825) p. 469.

[16] Ibid p. 477.

[17] *Edinburgh Review* vol. LXVII (1838) pp. 241–2.

[18] *Edinburgh Review* vol. LIX (1834) p. 357.

[19] *Westminster Review* vol. XIV (1831) p. 194.

[20] *Edinburgh Review* vol. LIX (1834) p. 348 (quoting Tufnell).

[21] *Blackwood's Magazine* vol. XXXV (May 1834), p. 845.

[22] *Edinburgh Review* vol. LXVII (1838) pp. 215–6.

[23] *Edinburgh Review* vol. LXVII (1838) p. 218.

[24] *Edinburgh Review* vol. CX (1859) p. 529.

[25] *Blackwood's Magazine* vol. CVII (June 1870) p. 750.

[26] *Edinburgh Review* vol. CXXVI (1867) p. 450.

[27] Ibid p. 452.

[28] *Edinburgh Review* vol. CXXVI (1867) p. 448.

[29] *Edinburgh Review* vol. CX (1859) p. 536.

[30] *Edinburgh Review* vol. LIX (1834) pp. 352–3.

[31] *Edinburgh Review* vol. CX (1859) p. 536.

[32] *Edinburgh Review* vol. LXVII (1838) p. 255.

[33] *Blackwood's Magazine* vol. XXXV (May 1834) p. 836.
[34] *Edinburgh Review* vol. LXVII (1838) p. 214.
[35] *Edinburgh Review* vol. CX (1859) p. 528.
[36] *Edinburgh Review* vol. CX (1859) p. 557.
[37] Ibid p. 551–2.
[38] *Edinburgh Review* vol. XXXIX (1824), p. 319.
[39] *Edinburgh Review* vol. CX (1859) pp. 536, 541.
[40] *Edinburgh Review* vol. LXVII (1838) pp. 245, 252.
[41] Ibid pp. 241–2, 245, 248–9.
[42] *Edinburgh Review* vol. LXVII (1838) p. 257.
[43] *Edinburgh Review* vol. CX (1867) pp. 422–3.
[44] S. Pollard (ed.) *The Sheffield Outrages* (Bath 1971) pp. xiii–xv.
[45] *Edinburgh Review* vol. LXVII (1838) p. 223.
[46] Ibid pp. 222–34.
[47] *Edinburgh Review* vol. CX (1859) p. 541.
[48] Pollard op. cit. p. xiii–xv.
[49] *Edinburgh Review* vol. CX (1867) p. 441.
[50] See R. Harrison, 'Before the Socialists: Studies in Labour and Politics 1861–1881' (London 1965 pp. 279–282) for an account of the hard-hitting speech by Prof. E. S. Beesly. Beesly was also the author of an article, in far less uncompromising vein, in this collection – *Westminster Review* vol. XX (1861).
[51] *Edinburgh Review* vol. CX (1859) p. 529.
[52] *Edinburgh Review* vol. LXVII (1838) p. 235.
[53] *Edinburgh Review* vol. CX (1859) p. 534.
[54] *Edinburgh Review* vol. CXXVI (1867) p. 426.
[55] Ibid p. 447.
[56] *Westminster Review* vol. V (1854) p. 123.
[57] *Edinburgh Review* vol. LXVII (1838) p. 257.
[58] *Edinburgh Review* vol. CX (1859) p. 459.
[59] J. B. Jefferys *The Story of the Engineers* (London 1945) p. 75.
[60] See E. Frow and M. Kalanka, 1868 *Year of the Unions* (London 1968).
[61] See Harrison op. cit. pp. 279–82. This point was made in Beesly's speech.
[62] *Edinburgh Review* vol. CXXVI (1867) p. 420.
[63] *Westminster Review* vol. XXXVI (1869) pp. 105–6.
[64] For a useful modern summary of the positive achievements of 'sectional' craft unionism, see E. J. Hobsbawm *Labouring Men* (London 1964) p. 323.
[65] *Edinburgh Review* vol. CXXVI (1867) p. 422.
[66] Ibid p. 425.
[67] *Edinburgh Review* vol. LIX (1834) pp. 354–5.
[68] *Edinburgh Review* vol. LXVII (1859) pp. 525–6.
[69] For a recent discussion of the problems of 'watersheds' and 'discontinuities' in nineteenth century trade union history see A. E. Musson *British Trade Unions* 1800–1875 (London 1972) esp. c.6.
[70] Clements op. cit.

[71] For a sympathetic brief account of the ending of Applegarth's union career, see H. Pelling *A History of British Trade Unionism* (London 1963) p. 73.

[72] On MacDonald, see R. Challinor 'Alexander MacDonald and the Miners' *Our History* no. 48, winter 1967/68.

[73] For recent discussion of the significance of this legislation see Musson op. cit. c.3.

[74] *Edinburgh Review* vol. xxxix (1824) p. 325.

[75] Ibid p. 329.

[76] *Blackwood's Magazine* vol. lxxix (1856) pp. 56–7.

[77] *Blackwood's Magazine* vol. lii (Nov. 1842) p. 647.

[78] *Edinburgh Review* vol. xxxix (1824) p. 335.

[79] *Westminster Review* vol. xliii (1845) pp. 453–4.

[80] *Westminster Review* vol. i (1852) pp. 78–80.

[81] *Blackwood's Magazine* vol. xviii (Oct. 1825) p. 477.

[82] Fetter, op. cit. p. 241.

[83] *Edinburgh Review* vol. lxxxi (1845) p. 513.

[84] Ibid p. 516.

[85] *Westminster Review* vol. v (1854) p. 133.

[86] *Fraser's Magazine* vol. I (1870) p. 511.

[87] For an interesting demonstration of how even imaginative writers consciously hostile to political economy shared the same basic hostile assumptions about trade unionism see P. Brantlinger 'The Case Against Trade Unions in Early Victorian Fiction' *Victorian Studies* vol. xiii, 1 Sept. 1969.

[88] *Edinburgh Review* vol. cxxvi (1867) p. 449.

[89] Ibid p. 552.

Art. III. 1. *Draft of proposed Bill for repealing several Acts relating to Combinations of Workmen, and for more effectually protecting Trade, and for settling Disputes between Masters and their Work-people.* Ordered by the House of Commons to be printed, 22d April, 1823.
2. *Considerations on Emigration.* London, 1822.

From the reign of Edward I, down to a very recent period, it has been the practice of the Legislature to interfere respecting the stipulations in the contract of wages between masters and servants : And as its deliberations have been, in most cases, guided by the advice of the masters, it was natural that it should interfere rather to promote their particular interests, than to treat both parties with even-handed and impartial justice. But the gradual advance of civilization, and the dissemination of sounder and more enlarged principles of public economy, having impressed all classes with a conviction of the general impolicy of such interference, it is now rarely practised. The experience of nearly five hundred years has shown, that while every attempt to set a *maximum* on the price of labour is oppressive and injurious to the workmen, it is of no real advantage to their employers : for it has been found, that the workman has invariably become more persevering, sober, and industrious, according as his freedom has been extended, and as he has been relieved from the vexatious restraints to which he was formerly subjected.

But, though the Legislature no longer interferes to dictate the precise terms on which masters shall buy, and workmen sell their labour, a set of laws have of late been much extended, and are now very frequently acted upon, by which workmen are severely punished for *combining together* to raise their wages, or to oppose their reduction. These laws, which seem to us to be in the highest degree partial, oppressive and unjust, had their origin in a dark and barbarous period. The dreadful plague that desolated England, in common with most other countries of Europe, in 1348 and 1349, having destroyed great numbers of the labouring poor, a greater competition took place for the services of those who survived, who, in consequence, obtained much higher wages. Parliament, however, instead of leaving this temporary rise of wages, to which the poor had an unquestionable right, to be reduced by the increase of population it must infallibly have occasioned, passed, in 1350, the famous act (23 Edward III.) for regulating wages. By this statute, labourers were obliged to serve for such wages as were

X 2

common in the districts in which they resided previously to the
pestilence. But as this gave rise to a great deal of cavilling, a
statute was passed two years after, fixing the specific amount of
the wages to be given to reapers, mowers, haymakers, thrashers,
&c., and to the more common and important classes of artificers. * A variety of subsequent acts were passed, to enforce
compliance with the regulations in this statute of wages, of the
spirit of which some idea may be formed, from the fact of its
having been made *felony*, by an act passed in 1425 (3 Henry VI. cap. 1.), for masons to confederate or combine together
to raise their wages above the statutory rate. And though this
brutal and barbarous law is no longer acted upon, it is still suffered to disgrace the Statute-book, and may be considered as
the parent stock—*fortes creantur fortibus*—from which, through
a long line of ancestors, the existing statute against combinations has been derived.

This statute (39th and 40th Geo. III. cap. 106.), after declaring all combinations to obtain an advance of wages to be
unlawful, goes on to enact, that any workman who enters into
a combination, either verbal or in writing, to obtain an advance
of wages, to lessen the hours or time of working, to decrease
the quantity of work, to *persuade*, intimidate, or, by money or
otherwise, endeavour to prevail on any other workman not to
accept employment; or who shall, for the purpose of obtaining
an advance of wages, endeavour to intimidate or prevail upon
any person to leave his employment, or to prevent any person
employing him; or who, being hired, shall, without any just or
reasonable cause, refuse to work with any other workman; such
workman shall, on the oath or oaths of *one* or more credible
witnesses, before *any two Justices of the Peace*, within three
calendar months after the offence has been committed, be committed to, and confined in the COMMON GAOL within their jurisdiction, for any time not exceeding THREE CALENDAR MONTHS;
or, *at the discretion of such Justices, shall be committed to some
house of correction, within the same jurisdiction, there to remain,
and be kept at hard labour, for any time not exceeding* TWO CA-
LENDAR MONTHS!

The extreme severity of this enactment must strike every one.
Justices of the Peace belong to the order of masters; and, however respectable individually, generally possess a full share of their
particular feelings and prejudices. To invest two of them with
the power of imprisoning workmen for three months, *without the
intervention of a jury*, is certainly entrusting them with an au-

---

* See the rates in Sir F. M. Eden's State of the Poor, vol. I.
p. 33.

thority very liable to be abused, and which, if it is to be exercised at all, ought to be placed in the hands of persons less likely to act under a bias. It is true, the workmen can appeal to the Quarter-sessions; but as this is only an appeal from one set of Justices to another, it cannot be of much importance. There are a variety of other clauses, discharging all workmen from attending any meeting for the purpose of combining, from contributing to defray the expenses incurred by persons acting contrary to this act, and compelling *offenders* to give evidence, &c. &c. under the above-mentioned penalties.

A very strong feeling has been spreading of late years, not only among the workmen, but also among the more intelligent and liberal portion of the masters, that the attempts to enforce the provisions of the Combination Act have done infinitely more harm than good. And in unison with this feeling, in the course of last Session, Mr Moore, member for Coventry, introduced the bill of which the title is prefixed to this article, into the House of Commons, for the repeal of the Combination Act, and of a variety of other acts regulating wages in particular trades. Instead, however, of confining his Bill to the simple repeal of the acts in question, and leaving to masters and workmen to enter into any kind of contract they pleased, Mr Moore has chosen to load it with a multitude of clauses which go to regulate the mode in which almost every possible transaction that can take place between the two parties shall be conducted ! These clauses are exceedingly confused and perplexed; many of them seem also to be in the highest degree preposterous and absurd; and while their adoption would be productive of more litigation than ever, there is no reason to think that they would tend in any considerable degree to lessen the irritation and disgust occasioned by the existing law. It is unnecessary, however, to enter into any particulars respecting the regulating clauses in the bill before us, as there can be no doubt, from what took place in the House when the discussion of the bill was postponed till next Session, that they will be rejected. We are most anxious, however, that that portion of the bill which goes to repeal the laws against combinations should receive the sanction of the Legislature. And we shall avail ourselves of this opportunity to lay before our readers the reasons on which we found our opinion, that such repeal would be of the greatest possible advantage to all classes of the community.

The observations we are now about to offer on the Combination Act, are meant to apply exclusively to the justice and policy of attempting to prevent *voluntary* combinations among workmen. That all attempts to extend combinations by violent means, or by one set of workmen endeavouring forci-

bly to hinder others from working at any rate of wages they
may choose to accept, should be immediately repressed by suitable punishment, cannot admit of a moment's doubt or hesi-
tation. But there is a wide difference between interfering to
prevent workmen from violently obstructing the business of
their neighbours, and interfering to suppress any *voluntary* a-
greement they may have made amongst themselves. The former is an obvious and direct breach of the peace; the latter
seems a mere harmless exercise of that freedom of action to
which every man is naturally entitled. Whatever may be the
ultimate consequences of a voluntary combination, there is
plainly nothing either *unjust* or *immoral* in a number of individuals agreeing together not to sell their labour—if they can
help it—below a certain price, or to work above a certain time
each day.

It shall, however, be our business to show, that the *consequences* of combinations are by no means such as to warrant their
prevention by law. Wages, like every thing else, ought always
to be left to be regulated by the fair and free competition of the
parties in the market, and ought never to be controlled by the
interference of the Legislator. 'The property,' says Dr Smith,
' which every man has in his own labour, as it is the original
' foundation of all other property, so it is the most sacred and
' inviolable. *The patrimony of a poor man lies in the strength
' and dexterity of his hands; and to hinder him from employing
' this strength and dexterity in what manner he thinks proper,
' without injury to his neighbours, is a plain violation of this most
' sacred property.*' (I. p. 188.) But it is obviously false to
affirm that workmen are allowed to dispose of their labour in
any way they please, so long as they are prevented from concerting with each other the terms on which they are to sell it.
Capacity to labour is to the poor man what stock is to the capitalist. But you would not prevent a hundred or a thousand
capitalists from forming themselves into a company, or *combination*, who should take all their measures in common, and dispose of their property as they might, in their collective capacity, judge most advantageous for their interests :—and why then
should not a hundred or a thousand labourers be allowed to do
the same by *their stock?* Of all the species of property which
a man can possess, the faculties of his mind and the powers of
his body are most particularly and emphatically his own : and
to fetter him in the mode in which he is to exercise or dispose
of these faculties and powers, is a manifest and flagrant encroachment on the most inviolable of all rights, and can be justified only by the most urgent and overwhelming necessity.

It is easy, however, to show that, in point of fact, no such necessity ever did or ever can exist. The wages of any set of workmen who enter into a combination for the purpose of raising them, must be either *below* the *natural* and *proper* rate of wages in the particular branch of industry to which they belong, or they must be *coincident with that rate,—or above it.* Now, it is clear that, in the first case, or when wages have been depressed below their natural level, the claim of the workmen for an advance is highly proper, fair, and reasonable; and it would obviously be the extreme of injustice and oppression to prevent them adopting any measure, *not injurious to the just rights of others,* which they might think best fitted to render their claim effectual. But a voluntary combination among workmen is certainly in no respect injurious to any of the rights of their masters. It would be a contradiction and an absurdity to contend that masters have any right or title whatever to the services of free workmen, in the event of the latter not choosing to accept the price offered them for their labour; and as the very existence of a combination to procure a rise of wages shows that they have not so chosen, and is a proof of the want of all concord and agreement between the parties, so it is also a proof that the *workmen are fairly entitled to enter into it*; and that, however injurious their proceedings may be to themselves, they cannot possibly encroach on the privileges or rights of others. Not only, therefore, is a combination harmless in itself, but when it is entered into for the purpose of raising wages that have been unduly depressed, its object is most proper and desirable. No master ever willingly consents to raise wages; and the claim either of one or of a few individuals for an advance of wages is sure to be disregarded, so long as their fellows continue to work at the old rates. It is only when the whole, or the greater part of the workmen belonging to a particular master or department of industry combine together, or when they act in that simultaneous manner which is in every respect equivalent to a combination, and refuse to continue to work without receiving an increase of wages, that it becomes the interest of the masters to comply with their demand. And hence it is obvious, that without the existence either of an *open and avowed,* or of a *tacit and real combination,* workmen would *never* be able to obtain a rise of wages by their own exertions, but would be left entirely dependent on the competition of their masters.

When workmen are allowed to combine, as in the case supposed, to raise wages that have been unduly reduced, the masters cannot expect to carry on their business by the aid of workmen obtained from other employments; for, by the hypothesis, the rate of wages, in the department in which the combination has taken place, has been reduced below its proper level, and, of course, none would leave others to enter into it. Neither could they expect that the workmen would abandon the combination, and return to their old employment at the former rate of wages; for though this might probably be the case with a small number, the majority would naturally betake themselves, in preference, to those businesses in which labour bore a higher price. These are plain and obvious consequences of a relative depression in the wages of any class of workmen; and as it could require no peculiar sagacity or penetration in the masters to discover them, and as they would also *feel* that their capitals could not be rendered available for the production of a profit or revenue without the labour of the workmen, the probability is, that they would, in general, be disposed to raise wages to their proper level soon after the formation of the combination, rather than defer taking a step which, it is plain, they must take in the end, until they had been compelled to do so from their inability otherwise to obtain the means of setting their capitals in motion. Every attempt to prevent combination in such cases as this is neither more nor less than an attempt to hinder the workmen from making use of *the only means* by which their wages can be speedily and effectually raised to their *just level.* It is committing injustice in behalf of the strong, at the expense of the weaker party !

We admit that the *object* of the *second* class of voluntary combinations, or of those in which the wages of the combining workmen are already equal to or above their natural and proper rate, is improper and unreasonable. Still, however, it is very easy to demonstrate, that there is no more cause for the interference of the Legislature in this case, than in the former. There is no good reason why workmen should not, like the possessors of every other valuable and desirable article, be allowed to set whatever price they please upon the labour they have to dispose of. The apprehensions formerly so prevalent about the injurious effects of *forestalling* and *regrating*, and the forming of combinations to raise the price of the necessaries of life, have now almost entirely vanished; and experience has invariably shown, that every market has been better supplied with every species of useful and desirable produce, and at a much less expense, according as legislative interference has been withdrawn, and a greater freedom of action allowed to the dealers and producers. And what ground is there for supposing that the relieving of workmen from restraint, and allowing them to concert measures in common, should have a different effect ? The merest tyro in economical science would not hesitate to ridicule all apprehension of famine, or even of a stinted supply of the market, from a combination of corn dealers, or of bakers, to raise the price of corn or bread : For he would feel assured, that there were a hundred chances to one that no such combination would ever be generally entered into; and that supposing it were, the moment prices had been raised ever so little above their natural rate, it would become the interest of a large body of the combiners to secede from the combination, and to throw their stocks on the market. But, if we can thus securely trust the supply of the most necessary articles to the unfettered competition of a comparatively small body of masters,—can any thing be more childish than to fear any bad consequences from leaving the market for labour to be supplied by the unfettered competition of the workmen ?—a body in which, because of its being infinitely more numerous, combination must be infinitely more difficult than among the masters. Assuming, however, that the mass of workmen occasionally combine together, it appears absurd in the last degree to suppose that their combinations should ever enable them to obtain from their masters more than a due share of the produce of their labour. That the masters would resist a demand for any greater portion, is certain; and the slightest glance at the relative condition of the parties must satisfy every one that they cannot fail to succeed in defeating it. The workmen always suffer more from a *strike* than their masters. It is indeed true, as Dr Smith has observed, that in the *long run*, they are as necessary to their masters as their masters are to them ; but this necessity is plainly far from being so immediate. The stock and credit of the master is in almost every instance infinitely greater than the stock and credit of his labourers ; and he is, therefore, able to maintain himself for a much longer time without their labour, than they can maintain themselves without his wages. In all old settled and fully peopled countries, wages are, unfortunately, seldom or never so high as to enable labourers to accumulate any considerable stock ; and the moment their scanty funds are exhausted, there is necessarily an end of the combination,—and instead of dictating terms, they must accept those that are offered to them.

But this is not all.—When workmen enter into a combination to enforce an unreasonable demand, or to raise wages that are *already up to the common level,* it is evident they *must lose* and can gain nothing by entering into an employment to which they have not been bred; while it is equally evident that a very small extra allowance will be sufficient to entice a large supply of other labourers to the business they have left. All the great departments of industry have so many and so closely allied branches, that a workman who is instructed in any one of them, can, without much training, readily and without difficulty, apply himself to the others : And thus the workmen who had entered into the combination would not only fail of their object, and be obliged to return to their work, but, owing to the influx of other labourers into the business during the period of the *strike*, they would be compelled to accept of a lower rate of wages than they had previously enjoyed.

For these reasons, we think it is impossible that any one who will calmly consider the subject can resist coming to the conclusion, that a combination for an improper object, or to raise wages above their proper level, must *cure itself*—that it must necessarily bring its own chastisement along with it :—And if the attention of workmen was not distracted by the interference of Government, they could not but perceive the close and intimate connexion between the offence and the punishment; and a very short experience would be sufficient to satisfy them of the mischiefs attending combinations to procure the gratification of an unreasonable demand, and would effectually hinder their wantonly engaging in them.

This statement is sufficient to show the fallacy of the opinion of those who contend, that if the combination laws were repealed, workmen would be every now and then leaving their employment, and that they would become insolent and overbearing. The experience of the United States is also conclusive on this point. No combination laws exist in that Republic; and yet, although the high rate of wages puts it into the power of every individual to accumulate stock, and consequently, if he pleases, to become idle, the workmen are particularly distinguished for their regular, frugal, and industrious habits. The truth is, that a *strike* is always a subject of the most serious concern to workmen ; and the privations to which it unavoidably exposes them, form a strong presumption that they are honestly impressed with a conviction that the advance of wages claimed by them is moderate and reasonable, and that the *strike* has been forced upon them by the improper resistance of their masters. Even in those cases in which wages are notoriously depressed below the proper level, workmen will always be shy about *striking*, and will resort to it only as a last resource. Such a proceeding instantly deprives them, and those who are dependent on their exertions, of their accustomed means of subsistence ; and in the event of their masters delaying for any considerable period to come to an accommodation, they are driven, from inability to support themselves, either to return to the business they have left, or to engage in employments to which they have not been bred, and which are not congenial to their habits. It is not, therefore, easy to suppose that workmen should often enter into a combination, and proceed to a *strike*, for the purpose of obtaining an unreasonable and exorbitant rise of wages. But if they should be at any time foolish enough to do so, there can be no question whatever that their efforts will be wholly impotent and ineffectual; and that, besides exposing themselves to great temporary hardship and distress, they will in the end have to accept the terms dictated by their masters.

Thus it appears, that if wages are at any time lower than they ought to be, a combination on the part of the workmen is highly proper and expedient, as being one of the best means of inducing their masters to raise them to their proper level. But if wages have already reached their natural limits, the self-interest of the masters will induce them to resist the combination, and the workmen will not obtain another farthing. The laws to prevent combinations are, therefore, either unnecessary, or unjust and injurious. They are unnecessary, whenever the rate of wages is as high as circumstances will permit; and they are unjust and injurious whenever it is below that level. Neither ought it to be forgotten, that whenever an attempt is made to control the operations of workmen, and to suppress their combinations by legislative measures, they uniformly ascribe to these measures an infinitely greater influence and effect than what really belongs to them. They look on them as being the exclusive cause of those reductions in the rate of wages, which must frequently be caused by changes of fashion, by a falling off in the foreign demand for their produce, and by other causes. The strong sense of their injustice, induces them to refer almost every real grievance with which they are affected to the same hated cause; and ultimately, the best institutions come to be viewed only as a part of a system which they conceive has inflicted on them much intolerable oppression.

Even though it were conceded that it is prudent and expedient for Government to interfere to put down a combination to raise wages above their proper level, the concession would be of no real value to the apologists of the combination laws; for the *result of the combination* is, in fact, the only test by which we can discover whether the advance of wages claimed by the workmen has been fair and reasonable, or the reverse. If Government were to refer to the opinion of the masters for information on the subject, they would be taught to consider the best founded claim for a rise of wages as unjust and ruinous: and if, on the other hand, they were to refer to the opinion of the workmen—an opinion which is just as deserving of attention as the other—they would be told that the most exorbitant and unreasonable demand was extremely moderate and proper, and that a compliance with it was imperiously required in the actual circumstances of the case. It is only by the fair and free competition of the parties in the market, that we can discover which of these opposite and contradictory assertions is most consistent with the truth. There neither are, nor is it in the nature of things, that there can be any other means of forming a correct conclusion on the subject. If the workmen are in the right, they will, as they ought, succeed in their object; and if they are wrong, they will be defeated. Every interference of Government in the decision of such questions, must obviously, therefore, be productive only of pure and unmixed evil. As they have no means of informing themselves of the real merits of the case, they must, if they act at all, necessarily act blindly and capriciously: But even if they had such information, it would still be most unadvisable for them to attempt to interfere; as it is certain that every combination for an improper object will be much better and more effectually put down without their assistance than with it.

We must not, however, fall into the error of supposing that combination is an instrument wielded only by the workmen in order to force up their wages. So far from this being the case, it is the favourite means to which *the masters* almost invariably resort, when they wish to reduce wages; and it is clear, that the smaller number of the masters, the close and intimate connexion subsisting among them, their superior intelligence, and the greater amount of their accumulated wealth, must render a combination on their part incomparably more injurious to their servants, than a combination among the latter can ever be to them. And yet, notwithstanding all the boasted impartiality of the English law, *the very same statute which punishes the poor workmen who enter into a combination, with a lengthened, and, in some cases, solitary imprisonment, allows the combining masters to escape, on payment of a trifling penalty of TWENTY POUNDS!!!* But the attaching of similar penalties to a combination of masters to those that are attached to a combination of workmen, would really do very little to render the operation of the law against combinations less grossly partial and unequal. An identity of penalties would certainly give equality to the *letter* of the law, but it would not touch its *spirit and principle,* which are, and always must be, decidedly unfavourable to the workmen. However much it may be desired, it will be found, on examination, to be quite impossible to make the provisions of the combination laws affect the masters as they affect their servants.

If we suppose, for the sake of illustration, that the workmen in the employment of an *individual* master combine together, and proceed to a *strike,* they become liable to all the penalties of the statute; while it is obvious that this same master might, in the absence of all previous intimation of his intentions, inform his workmen, at any moment he pleased, that he meant henceforth to take 10, 20, or 50 per cent. from their wages; and in the event of their refusing to accept his terms, he might instantly dismiss them, without its being possible to indict him for a combination! No one can doubt that it is essential to the best interests of the community that the masters should enjoy this power, and that any attempt to dictate the terms on which they should employ workmen, would stimulate them to transfer their capital abroad, and give a mortal blow to the manufacturing and commercial prosperity of the country. It is evident, however, that so long as masters are possessed of this power, so long should every individual amongst them be considered as forming, of himself, a *perpetual and indivisible combination against his workmen;* and if we are to control the proceedings of the one party, the plainest and most obvious principles of justice require that we should equally control those of the other! Generally speaking, it must be a constant object with every master to reduce the wages of his workmen to the lowest possible limit, as it must be a constant object with the workmen to raise them to the highest; and this is evidently a struggle in which the master has always very great natural and acquired advantages on his side. The most skilfully organized and perfect confederacy on the part of the workmen, can never enable them to act with the secrecy, promptitude, vigour, and decision of the single individual, or *combination sole*, to which they are opposed. The utmost injury, too, that a *strike* can do to the master, is to deprive him for a short period of the productive services of his capital; whereas when workmen are turned out of employment, they are either involved in instant indigence, or are obliged to depend for subsistence on the slender provision they may have accumulated as a resource in old age and sickness. And when such is the case, we ask, whether any thing can be more palpably and glaringly unjust, than to punish workmen for endeavouring *to meet combination by combination ?*—for availing themselves of the only means in their power for defending their interests against the unceasing attacks of their masters? For our part we do not hesitate to say, that it is greatly to be wished that combinations of workmen could be rendered more effectual, and that, consequently, the condition of the parties to the contract of wages could be brought more nearly to correspond.

But, as we have already observed, masters are very seldom satisfied with the tacit and unavowed, though powerful and efficient combination, which each forms against his own workmen. On the contrary, they frequently join together, and concert

4

measures in common, either to oppose the claims of the workmen for an advance of wages, or to enforce their reduction; and
while the comparative fewness of their number enables them to
combine easily, and in such a way as greatly to diminish the chance
of detection, it gives a degree of unity and energy to their resolutions, which can never be expected from the tumultuary, va-
cillating, and unsteady councils of the workmen. ' We rarely
' hear,' says Dr Smith, ' of combinations of masters, though
' frequently of those of workmen. But whoever imagines, upon
' this account, that masters rarely combine, is as ignorant of
' the world as of the subject. *Masters are always, and every-*
' *where, in a sort of tacit, constant, uniform, and sometimes open*
' *and avowed, combination, not to raise the wages of labour above*
' *their actual rate, and frequently even to sink them below it.*
' To violate this combination is everywhere a most unpopular
' action, and a sort of reproach to a master among his neigh-
' bours and equals. We seldom, indeed, hear of this combina-
' tion; because it is the usual, and, one may say, the natural
' state of things, which nobody ever hears of. Masters, too,
' sometimes enter into particular combinations, to sink the
' wages of labour even below their actual rate. These are always
' conducted with the utmost silence and secrecy, till the mo-
' ment of execution; and when the workmen yield, as they
' sometimes do, without resistance, though severely felt by
' them, they are never heard of by other people. '—*Wealth of
Nations,* vol. i. p. 100.

In proof of what is here stated by Dr Smith, of the effect of
combinations among the masters, we may mention the curious,
and, in this respect, important fact, that the average money wages
of type-founders in London are about the same (18s. per week), *
at this moment as in 1770. The type-foundery is a comparatively
limited branch of business, there being only about *ten* founderies,
great and small, in London. Such facilities of combination have
proved, of course, too tempting to be neglected; and the most
perfect and complete union has long subsisted among the masters.
All their measures are concerted in common; and their deliberations are conducted with as much secrecy, and their resolutions
prosecuted with equal constancy, and inflexibility of purpose, as

---

* The type-founders are paid by the piece; but 18s. a week is a-
bout the *average* of their earnings. Strictly speaking, they have got
two advances of wages within the last thirty years; but, from the
greater fineness and delicacy that is now required in the letters, the
workman is obliged to cast a great many more, in order to obtain
the same number of perfect ones. The advance was, therefore, required to keep his money wages from falling, and did not really raise
them.

those of the old decimal fraternity of Venice, to which they have not unaptly been compared. There is good reason, however, for thinking, that had it not been for the operation of the combination laws, the workmen might, by confederating together, and acting in concert, have made head against this combination, and forced their masters to raise their wages. But as the law now stands, any such proceeding would only serve to involve them in additional difficulties—to add persecution and imprisonment to the most squalid and abject poverty!

It is an admitted principle, that wherever competition is perfectly free, the rate of wages in those employments which are particularly noxious or disagreeable, must be elevated so much above the common level, as to afford a fair and reasonable compensation for the privations to which the workmen are exposed. The truth of this principle is too self-evident to require illustration; and as the business of the type-founders is of the most unwholesome and most disagreeable kind, their wages must, but for artificial impediments, have been comparatively high. The type-founders are constantly on their legs, with their heads over a furnace of nearly red hot metal, consisting of a compound of iron, lead, and antimony, the fumes of which are particularly deleterious. They are, in consequence, exposed to various diseases peculiar to that trade only, and which are reckoned so very destructive, that it is not unusual to exclude type-founders from becoming members of Benefit Clubs and other Friendly Societies. And yet, in despite of all this, from the facility with which apprentices may be obtained, and the almost insuperable obstacles which the combination laws afterwards throw in the way of the workmen leaving their employment and obtaining a rise of wages, it is a fact, that there is hardly one of the *more extensive* trades in the metropolis, and in which of course the combination among the masters is less complete, wherein, notwithstanding their superior healthiness and agreeableness, the rate of wages is not much higher than among the type-founders. The wages even of tailors are a full half higher! And we are informed that the wages of nailors, a species of employment which approaches pretty closely to that of type-founders, only that it is much more extensive, were the same in 1770 as those of the type-founders; but instead of remaining stationary, they are now about *double* the amount of the latter!

We know too that it is a common practice in many trades, when any of the workmen in the employment of a particular master either leave him, or are dismissed, to send a circular note to the other masters informing them of the circumstance, and warning them not to engage the individuals in question! On one occasion the saddlers of London and Westminster held a meeting, and publicly resolved, that ' *they would engage no jour-* ' *neyman saddler whatever, without first obtaining from his last* ' *master an account of his conduct during the time he was in his* ' *employ.*' This is combination in its worst and most offensive shape—combination not for the mere purpose of resisting a claim for a rise of wages, or of enforcing their reduction, but of proscribing every workman who may have, however unde- signedly, given offence to a master—And the fact, that such combinations are publicly avowed and vigorously supported, at the very moment that the workman who combines to raise his wages is prosecuted with as much rigour as if he had been guilty of the most atrocious crime, certainly forms a singular feature in the far-famed justice of England!

We should never have done were we to attempt to lay be- fore our readers a tithe of the information of which we are pos- sessed, respecting combinations of masters against their work- men. The following, however, may be regarded as affording a pretty fair specimen of the spirit by which such associations are generally actuated, and of the means to which they resort to carry their purpose:—

The paper-makers of Scotland were long, and, for any thing we know to the contrary, still are, engaged in an intimate union and confederacy, one of the principal objects of which seems to have been to keep down the wages of their workmen to the lowest possible rate. In 1799 this formidable confederacy resolved to take 2s. a week from the wages of their journeymen; and on the latter remonstrating, *the whole papermakers of Scotland were turn- ed out of employment by their masters on the same day!* After being deprived of their ordinary means of subsisting themselves for about three months, the masters agreed to take them back at the *old wages,*—a pretty substantial proof that the proposed reduction had not been necessary. In 1804, the continued relative lowness of wages in the paper-making business induc- ed several of the journeymen to leave it, and to seek employ- ment in other trades; but though no combination had been formed amongst them, the masters immediately held a meeting, and printed and published resolutions, in which, besides de- claring that they would give no increase of wages, they resolv- ed, that *the names of the journeymen who left their service should be published, the public at large cautioned not to receive them into any other employment, and the Justices of the Peace requested to proceed against them as vagrants!* The workmen continued to submit with exemplary patience for three years longer, to this unprovoked attempt to reduce them to a state of villen- age. And it was not till 1807 that they presented Petitions, written by Mr Sprot, Procurator-fiscal for the City of Edinburgh, humbly beseeching their masters to raise their wages. The supplication was indignantly rejected; and, in consequence, a large proportion of the men left their employment, and many of them entered into other businesses, while not a few emigrated to other countries. The confederated masters, however, did not even yet despair of carrying their point, and of forcing those whom they really seem to have considered as a species of ' hereditary bondsmen' back to their service. To effect this object, they entered into an offensive and defensive alliance with *the papermakers of England,* and resolved, in concurrence with the latter, that no master should, under certain specified forfeitures, allow his workmen any advance of wages, and that criminal informations should be filed against those who had withdrawn from their employment, in the Court of Justiciary !

We state these facts, not as forming matter of charge against the masters, but to show the practical bearing and real effect of combinations amongst them. That they should enter into such confederacies, is natural, and we really do not blame them for it: We are only anxious that the same freedom of combining should be extended to the workmen, and that each party should be left, without any interference on the part of Government, to support their respective pretensions as they think best. Hitherto the law has run altogether in favour of the stronger side; and we have yet to learn that a single master has been a-merced in the trifling statutory penalty for entering into a combination to depress wages, or to resist their rise. How, indeed, could it be otherwise, when one of the Judges* of the land has not hesitated to declare from the Bench, that any master who should concede the demands of his workmen, who had struck for a rise of wages, ought to be considered as an enemy to his country ! There is no meaning in language if this be not encouraging combination, and calling on the masters to confederate together to resist a demand which, for any thing that the Judge could possibly know to the contrary, might be perfectly fair and reasonable. The cruel and tyrannical conduct of many masters to those in their service, is not so much their fault as it is the fault of this unjust system of legislation. When we cast the poor workman bound hand and foot at the feet of his master, and tell the latter that he may trample on him with impunity, can we be surprised at his sometimes exercising this power? Does any one imagine for a moment that the master papermakers of Scotland would ever have acted as they did, had it not been for the confidence

---

* Mr Justice Best, at a trial at Chester in 1817.

placed by them in the *partiality* of the law, and a belief that, by
its assistance, they would be able to force their journeymen back
to their employment at the old rate of wages? It is the bane
of the combination laws that, while they encourage and prompt
the most humane and indulgent masters to resist an advance of
wages, even when the claim for it is well founded, they furnish
those of a different character, and who may be disposed to act
oppressively, with the means of indulging their vindictive feelings, and, in some measure, of dictating to the whole trade.
Instead of that kind, conciliatory manner which a master ought
always to exhibit towards the labourers in his employment, and
which, were the latter relieved from restraint, he would always find it *for his advantage* to exhibit, the combination laws
have done all that it was possible for any laws to do, to render him haughty, domineering, and capricious,—to impress
him with a conviction that he is of a superior *caste*, and that
the labouring poor neither have, nor ought to have, the same
rights as himself. The poor are sensible of this ignominious
treatment, and they naturally and deeply resent it. The combination laws have taught both masters and workmen to believe,
that there is one measure of justice for the rich and another for
the poor. They have thus set the interests and the feelings of
these two great classes in direct and hostile opposition to each
other; and have, in consequence, done more to engender a
deadly hatred between the different orders of society—to turn
the masters into petty despots, and the workmen into treache-
rous and rebellious slaves, than can be easily conceived or imagined by those who are not pretty intimately acquainted with
the state of society in the manufacturing districts. For the fair,
open, and candid proceedings of men honestly endeavouring to
advance themselves in society, and to sell their labour at the
highest price, the combination laws have given us nocturnal
meetings, secret cabals, and oaths of privacy!

In order to be effectual, legislative enactments must proceed
on some recognised principle of justice and utility; for it is absurd to suppose that the bulk of mankind will ever yield a willing obedience to a law which they consider repugnant to the
plainest principles of justice, and subversive of their own best
interests. Now, this is notoriously the case with the combination laws. Their object is to prevent the labouring class from
resorting to the only means by which they can maintain their
proper place in society, and protect themselves against the
combined efforts of those who have all the natural and solid
advantages of accumulated wealth and political influence on
their side. In consequence, there is scarcely a workman to be

found who does not consider it as a bounden duty to embrace every opportunity of acting in the teeth of their most positive enactments. All the means which the intelligence, the cunning, and the privations of workmen can suggest, for defeating and thwarting their operation, are resorted to from a thorough conviction of their gross partiality and unfairness. Unfortunately, however, the mischief does not stop here. The mere breaking through an unjust and absurd regulation, if it be a fault at all, is certainly one of a very venial description. The real evil consists not so much in what is *actually done*, as in what *it stimulates to do*;—in the contempt which it is but too apt to generate for all the institutions which have received the sanction of society, and which are necessary to its existence. Men of reflecting habits and dispositions distinguish between those laws which are either oppressive and unjust, or unnecessary and inexpedient, and those which conspire to secure the property, the liberties, and the rights of the different classes. However much such persons may deprecate the anomalous and absurd proceedings of legislators, they will give no countenance to the efforts of those who would not scruple, in order to get rid of a bad law, to subvert *all* the institutions of society. But the generality of men are not actuated by such motives. The odium which attaches itself to a partial and unjust law, provided, as in the case in question, its operation be very widely and generally felt, communicates itself to others. The poacher, who is as much persecuted and harassed for killing a hare or a partridge as if he had been guilty of the most atrocious crime, instead of being reclaimed by such harsh treatment, most commonly endeavours to *deserve* the punishment he receives, and becomes a robber and a murderer. Whenever we have made one bold and decisive step in opposition to one or other of the positive enactments of the law, our respect for the rest is necessarily very much weakened.—*C'est le premier pas qui coute.*—The flagrant injustice of a single part infects and contaminates the whole. The generality of men invariably lay the abuse of a principle to the charge of the principle itself; and because the Legislature have unjustly prevented workmen from combining together to raise wages, they may not be disinclined, should a convenient opportunity present itself, to revenge themselves by combining together to overturn the Legislature!

On every ground, therefore, both of justice and expediency, it appears to us, that the repeal of the combination laws would be an extremely wise and salutary measure. Until they are repealed, the terms of the contract between masters and workmen will never be adjusted, as they always ought to be, on the fair principle of free and unrestrained competition. We defy any one to show that these laws have been productive of a single good effect. That combinations of workmen, as well as of masters, may be, and sometimes are, formed for the accomplishment of improper objects, we readily allow. But we have shown that these combinations will, when let alone, inevitably cure themselves, and that the efforts of Government to suppress them are both uncalled for and unnecessary, and oppressive and unjust. Every individual who is not a slave, must be entitled to demand any price for his labour that he thinks proper ; and if one individual may do this, why may not fifty, or five thousand, demand the *same* price? A criminal act can never be generated by the mere multiplication of acts that are perfectly innocent. We are not to confound the power and the right to set a price on one's own labour, with the reasonableness of that price. It is the business of those who are the buyers of labour, and not of the Government, to decide whether the price set on it is reasonable or not. If they think it is unreasonable, they may, and they certainly *will*, refuse to buy it, or to hire the workmen ; and as the latter cannot long subsist without employment, necessity will oblige them to moderate their demands. This, then, is plainly not a case for public interference and official regulation. The maxim—*Nec deus intersit, nisi dignus vindice nodus*—is still more applicable in politics than in poetry. But here interference is as *unjust* as it is unnecessary. To take from workmen the power of demanding any price they please for their labour, and of withdrawing from their employments if they do not obtain it, is to deprive them of the power of freely disposing of the only property they possess, and is, in effect, inviting their masters to treat with them as they would treat with slaves. Neither can it be doubted, that the abolition of this partial and oppressive system of legislation would really be as much for the advantage of the masters as of the workmen. The former being capitalists, must necessarily be far more deeply interested in the preservation of the public tranquillity ; and it is, therefore, of comparatively great importance to them that every law or regulation, which, at the same time that it is essentially unjust, has a powerful tendency to irritate and inflame the great mass of the population, should be repealed. And that such is the real character, and such the effect of the combination laws, none can doubt. Whatever advantage they give the masters over the workmen, is *unjustly* given them ; though, by rendering the services of workmen in some measure compulsory, and preventing them from feeling the full force of some of the most powerful motives which stimulate men to be industrious, it may be questioned, whether they do not really render the *quantity of labour that is actually performed* dearer than it would be were they abolished. But, admitting that they do confer a real advantage on the masters, still it is plain that they can have no just title to what they obtain at the expense of another, and certainly not less valuable, part of the community: and it is farther plain, that Government cannot continue them in the possession of this unjust advantage, without alienating the affections, and exasperating the mass of the labouring poor, and, consequently, without greatly endangering the safety and tranquillity of the state, and paving the way for convulsions and bloodshed.

We have heard it said that the combination laws are advantageous, because they tend to keep wages down ! But it is a miserable error to suppose that low wages can ever be advantageous. If the condition of the labourers be depressed, the prosperity of the other classes can rest on no solid foundation. The labourers always form the great mass of the population of every country ; and whenever their wages are reduced to the lowest limits, they must of necessity subsist on the coarsest and scantiest fare. Men placed in such circumstances are without any sufficient motive to be industrious, and, instead of activity and enterprise, we have sloth, barbarism and ignorance. The example of such individuals, or bodies of individuals, as submit quietly to have their wages reduced, and who are content if they get only the bare necessaries of life, ought never to be held up for public imitation. On the contrary, every thing should be done to make such indifference be esteemed disgraceful. The essential interests of society require that the rate of wages should be elevated as high as possible— that a taste for the comforts, luxuries, and enjoyments of life should be widely diffused, and, if possible, interwoven with the national habits and prejudices. A low rate of wages, by rendering it impossible for increased exertions to obtain any considerable increase of comforts and conveniences, effectually hinders any such exertions from ever being made, and renders the labourer idle, sluggish, and indifferent. But the desire to rise in the world, and to improve our condition, is deeply seated in the human breast, and can never be wholly eradicated; and whenever wages have been increased, and new conveniences and enjoyments made attainable by the labourer, indolence has uniformly given way to exertion; a taste for these conveniences and enjoyments has gradually diffused itself; increased exertions have been made to attain them ; and ultimately, it has been thought discreditable to be without them.

It has, we know, been repeatedly affirmed, that high wages

are more productive of idleness and dissipation than of exertion; and that, if labourers can earn as much in three or four days as will support them a week, they will absent themselves during the remaining days from their employment. Nothing, however, can be more marvellously incorrect than these representations—more completely at variance with principle and experience. It is certainly true, that individuals will be found in every country and situation of life, who are careless of the future, and attentive only to present enjoyment; but these always form a very small and even inconsiderable minority of each particular class. Whatever may be the case with this or that individual, the principle of accumulation always predominates in aggregate bodies over the passion for expense. That the *amor habendi crescit quantum ipsa pecunia crescit*, is as certainly true of the labourer as of the miser. Industry, as Dr Smith has observed, is like every other virtue, *it improves in proportion to the encouragement it receives.*

If an increase of wages ever discourages industry, it must be the industry of the wretch who has previously been working for mere subsistence, or the forced industry of the indolent and the dissolute; and even to produce this effect on them, the increase must have been *sudden and transitory*, not gradual and permanent. We are warranted in affirming, that a steadily high rate of wages, never has had, and never will have, any such effect. The poor have, upon plain practical questions that touch their immediate interests, the same understanding, the same penetration, and the same regard to consequences as those who are rich. It is indeed a contradiction, and an absurdity to pretend, that if labourers are capable of earning, by an ordinary degree of application, more than is sufficient to support them, they alone, of all the various classes of society, will spend the surplus in riot and debauchery. They have the same common sense, they are actuated by the same passions, feelings and principles, as other men; and when such is the case, it is clear they cannot generally be guilty of such inconsiderate conduct. But, to lay aside general reasoning, does not the state of industry, in countries where the natural rate of wages is low, compared with its state in those where it is high, substantiate all we have now said? Have the *low* wages of the people of Ireland, Poland, and Hindostan, made them industrious? or the *high* wages of the Americans, the English, and the Hollanders, made them lazy, riotous, and profligate? Just the contrary. The former are as notoriously and proverbially indolent, as the latter are laborious, active, and enterprising. The experience of all ages and nations proves that high wages are the keenest

spur—the most powerful stimulus to unremitting and assiduous
exertion.   Wherever the rate of wages is high, workmen have
not only a considerable command over the necessaries and
conveniences of life, but also a considerable power of accumulation: And as few are so brutified as to be insensible of the
blessings of independence, they almost universally endeavour
to avail themselves of this power to emerge from poverty and to attain to opulence.   Every individual, placed in
such circumstances, *feels* that he derives a direct and tan-
gible advantage from the institution of the right of property,
and that otherwise he should not be able peaceably to enjoy
the fruits of his industry; and he consequently becomes personally interested in its support, and in the support of the public
tranquillity.   It is not when wages are high and provisions a-
bundant, but in periods when they are low, and the harvest less
productive than usual, that the manufacturing and thickly peopled districts are disturbed by popular clamours and radical
commotions.   Nor is this the case in Britain only, but in all
other countries.   *Dans aucune histoire, on ne rencontre un seul*
trait qui prouve que l'aisance du peuple par le travail a nui à son
obeissance. *   Whatever may be said or written to the contrary,
there cannot be a doubt that high wages are by far the most effectual means of promoting industry, and attaching the bulk of
the people to the institutions under which they live: while
they have the farther advantage of insuring a comfortable subsistence and good education to youth; and of preventing sickness and old age from being driven to seek a wretched asylum
in workhouses and hospitals.

Nothing, therefore, can be so signally disadvantageous, so
overwhelmingly disastrous to any country, as a permanent degradation in the rate of wages, or a decline in the opinions of
the labouring class respecting what is necessary for their comfortable and decent subsistence.   And in the absence of all other
reasons for their repeal, the fact, that the combination laws have
a decided tendency to reduce wages, ought to be held to be
conclusive of their impolicy, and of the propriety of abolishing
them.   No country can be flourishing when the rate of wages
is low, and none can be long depressed when it is high.   The
labourers are the sinews of agriculture, of manufactures, and of
commerce.   Their numbers are not estimated, like those of the
other classes, by hundreds or thousands, or even by hundreds
of thousands, but by *millions!*   It is by their labour that our

---

* Forbonnais, *Recherches sur les Finances de France.*   Tome i.
p. 111.

machinery is constructed and kept in motion; and it is by their
industry, ingenuity and frugality, that we are enabled to support burdens that could hardly be supported by any other
people. Every thing then that may have the slightest tendency
to depress their condition, or to sink them in the scale of society, ought to be most particularly guarded against. Those
who feed and clothe all the rest, ought themselves to be
' *well fed and well clothed.* ' The labourers are the *foundation* of the social pyramid; and so long as they are treated
impartially and fairly, and wages continue high, the foundation
will be stable; for so long will they be peaceable, orderly, and
industrious. But if we continue to enforce the provisions of the
combination act:—If we continue to treat the labourers as a degraded *caste*, and to prevent them from setting a price on their
labour, and from doing that which their masters are every day
in the habit of doing, the desire to avenge such barefaced injustice and oppression, will supplant the desire to save and rise
in the world, and they will infallibly become idle, dissipated,
and rebellious. The spirit of industry, by which they have
been so eminently distinguished, will gradually evaporate, and
with it the morals, prosperity, and tranquillity of Britain.

As to Scottish combinations, we scarcely know how to talk
of them,—because we are (that is to say, the author of this
article is) utterly unacquainted with the forms, and even the
very phraseology, of the law of Scotland; and there are some
things in the books which he has looked at on the subject so
extraordinary, that he is forced to suppose that he is altogether in a dream, although he must confess himself wholly unable to discover where the delusion lies. It is believed, however,
that the whole mystery is to be found in a principle of Scotch criminal law, which is explained very distinctly in the late learned
work of Mr Hume on that science. This principle seems to
be, that the Court of Justiciary, which is the supreme criminal
tribunal of that country, has power to declare any thing a crime
that it pleases, without precedent or statute. This maxim seems,
to an uninitiated person, to be as curious as any of the wonders
which it is used to explain. But it must of course be assumed
(though we have not met with any body who has been able to
point out the precise act), that Parliament must have conferred this authority by some special statute, and made that
delegation of its powers to this particular Court, which no one
ever heard of its doing to any other. He who reflects on
the Scotitsh law of combination, therefore, as a political economist, must begin by subduing his mind to the reception of this
principle as an ultimate fact; and then he must next reflect,

that when the catalogue of crimes depends merely on the opinion of a single tribunal, composed of a small number of individuals, it must vary according as the persons or the views of these individuals change. Thus prepared, he may stomach the following statement of a chapter of Scotch Criminal Law, which is taken entirely from the learned work that has been already named.

It appears that, in the year 1808, combination was adjudged *not* to be an indictable offence in Scotland. The combination statute was held not to apply to that country; but in that year, certain journeymen papermakers were brought to trial at common law. This was the *first* instance in which the judgment of the Court of Justiciary was fairly demanded on such a case. ' For, ' says Mr Hume, ' though stated ' in certain libels' (indictments), ' the matter *had not been* ' *deliberately considered on any former occasion.* ' * The Court was of opinion, and accordingly pronounced a legal judgment declaring,—that *combination was no offence;* that is, no offence for which an indictment lay in a Scotch Criminal Court. If this judgment had proceeded simply and firmly on the principle, that since there was no statute, and no precedent, for declaring the union of workmen to be a crime, it was not the province of a court of law to make one, it would have stood upon sure and intelligible ground. But it appears that this view was taken by nobody, at least on the Bench. It is stated, that the majority of the Judges held combination not to be criminal, merely because it ' did not imply that degree of ' *baseness or depravity* in the confederates which were essential, ' in the opinion of these Judges, to the notion of an indict- ' able crime. ' As to the views of the rest of the Court, it is fortunate that we can state them in the words of the author we have already referred to ; because, otherwise, we should certainly not have been able to conjecture upon what grounds *a court of law* should enact a particular arrangement, the expediency or inexpediency of which depends merely upon delicate principles of commercial policy, to be not only of a criminal character, but so criminal that the man who was accessory to it, should be liable to be apprehended and punished without the slightest previous intimation that what he was doing was wrong. But the following, it seems, were the judicial views of those who thought that this was an indictable offence. Before quoting them, we must request the reader to observe them narrowly, and to endeavour to ascertain, as he is going along,

---

* Vol. I. p. 489, Ed. 1819.

whether combination was to be punished, because it was *a fraud*,—or an *infringement of the liberty of the subject*,—or *extortion*, or the *setting up of an arbitrary government*,—or *sedition*,—or *treason*.

' Three of the Judges dissented from this judgment,—and on
' these grounds : That a combination to raise wages by the sud-
' den striking of work, is a measure of a compulsive character,
' and implies a deliberate and mischievous purpose to distress
' the employer and the public : That by means of such pro-
' ceedings, labour has *a false price* affixed to it, *in defraud of*
' the buyèr, and to the great prejudice of manufacture and
' trade : That they are an infringement of the freedom of the
' market, which it is one of the main objects of policy in every
' state to secure : That they are no less *an infringement of the
' freedom of the subject*, which does not consist in liberty of per-
' son only, but of conduct,—in the right of doing as one pleases,
' in all matters not commanded or forbidden by law ; and,
' among others, that of hiring out one's service, to whom and
' on what terms one chuses : That an *extortion* is here practised
' against the employer and the public, and this by means which
' strike at the vitals of order and civilized society, and truly
' amount to *an usurpation of sovereign authority ;* in as much as
' there is here an attempt *to set up an arbitrary and uncontrol-
' lable dominion in the State,* which shall enforce, at its own plea-
' sure, what the legislature have never thought advisable to at-
' tempt : That any association which aims at power or perma-
' nency, or proposes to do its work by means of such instruments,
' requires his Majesty's authority, and, without it, is *downright
' usurpation;* and *that to discipline multitudes into common mea-
' sures, even in what is innocent, is an interference with the rights of
' Government,* which is justly regarded with jealousy in all well
' regulated states, and is permitted, if at all, with circumspec-
' tion, and under precautions : That we have, in the present in-
' stance, the creation of an engine of prodigious power, readily
' convertible to the purposes of *sedition and democratic oppres-
' sion,* and to favour, according to the pressure of the times, the
' projects of *designing demagogues,* or the vices or follies of the
' rash or turbulent : That such confederacies tend, in the ex-
' ample, to the highest and most extensive mischief; and as the
' thing is thus marked, not with one, but with many of the pro-
' per characters of a crime (for a corrupt and malignant heart
' is nowise indispensable), so, according to the settled principles
' of our practice, *it falls under the wholesome correction of our
' common law, and may competently be chastised with a suitable
' and seasonable censure,* before the evil grows too strong, and

' spreads too far to be subdued, *without the help of statutable and*
' *extraordinary means.*' *

This being the state of the law, we must suppose that there
are, of course, no Bible Societies in that part of Great Britain called Scotland; because the people of that country are
extremely loyal, and it seems that there, ' to discipline mul-
' titudes into common measures, *even in what is innocent*, is
' an interference with the rights of Government,' and falls
under that ' *wholesome correction,*' by which the office-bear-
ers may be imprisoned or transported, or scourged, ' without
' the help of statutable and extraordinary means.' These
doctrines, however, did not go down in the year 1808. The
lieges were judicially told, in October of that year, that
Combination, notwithstanding these strong and legal considerations, was not an indictable offence. But the workmen,
if any, who were induced, by this decision, to resist their
masters with their own weapons, soon found themselves in
a trap; for it seems, that, before three years had passed,
combination *had become* a crime. Some shoemakers were
indicted in the beginning of 1811; and although there were
other objections to the indictment, which saved them from being tried, it appears that the Court had, by that time, so far
changed its views as to intimate an opinion that the prisoners
had been guilty of a punishable offence.

Still, however, there was no actual conviction. Therefore, †
' a further *experiment* was made,' by indicting some journeymen cotton-weavers. These persons were tried and found
guilty; and had an opportunity of knowing something of the
wholesome correction of our common law. The several pan-
nels ' had sentences of imprisonment in proportion to their re-
' spective degrees of activity in the cause, *for four*, *nine*, *and*
' *eighteen months*, *till they should find caution to keep the peace*
' *for three years.*' (Hume, vol. i. p. 491.) It was stated, not as
the essence, but as a mere aggravation of the guilt of these persons, that, in furtherance of the combination, they had been
guilty of violence and other outrages. The simple combination, *by striking work*, was held to be enough, though they were
convicted both of this and of the aggravation. But in the next
case, which occurred in March 1813, a workman was expressly
found ' *not* guilty of any of the acts of violence, intimidation or
' extortion charged;' and he was *punished for simply combin-*

---

* Hume, Vol. I. p. 489. Ed. 1819.
† Hume, vol. i. p. 490, ed. 1819.

ing. In all these cases, it had at least been required that the
men should have struck work. This at the least was thought
to be necessary, as the palpable overt act by which combination is generally known, and by which alone it generally proves
injurious. But even this was speedily dispensed with; and, in
the year 1818, two colliers were convicted for their accession to
a combination, in the course of which there had been no violence, or intimidation, or extortion, *or actual striking of work,*
but simply an intimation to the masters, that if their wages were
not raised, they *would* strike. It was held that ' *a threat* to
' strike work is a true and substantial compulsory measure. '

Thus, in the course of nine years and a half, did the law of
Scotland, administered by a Court having the power to declare
new offences, vibrate between combination effected not merely
by striking work, but by great violence, being no crime at all,
and its being a crime, when effected by simple union, even without
any striking whatever. Within this period, the paper-makers,—
though accused of combination accompanied by violence,—were
found innocent; and the weavers, though accused of combination without violence, were imprisoned from four to eighteen
months. The reflection with which this history is closed by
the learned author, from whom we have taken it, is in these
words. ' This *new* point of dittay seems, therefore, now to be
' thoroughly established ; *and it furnishes another illustration*
' *of the character of our common law, and of its power to chas-*
' *tise, of its own native vigour, all wrongs and disorders, as the*
' *state of society brings them forth, which are found to be mate-*
' *rially dangerous to the public welfare.* ' We can add nothing
to this, except that one of the Judges (the late Lord Meadow-
bank), after giving an exposition of the evils attending a combination of workmen, suddenly changes the whole of his reasoning, when he comes to speak of the other combination out of
which this one invariably grows, and lays it down in direct
terms, that ' the combination of *masters* is in general *beneficial*
' to the public, and to the workmen they employ. ' * We apprehend our readers will consider this as a sufficient specimen
of the law of Scotland with respect to Combinations—and shall
only add, that if the definite, and comparatively mild statutes of
England are now to be repealed as unjust and oppressive, the
recent and variable rigour of the Scottish common law, on this
subject, must at the same time be corrected.

Besides the unjust and oppressive restraints laid on workmen
by the combination laws, a variety of statutes have been passed

---

* Report of Speeches, Burnett's Criminal Law, Appendix, p. 37.

to prevent them from emigrating, and even to hinder them from exporting any portion of the produce of their industry, when in the shape of machinery, to other countries. Thus, it is enacted by the 5th Geo. I. cap. 28, extended and confirmed by the 23d Geo. III. cap. 13, that any person who shall ' contract with, ' entice, persuade, or endeavour to persuade, solicit or seduce, ' any manufacturer, workman, or artificer in wool, mohair, ' cotton, or silk; or in iron, steel, brass, or other metal; or ' any clockmaker, watchmaker, or *any other* manufacturer, ' workman, or artificer in any other of the *manufactures* of ' Great Britain or Ireland, *of what nature or kind soever*, to go ' out of this kingdom into any foreign country not within the ' dominions of the Crown, is liable to be indicted, and to forfeit ' 500*l.*, to suffer imprisonment for twelve months, and until the ' forfeiture is paid; every subsequent offence being further pu- ' nishable with 1000*l.* penalty, and two years' imprisonment. ' It is also enacted by the same statute, that any artificer who shall have quitted the kingdom and settled in a foreign country, and who shall not return within six months after warning given him by the British ambassador where he resides, shall be deemed an alien, shall forfeit all his goods, and be made incapable of receiving any gift or legacy !

Before an emigrant can pass the customhouse, he must be furnished with a certificate, signed by the churchwardens and overseers of the parish. This certificate certifies and declares, that ' the bearer is not, nor hath ever been, a manufacturer or ' artisan in wool, iron, steel, brass, or any other metal; nor is ' he, nor hath he ever been, a watchmaker, or clockmaker, or ' any *other artificer whatsoever*. ' And to establish the authenticity of this document, it must be signed by a Justice of the Peace, certifying that Messrs so and so are the churchwardens and overseers of said parish !

With respect to machinery, it is enacted, by the 14th Geo. III. cap. 71, that if any person exports any tools or utensils used in the silk, cotton, linen, or woollen manufactures, he forfeits the same and 200*l.*; and the captain of the ship having knowledge thereof, likewise forfeits 200*l.* The punishment for this offence was further increased by the 21st Geo. III. cap. 37, which, besides the penalty of 200*l.*, subjects the offender to imprisonment for twelve months; and by the 22d Geo. III. cap. 60, the penalty is increased to 500*l.*, exclusive of the imprisonment !

The extreme hardship of these regulations is obvious. What can be more oppressive than to prevent an artisan from carrying either his labour, or the produce of his labour, to the best market? Why should he be forced to remain in this country, if he supposes he can improve his condition by removing to another?

All the best writers on public law agree in opinion, that it would require very strong reasons to justify the government of a free state in restraining the emigration of its subjects. * The Romans granted full liberty to any one who chose to withdraw from under their government; a privilege which Cicero justly regarded as of the highest importance, and as being essential to the preservation of the public freedom. *O jura præclara, atque divinitus, jam inde a principio Romani nominis, a majoribus nostris comparata —— Ne quis invitus civitate mutetur, neve in civitate maneat invitus. Hæc sunt enim fundamenta firmissima nostræ libertatis, sui quemque juris et retinendi, et dimittendi, esse dominum.* (Orat. pro L. C. Balbo, cap. 13.)

The disadvantages to which individuals are subjected in their native land must be very great indeed, to render force and unjust restraints necessary to retain them in it. All our prejudices and affections are in favour of the country of our birth. It is endeared to us by the tenderest ties.—The sea which the emigrant has to pass appears, to use the words of Mr Malthus, like the separation of death from his friends, his kindred, and the companions of his former years. And except when a spirit of enterprise is added to a strong sense of the evils of poverty, and a lively expectation of being able to escape from them in another country, few will be disposed to snap asunder the ties which bind them to the homes of their fathers, but will

    ‘ Rather tamely bear the ills they have,
    Then fly to others which they know not of.’

But the restraints on the emigration of artisans are as impolitic and inexpedient as they are unjust and unnecessary.—Whenever population is redundant and the wages of labour depressed, every facility ought to be given to emigration. Were it carried to a considerable extent, it would have the effect, by lessening the supply of labour in the market, to raise the rate of wages, and to improve the condition of the labourers who remain at home. Nor, while it would produce these good effects, is there the least risk that it could be carried too far, or that the supply of labourers could be injuriously diminished: For, the rise of wages that must always follow every considerable emigration, would not only stimulate the principle of population, but would

---

* See Grotius par Barbeyrac, Tome I. p. 306. Puffendorff par Barbeyrac, Tome II. p. 600. Burlamaqui's Political Law, p. 119, Eng. Trans.

also weaken the motives to emigrate, at the same time that it would give new strength to the natural repugnance which every one has to leave his native country. Government, indeed, by giving bounties and encouragements to emigrants to Canada, South Africa, and Van Diemen's Land, has recently acknowledged the justice of this reasoning. They have acknowledged that emigration is not only harmless, but that it ought, in certain cases, to be artificially promoted. And having gone thus far, they are bound in consistency to propose the repeal of those vexatious restrictions which prevent its being carried on freely.

But then it is said, that the places to which Government have authorized and encouraged emigration are subject to the Crown of Great Britain, and that there is a wide and material difference between allowing artisans to carry their industry from one part to another in our own dominions, and allowing them to settle among foreigners, and to become the instructors of our rivals and enemies! Surely, however, no one can be so silly as to suppose that even a fourth part of those who emigrate to Canada have any intention of continuing there, or that they can be detained in it a moment longer than they please. The artisans who are desirous of settling in the United States go to Canada, because they are not permitted to sail directly for the place of their destination. When there, they avail themselves of the earliest opportunity of crossing the frontier. And the result of the whole is, that in despite of penalties, imprisonment, forfeiture of property, and the certificate of churchwardens and Justices, there is not a single village in the United States which does not swarm with English artificers! Our regulations fetter emigration; but they are completely ineffectual for the intended purpose of checking it altogether, and of preventing our artisans from finding their way to foreign countries;—while, by forcing them to take a circuitous route and increasing their expenses, they cause the emigration of those who have saved a little capital rather than of those who are comparatively poor, and whom the country could have most advantageously spared.

The unconditional repeal of the laws preventing emigration could not occasion any considerable influx of British artisans into the Continent. The lowness of wages in the Continental States, the difference of customs and habits, and above all of language, are obstacles to extensive emigration which it is almost impossible to overcome. There are really no grounds whatever for thinking that the utmost freedom of communication between this country and the Continent could do more than facilitate the emigration of such of the better educated and more aspiring class of our artisans as are able to act as overseers; and all the harshness and severity of the existing restraints is insufficient to prevent such persons from dispersing themselves over every quarter of the globe. At this moment all the principal cotton factories of the Continent are furnished with English overseers and machine-makers. On Mr Augustus Lee, of the house of Phillips and Lee, of Manchester, being asked by the Committee of the House of Commons, appointed in 1816, to inquire into the state of the children employed in our factories, whether the machinery used in the cotton factories at Rouen and Paris was inferior to ours, he answered, ' *I saw some* ' *mills with machinery better than the average of ours, and the very* ' *latest improvements.*' He further stated, that the principal factories in France were furnished ' with English overseers and machine-makers, ' and that he had frequently met with them in Prussia.—(*Report*, p. 345.) As corroborative of Mr Lee's statement, we may mention, that M. Marcel de Serres, the author of the very valuable statistical work on Austria, in giving an account of the great cotton factory at Pottendorff, near Vienna, states, that the superiority of its yarn is owing to the excellence of its machinery, which was constructed under the direction of the skilful English engineer, Mr ———. And he adds, that there is hardly a factory in the empire, of any considerable extent, where Englishmen are not to be met with. —(Tom. ii. p. 88.)

We have here a striking and unanswerable proof of the inefficiency and absurdity of the restraints laid on the free emigration of artisans. The encouragement given on the Continent to those whose education and attainments fit them to direct the construction of large manufacturing establishments, or to superintend them when constructed, will always prove an overmatch for the pains and penalties of our law, and will procure them a sufficient supply of masters qualified to teach them all our arts. Our regulations are, as we previously observed, really operative only on the poor and ill-educated class of artificers, whose emigration would be equally advantageous to themselves and the country. It is to the United States only that such persons can emigrate; and by preventing their direct transit to that country, and by obliging them to reach it by a comparatively lengthened and difficult route, we do them and ourselves a real injury. Supposing, therefore, that the principle on which the restrictions on emigration are founded were as just and liberal as it is unjust and oppressive, still it would be true that the restrictions are either useless or pernicious:—

They are useless, because they cannot effect the object they have in view; and they are pernicious, because they prevent the e-migration of those whose emigration would be a benefit.

The observations we have already made are sufficient, of them-selves, to show the impolicy of the statutes preventing the ex-portation of Machinery. Of what possible use can it be to pre-vent the exportation of any article, when we cannot prevent the emigration of the artisans by whom that article is manufac-tured? Our restrictions are not really injurious to our foreign rivals, but to ourselves. The superiority to which we have at-tained in manufacturing industry, is owing partly to the com-parative freedom of our constitution, to the absence of all op-pressive feudal privileges, and to our greater security of pro-perty and of personal liberty, and partly to the advantages of our situation and our abundant supplies of coal. Most certainly we have not risen to opulence by the aid of restrictive laws and pro-hibitory regulations, but in despite of them. Instead of accele-rating, they have clogged and retarded our progress. Were the freedom of industry established, our artisans would, at no dis-tant period, become the makers of machinery for every coun-try in the world. Nor would this be in the least degree injuri-ous to our own manufacturers. They would then, as now, en-joy all those moral and natural advantages to which their pre-sent prosperity is entirely owing; while a new source of wealth and fortune would be opened to support and enrich another, and a very numerous class of their fellow-citizens. Our prohibitions do not prevent the French and Germans from obtaining the very best machines. No such thing. Their only effect is, to deprive our artisans of the opportunity of producing them, and consequently of the profit they would make on their sale, or, which is the same thing, to impoverish them for the sake of enriching the artisans of Normandy and Saxony!

Parliament has wisely resisted repeated solicitations to pro-hibit or fetter the exportation of cotton yarn: and it has done so on the ground, that such a prohibition would contribute in-finitely more to encourage the factories on the Continent than to increase the sale of British cotton goods. Now the case with respect to machinery is precisely similar. By prohibiting its exportation, we do not increase the consumption of British ma-nufactures on the Continent; we only force the inhabitants to construct machines for themselves, and to become our rivals and competitors in a branch of industry of which we should otherwise enjoy an almost exclusive monopoly!

Art. III.—1. *On Wages and Combinations.* By R. Torrens, Esq., M.P. 8vo. London: 1834.

2. *Character, Object, and Effects of Trades'-Unions.* 8vo. London: 1834.

3. *Trades'-Unions and Strikes.* 12mo. London: 1834.

4. *The Tendency of Strikes and Sticks to produce low Wages.* By Harriet Martineau. 12mo. Durham: 1834.

THE publications which we have enumerated at the head of this article are only a selection from amongst those which the present crisis in the history of our labouring population has called into existence. Not that the combinations at present subsisting among workmen in various branches of industry, and the Unions into which they are formed, appear to offer any new features of real danger, which should render them subjects of greater apprehension to the community than former associations of the same nature, which have long lasted, and frequently assumed for a time a threatening aspect and character. But they have acquired additional interest in the eyes of all, and in those of the timid great additional importance, from the turbulent state of so large a portion of the manufacturing population in France; from the new language held by their leaders; and, above all, from their approximation towards the co-operative doctrines which a few zealous speculators have so long preached, and with such little success. Until within the last few years, Unions among workmen had no other ostensible object than that which was the real one,—the establishment or maintenance of a fixed rate of wages in a particular employment. Now the writers and orators of these associations often assume a higher tone; they proclaim war against capitalists in general; and hold out the grand project of dividing profits among that class of producers which at present furnishes labour and receives wages,—a project which of course implies a complete social as well as political revolution. For our parts, we believe these visionary schemes, and the applause they have met with, rather to betoken the failing hopes and desperate condition of many of the combinations, the supporters of which require to have their expectations kept alive by extravagant delusion. Those Unions which have been most successful in effecting their immediate object of raising wages, and have consequently been most injurious to our manufactures, and most detrimental to the trade of the towns in which they were established, have always wrought in comparative silence, and confined their exertions to the accomplishment of their particular design, avoiding, above all things, political discussion.* All schemes of a more extended character have hitherto signally failed; and when experience shall have accumulated more materials, it will no doubt be a service to the public, if some writer, as well qualified for the purpose as those we are now reviewing, will present us with a sketch of the circumstances and causes of their failure; of the decline of those various co-operative societies which have been established in London and elsewhere; and of the recent unsuccessful attempt, on the part of the Derby workmen, to establish mills of their own, and commence trading as capitalists. But the late overtures of alliance between the Lodges of the Unions and the zealots of the levelling school in politics, have, of course, given an apparent degree of importance to the former, and attracted more general notice to their proceedings. Above all, however, the recent great strike among the tailors, in London and its vicinity, which lasted more than two months, by bringing the inconvenience of the present differences between masters and men home to the feelings of every one who wears a coat, has had the effect of drawing public attention, in an unprecedented degree, to the subject before us.

The work of Colonel Torrens is chiefly valuable for its exposing, in a clear and forcible style, the fallacy of maintaining that combinations, whether among masters or men, can regulate wages,

---

* It is said that at a recent and famous Liverpool election, the members of a trade agreed to divide their suffrages equally between the candidates, and that the sum of L.1600 was in consequence received and paid into the common stock.

except for a very limited extent in time or space. His reasonings bear the same relation to those of more practical writers on the subject, which the deductions of pure mathematical science bear to their evidences in the operations of nature. It is both curious and instructive, first to trace the unerring principle, and then to examine the obscure and tortuous ways in which the problem is circumstantially worked out, and that same result produced in real life at which the philosopher had arrived by abstraction within the walls of his closet. But we have space only for a very brief analysis of the Colonel's arguments.

Suppose, to take the most favourable case of combination among the masters, that in all trades a forced reduction took place, and in all trades an increase of profit followed. The necessary result—if that increase is to be maintained—must be, that all the additional income of the masters must be spent unproductively. The first who should employ part of his profit as additional capital, must bid for fresh hands, must consequently raise wages, and break up the combination. By working out the details of this principle, and tracing the phenomena which would appear in combinations limited to particular trades, the writer has shown convincingly, to use the words of his conclusion, ' that an effectual combination for the reduction of wages ' cannot by possibility exist.'

To pass to the effects of a combination to raise wages : The maximum of wages, in any given time or country, we must assume to be that point above which wages cannot rise, without reducing the lowest rate of profit at which the capitalist can continue the work of production. Suppose the actual rate of profit to be 10 per cent ; the lowest possible rate of profit 7 per cent. The labourers, by combining, might reduce profits 3 per cent before production would cease. But the moment in which the number of competitors for employment increased, or the moment in which foreign competition lowered the cost of the article to the consumer, would see the ruin of the combination begun. In the first case, wages would fall and profits rise ; in the second, wages would fall and profits remain stationary. And this is the only practical view in which the question affects the industry of England; for no Union among the workmen can check the pressure of their own numbers on the means of employment, or the pressure of foreign production on the markets for English commodities.

The last position requires a more detailed examination ; as it has been argued, that high wages in England can never influence our foreign trade, as long as the rate of profits falls in proportion to the rise of wages, and prices consequently do not increase. Profits being by the supposition 10 per cent in the first instance, the English master's profits fall to 7 per cent, the French master's remain at 10. The Frenchman cannot lower his prices without lowering his profit; he will not, therefore, lower his prices for the sake of an extended market, for the plain reason that he can make 10 per cent on his capital in any occupation. This reasoning is strictly and philosophically correct, upon the suppositions which it assumes. But the fact is, as Colonel Torrens has shown, that in the case of manufactured articles into the production of which fixed capital largely enters, the rate of the Frenchman's profits would rise, while his prices fell, if he could gain a more extended market. Suppose, as before, that 10 per cent is the rate of the Frenchman's profit, of which 5 per cent is the return to his fixed, 5 per cent to his floating capital. Suppose also, that his fixed capital, his mills, machinery, &c. are capable of being employed to produce a far greater quantity than they now do, without the cost of working them being materially increased. In this case, the Frenchman, in order to undersell the Englishman, consents to reduce his profit to 8 per cent on his first cargo of goods : he may now double the quantity produced, and obtain 8 per cent by *expending his floating capital only* in this second speculation ; that is, 3 per cent more than his previous rate of profit. Thus the Colonel is correct in asserting, that ' it ad-' mits of the strictest demonstration, that if additional quantities of ' raw material can be worked up without incurring an additional ' expense for buildings and machinery, the manufacturers of the ' country in which the rate of profit is comparatively high, will ' have an interest in lowering their prices in the foreign market, ' so as to beat out the fabrics of the country in which the rate of ' profit is comparatively low.'

With combinations of masters we have little to do at present; inasmuch as all allow that the dangers which now threaten our industry, proceed from another quarter. It is remarkable that some of the greatest authors in the science of political economy, should have agreed in maintaining that such combinations are far more general and more permanent than those among the men. Having made their observations at a period when the laws against the latter were still in force, and conscious of the unjust principle and ineffective character of those enactments, they seem to have written rather as advocates of the labourers, than as impartial observers. The sentiments of Dr Adam Smith on this subject have often been repeated. M. Say, too, maintained that masters had far greater facilities than workmen for combining : not partially only, but so as to regulate wages generally by their monopoly. But more recent experience must moderate the respect which we pay to the authority of names, however deservedly distinguished in this branch of knowledge. It should seem that neither these writers nor their followers had sufficiently estimated the peculiar control which the fluctuating nature of demand exercises over the resolutions of master manufacturers. If the demand for the goods which they produce pressed upon them in a regular and continued stream ;—if their business was nothing more than the making a steady profit on transactions, the amount and recurrence of which were as regular as the seasons and markets (in a long average of years) of the agriculturist,—then it is evident that they might, with much greater ease, enter into such a tacit confederacy as Dr Smith has described, not to raise wages above a particular level. They might then always calculate the amount of loss to be incurred by desisting from working their mills or their mines for a certain time, and subdue the resistance of their workmen by irresistible force. But the fact is, on the contrary, that the very essence of a master's business, in most of our manufactures, is speculation. He has no power to regulate the amount of orders he may receive, or the time at which they may come. Should a combination be ever so regularly formed, for instance, between the masters of a particular town, a sudden order coming on one of them, and requiring immediate execution, would be sufficient to induce him almost perforce to relinquish the Union, to call in fresh hands, and to offer higher wages. The individual artisan's employment being (however liable to fluctuation) far more regular, *on the whole*, than the profits of the individual master, he can calculate the supposed gain to be made, and the loss to be incurred by a strike, far better than the latter can do. Add to this, that Dr Smith's sanction of public opinion, which he supposes to bind the masters together, is a very weak preventive indeed against the strong stimulus of jealous competition. The committee of a Trades' Union may govern the operatives by intimidation ; the committee of a Masters' Union have no better resource than the censure of their own body, against which the ' nummi in arcâ ' afford a very sufficient consolation.

Another reason which strongly militates against the possibility of effective combinations among the masters, supposing them shortsighted enough to believe that such combinations would eventually increase their profits, is to be found in the large amount of stock which each of them has invested in fixed capital, and the loss which is incurred by leaving it unemployed. The reasoning of Colonel Torrens, with respect to the effect of foreign competition, in underselling goods produced by high wages, is equally applicable here. For the same reason which, on the former supposition, would induce the Frenchman to submit to low profits in the first instance, in order to increase his speculations, the rival manufacturer, in the present case, would be willing to give high wages, and win from the combiners the supply of the market. He would gain on his fixed capital more than he would lose on his floating capital. Hence in trades in which circulating capital is chiefly required, combination may and does take place with much greater facility among the masters; each has less temptation to overbid the other in the labour market; because any raising of wages is attended with much greater loss to him, than to the manufacturer whose capital is chiefly fixed. Therefore it is extremely probable that tacit combinations, of the nature described by Dr Smith, do frequently for a time raise profits in such employments above the ordinary level, to which the influx of fresh capital must speedily reduce them. This, perhaps, chiefly takes place in trades in which manufacture and retail dealing are combined; in which the producer disposes of the object produced to the consumer. Whether the journeymen tailors, on the occasion of their recent strike, were unreasonable or not in their demands (that they were so, few will hesitate in supposing, when it is known that the wages generally received in that trade, and which they struck to increase, are the same in 1834 as they were in 1815, when the prices of most necessaries were a third higher), there is no doubt that among the better masters—those who enjoy the monopoly profits which fashion gives—there is a combination, and that wages are in fact regulated less by supply and demand, than by the balanced leagues of employers and men. It is the consumer who really suffers, and in truth voluntarily suffers, as he is content to make to fashion the sacrifice of almost all the pecuniary saving which the general fall of prices ought to have secured him. But with manufacturers the case is widely different. Shops may be shut, and the capital usually laid out in wages, remain in the owner's pocket for a while; but factories cannot stand idle, or mines remain empty, without very serious loss. The old capitalist may hold out for a time, whether he endeavour to reduce wages, or to resist reasonable demands for raising them: the speculator cannot; he has been at a great expense, and cannot forego the return; he will therefore inevitably underbid his competitor, by offering higher wages, until he reduces himself to the average rate of profit on his fixed and circulating capital together, which must eventually fix the maximum limit of wages.

To imagine, therefore, that a combination can exist to lower wages, we will not say among master manufacturers generally, but even among those of any trade in any single town, is a delusion. Most advantageous it would be to all, could it become generally known that such is the case. The general

perception of this one truth in commercial science, would save
more suffering to the unfortunate operative, and his unhappy
family, than the acquisition of any of those chimerical objects
they now seek to attain. For it is important to observe, in justice
to all parties, that many of the most obstinate Strikes of which
the history has been recently before the public, and some which
are animadverted upon as acts of great injustice on the part of
the Unions, were, in fact, begun by the masters, not by the
men. We are aware that these instances are exceptions; that,
especially of late years, the Unions have generally commended
turns-out when trade has been brisk, and wages naturally high :
although any reader, from the first pages of the little pamphlet
of Miss Martineau, would be induced to suppose the contrary.
From a wish, we suppose, to address the men in conciliatory
language, she condoles with them as a suffering race, who are
induced to strike by the depression of their wages to the lowest
possible point. Surely it was not necessary for her thus to represent the exception as the rule; nor will men of intelligence be
attracted by an exaggerated statement of their case, while men
of no intelligence will be captivated by the representation, but
wholly neglect the moral. But *some* combinations, as we have
said, have been occasioned by the inevitable lowering of wages.
The great Strike among the spinners, in December, 1830, (by
which fifty-two mills and 30,000 persons, according to the statement of the author of the second and third pamphlets on our
list, were thrown into idleness for ten weeks,) occurred, we believe,
in consequence of the masters having lowered wages, which happened, from some accidental cause, to be higher at Ashton and
Stayley Bridge than in the neighbouring district. In 1829, their
turn-out in Manchester was occasioned by a reduction, the necessary consequence of the depression of trade in the spring of that
year. The famous Kidderminster Strike, in 1828, originated in
the same cause. Undoubtedly, in none of these cases were the
masters wilfully combining : they were merely endeavouring to
save themselves from loss, or rather, to divide the loss between
themselves and their men. But so long as the latter are under
the erroneous impression, that their employers are everywhere in
a confederacy against them, it would be too much to expect,
that they should not adopt the same weapons, in what they must
consider a case of self-defence. To endeavour to remove this
impression, should be one of the first objects of those who seek to
instruct the working classes; not to encourage the delusion, as
interested men have done, when, in endeavouring to force on the
manufacturers their projects for limiting the duration of labour—
projects which, whatever may be their value, can never be carried

into effect without lowering real wages until ' seven halfpenny
' loaves are sold for a penny, and the three-hoop'd pot has ten
' hoops '—they fraternize with the delegates of Trades'-Unions,
and join in the common cry against the avarice of capitalists.

It is of equal importance to show, as all the authors whose
productions are now before us have endeavoured in different ways
to do, the manner in which a Strike among the workmen almost
invariably counteracts itself.   Not only are high wages, when
enjoyed for a time, in consequence of a successful Union, usually
followed by a slack trade, and diminished employment ; but a
still more valuable lesson may be learned, by observing, that the
nominal high wages are in truth subject to proportionable deductions, occasioned by the consequences of the Strike.   They are, in
fact, reduced (as nearly as in so difficult a calculation it is possible to conjecture) to that amount at which the necessary regu-
lators of wages—supply and demand—would have fixed them.
This point, perhaps the most important which can be discussed
with reference to Trades'-Unions, we have nowhere found so well
stated as in the second pamphlet on our list ;- the author of which
(Mr E. Tufnell) has qualified himself for its elucidation by a very
extensive acquaintance with the condition of the several branches
of our manufacturing industry, and sums up the evidence with
equal intelligence and impartiality.

' Where the workmen have succeeded in compelling their employers
to raise wages, they have equally failed to derive benefit, or even to escape
injury from the change, though it is of course more difficult in this case
to trace the means by which this effect has been produced.   It has either
arisen from the high wages attracting more labourers to enter the trade
in which they have been given, than can be supplied with work, and who,
consequently, must be supported by those who get work, else the competition of their numbers will beat down the advance that has been obtained ; in both which cases, the advance, or more than the advance, is
instantly lost : or it has arisen from the expense of maintaining the
various burdens which a combination entails, such as clerks, secretaries,
delegates, meeting-rooms, &c.—from the falling off of consumption, in
consequence of the increase of price ; and, therefore, less being manufactured, and less wages distributed among the body of the Unionists,—
from the driving away of the manufacture to other places,—from some
one of these, or other causes, the advantage vanishes in the moment of
expected fruition, and generally leaves the workmen in a worse state than
before.'—P. 76.

When, therefore, it is asserted, that the Spinners' Union, for
instance, and one or two others, have, in fact, eventually and
permanently raised the rate of wages in their respective trades,
this is the true answer—that the actual receipts of the workman
are no greater than his natural wages would have been ; the rest

is absorbed in what may be called the expenses of collection.
These expenses, or deductions, have been stated to amount in
some Unions to twenty per cent, besides occasional levies, and
this statement we should think below the mark.

' By the evidence of a large Glasgow manufacturer, given before Parliament last session,' (says Mr Tufnell,) ' it appears that the spinners in
that town have applied part of their funds towards paying the emigration
expenses of some of their class, and in this way have got rid of one-
eighth of their numbers.'—P. 96.

Here is an instance of a body of men uniting to raise wages,
and then devoting the excess of those wages to the greatest service, perhaps, which, in the long run, they could render the
country, as well as themselves.   But is it not probable, that had
they not procured the emigration of one-eighth of their number,
the whole would have found work at wages lower than the combination rate by a less sum per man than that actually contri-
buted towards their emigration fund?   The same problem might
be worked out in many ways.   The chief laws of political economy, however darkly they may lead to their result, are as unchangeable as those of nature ; and it would be as possible to make the
quicksilver in the thermometer expand beyond the temperature of
its atmosphere, as to fix wages at any other rate than that at
which they would fix themselves, if undisturbed either by Unions
or Acts of Parliament.

But the workmen go still farther, and lower wages beyond the
natural limit, in their attempts to raise them ; by the almost incredible expense entailed upon them under the sort of organization
which it is their pleasure to form.   Societies must have officers ;
officers must be supported out of the common funds ; and their
support must be, like that of other placemen, on a scale sufficient
to render their offices worthy of acceptance.   Thus a large body
of men is interested in what is called in commonwealths the maintenance of established order ; that is, the maintenance of the system which gives them dignity and profit.   Hence, in the accounts
of the Trades' Unions, from which many extracts lie before us,
we find something equivalent to most of the items of a nation's
expenditure.   They have their public creditors in the parties out
of work, who claim to be supported out of their funds.   Their civil
list, and their army and navy estimates,—the effective part of their
disbursements—are represented by the sundry items of the necessary expenses of committees, stationery, newspapers, and advertisements.   Their Parliaments, like those of America, are paid,
and at a pretty high rate too.   An account of one of the most
remarkable of these, the Spinners' Union Parliament, which met
in the Isle of Man in 1829, to frame laws for the three kingdoms

on that neutral ground, will be found in the early pages of Mr Tufnell's first pamphlet. They have their courts of justice too. ' I have known an hundred pounds spent in six weeks,' says a writer in a Yorkshire newspaper, ' in deciding the disputes of in- ' dividuals.' Finally, if governments have their coronations, their regalia, their palaces, and household troops, the Unions, too, are of opinion that the splendour which surrounds authority is one of its chief recommendations in the eyes of the governed ; and they show a noble disregard for economy in trifles, in the sums which they lavish on ' expenses for furniture in the hall, gas ' pipes, chandeliers, painting president's chair, new top and side ' curtains for president's chair,' for axes, emblematic devices, and robes of office. But for one of the articles most prominent in these financial estimates we confess we are at a loss to find an exact parallel in those of any exchequer except that of the King of Yvetot, of whom his poet sings,

> ' Il n'avait de goût onéreux
> Qu'une soif un peu vive ;
> Mais en rendant son peuple heureux
> Il faut bien qu'un Roi vive.

' We have before us,' says Mr Tufnell,* ' a statement of the half ' yearly expenses of all the lodges of the Union of Mechanics in ' England, Scotland, and Ireland ; in all of them the charge for ' *committee liquor* is large, and in some the chief item in the ' accounts; so that we may apply to the Unionists literally the ' words of the prophet, " he that earneth wages earneth wages to ' put it into a bag with holes." '

These fooleries, however unimportant they may seem amongst the graver matters of the great question now agitated between capitalists and operatives throughout the country, are of too serious consequence, in reality, to be passed over so lightly as they may at first seem to deserve ; because a full exposure of the wasteful extravagance on which the funds of the latter have been squandered, by the very men who have incited them to make such heavy sacrifices, will probably have more effect than any other argument in convincing readers of the working classes of the futile nature of these associations. In these intestine wars, the great body of mechanics fall under the influence of small côteries of artful or turbulent men ; and the desire of such paltry distinc- tions and emoluments as a Trades' Union has to bestow, operates in raising up a succession of agents to direct to mischief the en- deavours of the united body. Many, however, among the leaders

---

* Trades'-Unions and Strikes, p. 32.

have been of a very different character ;—men who have acquired
influence over their comrades from a reputation of steadiness and
honesty, and of extensive acquaintance with the economy of their
trade. It is on such men that writers who compile treatises
like those before us, for popular circulation, must hope to make
an impression. Many too hastily conclude, that, because such
treatises do not appear to acquire an extensive circulation among
those to whom they are directed, they are therefore useless ; and
that no argument except that of the passions ever makes a strong
appeal to the multitude. But the seed falls silently, and if in a
vast majority of instances the ground refuses to receive it, in
those few in which it penetrates, the means are thus afforded for
the productin and extension of the plant. The small thinking
class will ever exercise a decided influence over the multitude ;
more powerful, perhaps, in the long run, for good than for evil.
These are the men on whom the education of circumstances, and
the education of books, are not thrown away. That there are
many thousands of such men among our working population in
every department—men whose intelligence and activity of mind
are of the highest order—no one who has paid any attention to
the history of these recent agitations will venture to deny. When
these are gained over, and a majority of the best informed
mechanics, the reign of the Unions will soon be at an end. In
many of those who have exercised the greatest influence in recent
Strikes, such a change has already taken place. Among the most
remarkable of the leaders whom these events have called into authority, was one who almost wholly controlled and managed the
great turn-out among the clothiers at Bradford in 1829. The
account which this individual (John Tester by name) has sent
forth of the unsuccessful combination which he commanded, has
supplied Miss Martineau with great part of her materials for the
little publication named at the head of this article. We believe
it is only doing him justice to say, that under his direction it
was carried on with better temper, better order, and less extravagant expenditure, than has been often exhibited in similar emer-
gencies. Yet this man wrote at the end of the Strike, ' If I do
' not procure employment in a week or two, I shall be without
' the means of subsistence ; but this will not induce me to ask
' employment of the Bradford manufacturers. Not that I owe
' them any ill-will, wish them any harm, or shall ever think
' of treating them disrespectfully. My only motive is, I have
' heard some of them say they should like to have the pleasure of
' refusing me work, and I am determined they shall never have
' that pleasure.' Well may the authoress add,* ' It is a matter

---

* Strikes and Sticks, p. 17.

' of deep concern, not only to the people of Bradford, but to
' the whole of society, that such feelings should ever arise be-
' tween those who must go hand in hand if either are to prosper.'
This person, whose intelligence and dexterity are evidently such
as no education could give without great personal abilities, has
now not only completely changed his views on the subject of
Trades' Unions, but time and retirement have so operated on
him, as to smooth away all the irritation of party feeling, which
he had so long shared as well as directed ; at least, if he is the
author of two letters published in his name, which we find in the
Leeds Mercury (for June 7 and 14). We have no other authority for their genuineness than the character of the journal in
which they appear, and the tone of truth and soberness which
pervades them ; but believing them to be his productions, we do
not hesitate to say, that such good as can be done in this crisis
by the dissemination of pamphlets would be better furthered
by a cheap reprint of these letters, than by the circulation of
any tracts to which men belonging to other classes had set
their hands. They possess all the advantage which clear and
plain language can give, and the writer appears in the form which
finds most favour in the eyes of all men ;—in that of an equal,
who neither flatters nor threatens his readers, but who simply
states the result of his own experience—an experience of which
all must acknowledge the extent. ' If,' says he, ' any advantages
' are to be obtained—if any benefit can be secured—if any im-
' provement is to be effected—if any good may be achieved by
' the working classes of society, from strikes or combinations, or
' Trades' Unions, or any association of a similar description, some
' at least of these advantages must most assuredly have been visi-
' ble to me. On the other hand, should associations of this kind
' be injurious, and calculated to produce misery and suffering to
' those for whose benefit they profess to be intended, it is alike
' impossible the whole of the evil should have escaped my notice.'
No one can have had more opportunities of remarking the profligate expenditure of the committees which govern the Unions.
On this point, he gives the following details :—

' Of two hundred pounds paid as entrance-money into the Trades'
Union nearly two years ago, I calculated that L.60 were spent in *rega-*
lia; L.100 in eating, drinking, and wages for the Union's committees;
leaving only L.40 for the purposes originally contemplated by the members. Perhaps some one, wiser than myself, will explain to you in what
way your condition in life can be improved by the joint possession of
swords, death-scenes, gowns, banners, battle-axes, and large empty boxes,
like military chests, with a number of devices, of which no one knows the
meaning. The bare mention of committee expenses reminds me of
various scenes of profuse expenditure and wanton waste, and worse than

beastly gluttony, which I have witnessed, and always with feelings of disgust. . . . . . I am aware that professions are made by the advocates of the new system, which may be aptly called the nonsense system, that all these expensive feastings are abolished, and that every thing is conducted upon the least expensive scale. But notwithstanding these pretensions, the money is still wasted by committees as much as ever, only in such a way as to keep the great majority of members in the dark on the subject. The method generally adopted is this. The secretary, president, and other leading men, swill the committees and auditors with beer, and these in their turn pass the accounts with little or no examination. If peculation be discovered, it is connived at, and a favourable report issued to the members. . . . . . The instances of mal-appropriation of money, which I could enumerate, would surprise you ; and the various sums, if added together, amount to many hundreds of pounds. . . . . . Some few, by carefully preserving the money their wits enabled them to secrete from the general stock, have been able to commence business on their own account, and to take a part in that manufacturing tyranny which a short time before they had so loudly and vehemently denounced. . . . . . The most rigid economy is professed. Your officers declare to you that they work for nothing, notwithstanding which, your money is thus shamefully and profusely wasted. A person from the west of England attended, a short time ago, a Grand Lodge Meeting in the North, and his expenses of attendance were little less than L.30. It was really amusing to read some of the items in his extraordinary bill. There was so much for the purchase of an umbrella, to replace one lost upon the road ; so much per day during a number of days, during which, after his return, he was unable to work, from the great fatigue of his journey !'

We see, by the way, that a speaker, at one of the late Leeds Union meetings, charged John Tester himself with having left the Bradford Union with L.36 of its money in his pocket. The charge, we hope, has no foundation ; but if it has, it only places the writer in the situation of a king's evidence revealing a conspiracy. We have only room to quote one of his anecdotes, which illustrates our former statement, as to the necessary deductions from the high wages obtained by a successful combination :—

' Six years since, the Combers of Leicester turned out for a considerable advance, and after expending nearly L.2000, they attained the object of their wishes. But mark what follows :—At the commencement of that strike, there were less than 600 combers in the town, and at the conclusion of it more than 700. At the beginning we had all full employment ; at the termination, between one and two hundred must be supported without work, or they would go and turn in. Continual disputes took place between the employed and the unemployed ; the latter accusing the former of selfishness, and the former accusing the others of idleness and unwillingness to work. Eight-and-twenty shillings per week were allowed me for the exercise of my powers of persuasion, to keep these two parties from an open rupture, and in this way to do the best I could for the interest of both. Alas ! I saw most clearly that the wages could not be maintained, and voluntarily resigned my well-paid but unenviable situation, and left the town. Wages fell immediately, and men were soon working at a lower price than ever.'

Before dismissing the subject of the expenses entailed on workmen by their Unions, it may not be unimportant to notice the sums which they lavished last year in support of Lord Ashley's bill for the regulation of labour in factories. The principal part of the former evidence, before Mr Sadler's committee, had been furnished by parties in connexion with the leading body of the Clothiers' Union. This is not the place to discuss the important question which that measure involved—the question, namely, whether the law can or cannot interfere, with advantage, to control the duration of labour, or the internal discipline of factories ; whether the waste of health, and strength, and youthful happiness, which those factories undoubtedly occasion, can be diminished or no, without causing distress and suffering, far greater in amount, by the ruin of productive industry. No doubt can be entertained of the pure and humane motives which actuated most of its chief supporters. But while the philanthropists promoted it from principle, and conservative politicians, in hopes to break up the influence of the Whig party in the manufacturing districts, there is reason to suppose, that ' canny Yorkshire ' saw in it the commencement of a hopeful scheme for obtaining equal pay with less labour. Its chief agents were, therefore, loudly cheered on by all that designing class among the operatives, who have undertaken the great experiment of forcibly raising wages. By them it was considered only as one mode of effecting what the Trades' Unions seek to obtain by other means,—the absolute destruction of the capitalists, or their complete subjection to the committees of their workmen.

Accordingly, the Unions which then existed were set in active motion to promote the bill of Lord Ashley. ' A penny for Time ' Bill,' (alluding to charges incurred in sending delegates to London, and other disbursements, in furtherance of this object,) ' con-' stituted a regular item in the contributions to the Lancashire ' Trades'-Union.' Mr Tufnell (himself a factory commissioner) has given, we believe, a tolerably correct representation of the reasons which induced this body to take up the cause so heartily.

' From the evidence relating to the cotton trade, taken before the Factory Commission, it appears that the spinners were invariably the strenuous, and in many cases the only supporters of the Ten Hour Limitation Bill. It is also shown, by the Report of the Commission, that the spinners are nearly the sole employers of the children, and consequently answerable for the cruelty, if any there be, in their treatment. Why, then, it may be asked, did they not leave the promotion of this bill to those of their fellow-workmen, who could support it with a decent regard to consistency? Those, who have not penetrated their secret motives, may think this surprising; the circumstance, however, admits of an easy solution.

' The effect produced by the Spinners' Union, affords an explanation of this anomalous conduct. It has been before stated, that the high wages given in this business, cause a greater number of persons to enter it than the trade can employ, and that those superfluous labourers receive a weekly stipend from those who are in work, to prevent them from engaging themselves under the combination prices. The Union calculated, that had the Ten Hour Bill passed, and all the present factories worked one-sixth less time, one-sixth more mills would have been built to supply the deficient production. The effect of this, as they fancied, would have been to cause a fresh demand for workmen; and hence, those out of employ would have been prevented from draining the pockets of those now in work, which would render their wages really, as well as nominally high. Here we have the secret source of nine-tenths of the clamour for the Ten Hour Factory Bill; and we assert, with the most unlimited confidence in the accuracy of our statement, that the advocacy of that bill amongst the workmen was neither more nor less than a trick to raise their wages—a trick, too, of the clumsiest description; since it is quite plain, that no legislative enactment, whether of ten, or any other number of hours, could possibly save it from signal failure.'

It is not an easy matter to speculate on the doctrines or objects of Mr Sadler, or upon the view which he may now take of this great interlude in his unsuccessful dramatic performances at Leeds. But we should think Lord Ashley, for whose character and motives we entertain sincere respect, must look back with some degree of compunction on his connexion with those with whom he then associated, now that their wishes and plots have been more fully brought to light.

This is the point —namely, the enormous expenses which necessarily accompany the most successful combination—which we should wish to see most strongly insisted on by the numerous writers who are now endeavouring to instruct our industrious artisans in the real elements of their prosperity. So sanguine are the anticipations with which they invariably look forward to the result of a contest, that the history of ten unsuccessful Strikes, and of the misery, the debt, the demoralization which they have produced, would probably be listened to with less interest than the exposure of the real state of facts in a single case where similar efforts have proved successful.

As to the extent of the mischief which these Unions have done, and are still doing, to our manufacturing population, we confess we do not quite entertain the dark apprehensions with which many reasoners consider this subject. We have a confidence, not easily to be shaken, in the versatile and elastic character of British industry : we believe, too, that the unrivalled steadiness of our men—that very circumstance which makes their Strikes so stub-born, so lasting, and so peaceable—will prevent them from being hurried by passion into excesses, which can only produce lasting injury to themselves and their employers. It cannot be denied that Trades'-Unions may exist and flourish along with a flourishing trade, so long as their demands are not unreasonable, and their leaders uninfected with the levelling fancies which now beset them. This has been the case for many years, for example, in the spinning trade, in many respects the most important branch of our industry ; inasmuch as most of the processes in the cotton manufactory are necessarily dependent on it. Mr Babbage has drawn a very discouraging picture of the state to which the repeated Strikes of the workmen have reduced that an-cient and staple branch of British skill, the cutlery of Shef-field. It appears that this town is fast losing its long vaunted pre-eminence ; that in some of the finest articles of steel fabric, France, with her high-priced iron, and her half-developed industry, is said to be already superseding England in the foreign market ! In many other towns the effects of multiplied combinations are more or less conspicuous. Many of the most respectable manufacturers at Derby, Manchester, and other places, are supposed to be plan-ning the abandonment of their factories; less from actual loss than from the constant annoyance to which they are subjected by the unreasonable demands and rude dictation of the committees.* Not content with fixing the rate of wages, these bodies decide on the fitness or unfitness of men to be employed, on the hours and divi-sion of labour ; and the punishment for every infraction of their laws, inflicted frequently without any notice, is a turn-out. The men cannot wonder if, under such circumstances, the respectable portion of their employers, those who wish to deal fairly with them, are gradually driven to relinquish the contest; and that their

---

* It must, however, be confessed that this threat has been too often repeated to produce much effect on our minds. As long ago as 1807, the late Sir Robert Peel declared in Parliament, that in consequence of the combinations then existing in the cotton trade, ‘ there were many ‘ men of property who seriously thought of moving themselves and their ‘ capital to some other country where their property would be better pro-‘ tected.’ The subsequent extension of the greatest manufacture in Eu-rope has sufficiently answered these predictions, although uttered by one of those most conversant with its details.

place is supplied by adventurers of inferior capital and character, who may be willing to bow to the Unions for a while,—waiting for the first opportunity of obtaining the upper hand, and practising exaction in their turn.

There are many alleviating circumstances which have accompanied the recent extension of the Unions. One of these is, the impulse which they give to the ingenuity of the masters in the production of new machinery. High wages and dictation infallibly sharpen the wits of the masters and their agents. ' Corn laws and combinations,' says Colonel Torrens, ' have pro- ' duced the same effect, of causing machinery to be employed in ' this country more extensively than it otherwise would have ' been.' We must refer to a very interesting section of Mr Tufnell's pamphlet (the second on our list) for an account of Mr Roberts's self-acting mill; of the employment of steam-power in raising materials for building; of the wool-combing machine; and of others, which have been introduced into general use within the last four or five years by masters at variance with the Unions in those trades. Undoubtedly similar machinery would eventually have been discovered and employed without such a stimulus. But it is well remarked by Mr Tufnell, that ' the obvious ' result of this forced and premature adoption of new machinery ' is to displace labour with inconvenient rapidity ; and, instead of ' improvement proceeding by those gently varying gradations ' which characterise its natural progress, it advances, as it were, ' *per saltum*, and comes upon the workman unprepared for the ' change which his course of life must subsequently undergo.' The new engines are put in action, not to meet the gradual extension of demand, but to replace the unnatural deficiency in the supply of labour. How slowly, where no particular cause exists to accelerate the operation, labour is displaced by the invention of new machinery, may be calculated from the well-known fact, that in 1830 the number of hand-looms at work was nearly the same as it had been in 1820, after ten years of competition with the giant strength of the power-loom.

In the unfortunate state of hostility which at present subsists between the employers and workmen in so many districts of our empire, no victory obtained by either party can be regarded with satisfaction. Whichever side wins can only do so at the expense of much suffering and distress among parties, whom the natural fluctuations of trade expose but too often to calamity. But such have been of late the tyrannical and unjust demands of some of the Unions, that we must be permitted to hope that the recent defeats they have encountered will eventually prove of service to the country. All seem agreed, that the dissolution of the late combinations among the tailors in London, and the clothiers at

Leeds, was justly provoked by their unreasonable conduct. But a difference of opinion has arisen, whether or no the masters have acted rightly in requiring from men, on returning to work, a written renunciation of their Union. It is said, and with justice, that to deprive the mechanic of the right of combining, which the legislature has recognised, would be an abuse of authority on the part of the employer. Whatever the real effects of Trades'-Unions may be, it is quite impossible that, while the liberal professions. maintain among themselves a minimum rate of remuneration, and while all the landed proprietors in the country are combined in one great Union against the consumer, with Parliamentary enactments at their back, any argument can be employed to convince the workmen that they act with injustice, in endeavouring to raise wages by the best means in their power. Nor are these organized associations without some utility. They have occasionally exercised a beneficial interference with regard to the admission of apprentices. They have not unfrequently prevented masters from taking an unfair advantage of their workmen's necessities ;—for example, in cases of piece-work, by increasing the size of the blocks in calico-printing. Many other instances might be pointed out in which the men have protected themselves from injustice by their Unions ; and nothing can be more visionary than the apprehensions which some profess to entertain of the general association of the working classes throughout the empire. To unite in one body, for the purpose of fixing the rate of wages, the calico-printers and spinners, who make 30s. a-week, with the poor weavers, whose toil can often hardly procure them seven, would require power and contrivance such as no human authority could command. The regulations proposed at the convention of the defunct National Association at Manchester, (in June, 1830, when twenty trades sent delegates,) will afford to any one who consults them abundant evidence of the hopelessness of such a project. On these grounds, and also because it may appear impossible to put down a Union by exacting declarations from its members, it is urged that the masters should be content to readmit the men to employment without the requisition of any pledge. We are, nevertheless, of opinion that the masters have, in the present emergency, acted rightly. Although an extorted pledge be in itself of little value, yet the disgust and weariness of the men themselves at combinations, which have involved them so deeply in debt and distress, will give it additional force ; many will abide by it on principle ; many more, perhaps, as a sufficient plea to excuse them when they are solicited to reconstitute their Union. And should the present associations be broken up, no fear need be entertained lest, when any real occasion occurs on which they may be of service, there should be a difficulty in organizing fresh ones.

Be this as it may, we apprehend that Government ought on no account to interfere, unless, without any restrictive legislation, additional protection can be afforded to the persons and properties of manufacturers, and of operatives who desert the Unions. Some suggestions of Mr Tufnell on this subject may be worthy of attention ; for instance, that of giving to the police a power to apprehend persons stationed to ' picquet' the mills of refractory masters,—although it is evident that there would be considerable difficulty in justly exercising such authority. The appeal which is given to the Sessions, in cases of summary conviction under the present combination laws, is productive of much mischief; as time is thereby afforded for the Unions to put their funds into action, and to intimidate or buy off adverse witnesses. But here also it is difficult to suggest a remedy which should not interfere unwarrantably with the liberty of the subject. The resolution which has been lately adopted in so many instances by parish vestries to refuse relief to any applicants who belong to a Trades'-Union in an actual state of turn-out, is obviously no less demanded by common justice to the rate-payers, than by sound policy. But it is vain to expect that any discouragement, either by the laws or by the higher classes, can disarm the Unions of their mischievous tendencies. Our chief reliance must be on the accumulated experience of unsuccessful Strikes, and on the slow but steady progress of sound commercial knowledge among the people.

ART. XIII.—1. *Three Lectures on the Rate of Wages, delivered before the University of Oxford, in Easter Term,* 1830. *With a Preface on the Causes and Remedies of the present Disturbances.* By Nassau William Senior, of Magdalen College, A. M. ; late Professor of Political Economy.—1830.

 2. *Correspondence between the Right Hon. R. Wilmot Horton and a Select Class of the Members of the London Mechanics Institution, formed for investigating the most efficient remedies for the present distress among the labouring classes in the United Kingdom; together with the Resolutions unanimously adopted by the Class. Also a Letter from the Right Hon. R. Wilmot Horton to Dr. Birkbeck, President of the Institution : and his Answer.*—1830.

 3. *The Life and History of Swing, the Kent Rick-burner.* Written by himself.—1830.

IF Noah and his family, when they came out of the ark, had held a council upon the best way of providing themselves with the comforts of dry land, it would have been a strange line of argument for one of the household to have pointed to the stock in trade which had escaped the deluge, and have said, " This is a plough ; and by harnessing the clean beasts to it, you would do six times as much work as with a spade ; therefore break the plough, and take the spade. Your wife too has a spindle, with which she can spin so many threads an hour ; but I could show her a way, that would not spin half as much. Let us be machine-breakers ; and then we shall all be comfortable."

This would be such gross absurdity, that it is hardly practicable to set about stating wherein the absurdity consists. It is like a man's cutting off his legs, in order that he may have the pleasure of hopping upon crutches. Noah's brief answer would be, that he worked to *have;* and that the more he had, the better. The wildest enemy of machinery would never dream of executing such a principle in his own immediate concerns ; or of taking the worse instrument when he might take the better, for the simple pleasure of having more to do. The case, therefore, does not present a parallel to the existing question on the subject of machinery.

Take, then, another state of mankind, as for instance Abraham's ; who had men-servants and women-servants, and a steward to look after them. Now if the steward had proposed, that the men should be set to dig instead of plough, and the women weave cloth with their fingers instead of using the best piece of loom-machinery the country was acquainted with, and that the reason for all this was, that without it there would be no possibility of keeping them in employment,—the answer of Abraham would be much the same as Noah's, but with the addition, that if their work could be saved in one way, he would be answerable for finding them work in some other ;—that if the women could make two pieces of cloth instead of one, his wife should wear two at once, or else wear one that by its beauty should take as much making as two.

But if the steward was an obstinate person, and had an anti-machinery maggot in his head, he might reply, that if each servant could do twice as much as before, it was evident only half the number would be wanted, and therefore half must be either sold to the Midianites, or left to perish in the desert, which would be very hard upon the individuals. To which his master would reply, that if the gift of doing double work should fall on all of them at once as from the clouds, there might be some possibility of a part of them being an encumbrance ; but if there was any thing gradual in the operation, he, the master, would be answerable for work springing up for them as fast as they could find the means of doing it, and that not a hoof should be left behind in consequence of improvements in the method. And if the master, as there appears no reason to doubt, was fond of seeing every body satisfied about him, he would take an opportunity of representing to his people and followers, that it would be hard if the improvements did not in some degree turn to the advantage of every one of them ;—that if there was more corn by ploughing than by digging, there must needs be better feeding for themselves, their wives, and their little ones ; and that if cloth was easier made and more abundant, it was scarcely possible that the result should not be that the children would come by three shirts a-year instead of two. There would be no doubt that a principal portion of the advantage would fall to the share of the rich master and his immediate relatives ; but it would also be certain, that the servants down to the lowest would be better and not worse for the alteration, and that they would be unreasonable if they raised a hue-and-cry against the change.

This then, if any body has thought worth while to follow it, appears to let into the whole secret of the good and evil of machinery. It is a good to every body, working classes included, if only it does not come so rapidly as to throw great masses of people out of employment, faster than the consequent demand for hands in other branches can take them up. If the community in general by dint of machinery get a piece of cloth for six shillings instead of ten, they will to a certainty expend the four shillings in something else that they would not have expended it in before ;—unless it can be proved that they will throw it into the sea. If therefore there is a diminution of employment for cloth-makers to the amount of four shillings (which is undeniably the case), there is at the same time an increase of expenditure on some other arts and crafts to the same amount. But if other arts and crafts are affected in a like manner by machinery, each of these throws an increase of expenditure on some others, among which the craft of cloth-making will undoubtedly have a share. And if wages fall when employment is diminished, they rise when it is increased. So that provided only the introduction of machinery be gradual and general, there is an evident tendency towards a balance ; and though nobody can say that the balance shall be so complete as to leave every thing exactly as before, it is plain that the final alteration is the *difference* of the particular alterations, and not the *sum*. But all this time, there is a clear gain to the consumers at every step, of the whole amount of what is saved in each instance by machinery,—or what in the case of the cloth was represented by four shillings. So that while the effects upon the different operatives, in respect of their quantity of employment, go on balancing and counteracting each other, and are in the end next to none at all,—the gains of the consumers (of whom the operatives make part) go on increasing and accumulating by every particular addition. Or to turn the subject the other side up, if machinery of all kinds in all places could be annihilated at once by an Act of Parliament or a thunderbolt, the quantity of employment for operatives would on the whole be just what it is now ; but the operatives would take their share, with every body else, of the consequences of cloth being made with fingers instead of with a loom. That is, they would wear just so much cloth, and of such quality, as could be made with fingers by the exertion of the same time and labour which make what they now wear from the loom ; and the same in other things. And note further, that this includes only the home trade. But if ever foreign commerce should cease to be prohibited by Act of Parliament, then there must be taken into the account all the good things that might be obtained from foreigners in exchange for the products of machinery, and the share which the operatives would have in these good things by dint of the increased employment which would be created by the demand for manufactured goods.

The blunder therefore of desiring to put down machinery, is in the main and in the long run the same as the contemptible fallacy of restrictions upon trade, which is pressed upon the operatives by the supporters of the Corn Laws. The apparent gain made at every step of restriction either on trade or on machinery, is balanced by an equal loss to some other portion of the industrious classes somewhere else, and there is a clear unbalanced loss of the amount in question to the consumers in the aggregate besides. But the operatives are to be persuaded, that if John, Thomas, Richard, and Henry, get sixpence each, by at the same time taking twopence out of the pocket of each of the other three, John, Thomas, Richard, and Henry make a gain; and not only this, but they do so if John, Thomas, Richard and Henry in their quality of consumers, lose another sixpence among them every time besides. This is the sum and substance of the system that calls itself *protection to trade.* It is a plan to set every body to rob the rest, and count the plunder as a general gain. The subject, as relates to trade, has been examined at length in a former article*, under the illustration of the monkeys in Exeter Change who chose to feed out of each other's pans; where it was shown that the land monopoly is the great baboon of all, for whose benefit the lesser apes are persuaded to aid in keeping up the fraud.

Machinery then, like the rain of heaven, is a present blessing to all concerned, provided it comes down by drops, and not by tons together; and any thing which prevents its free and expanded operation, has an effect of the same kind as would be produced if the rain could be collected into water-spouts. It remains therefore to be seen, what laws and human institutions have done towards securing the free diffusion of the advantages derivable from God's gift of ingenuity to man. And here the first thing apparent in our own country is, that the aristocracy have made a law, that no use shall be derived from it at all. They have determined by Act of Parliament, that men may invent as many machines as they think proper, but shall not be allowed to sell the produce; or which comes to the same thing, shall not be allowed to sell for what is wanted in return. The whole misery about machinery,—every atom and fragment of suffering, alarm, and wretchedness directly or indirectly consequent thereon,—are the pure and necessary result of the gross fraud and half-witted idiotic cruelty perpetrated by the n.ajority of the landlords upon the rest of their

---

* Article on Free Trade, No. XXIII.

own order and of the community. The compiler of this is a landlord; he has a qualification for a county; but he is not such a dolt as to believe that he is gaining by the profligacy of the Corn Laws, even if he had no other objection to the fact. Like every body else, he has ben obliged to reduce his rents; but he did it with a stipulation, that they should be raised again on the removal of the Corn Laws. All rotten sheep are his to pay for; complaint and misery, the fit consequences of cruelty and injustice, are in every department both of the live stock and the dead. And in addition to this, he has to struggle with the impossibity of putting his children into any calling they can live by. His only hope is that what ' Swing' leaves, the poorrates may speedily swallow; and if the operation be but quick and general, the result may be some comfort for his posterity. It is a hard case that there should be no hindering men from ruining others, except by their finding out that they have ruined themselves; but if it is so, there is nothing to be done but pray for the quickest completion of the process.

It will probably be answered, that the distress just now is in the agricultural districts; and how can it be shown that this would be helped by the removal of the Corn Laws? Easily; as any person may see who has not a reason for blindness in his pocket. When the quantity of food procurable is limited by law, and the population has increased till it presses against this limit, there is no difficulty in seeing that the misery thus produced must extend itself to the agricultural population as well as others. Only a given quantity of agricultural labourers can be wanted to raise a given quantity of corn, and therefore, since all other employments are equally circumscribed, the increase above the given quantity must be starved on the same principle that puppies are drowned; and the starved puppies are what the landlords call superfluous population. They make a law that there shall not be food for more than a certain number, and therefore the rest shall be executed as superfluous. But if this is to be the case with dogs in general, it is clear that the agricultural breeds can have no prospect of escape. The plea that the sufferings of the agricultural labourers would be increased by the removal of the Corn Laws, is therefore only one of the juggleries by which those who have more cunning impose upon those who have less. It might not give instant relief, or there might even be an increase of pain on the commencement of the process, especially if gone about too precipitately; as is the case in the cure of a broken leg. But the great cause of evil would be removed, without which there is no question but of the sufferer's being left to die. The plea therefore is one of those subterfuges, which no educated man puts forward with a grave countenance without having an interest in its success.

But to the less educated classes,—to those who have not been in the habit of considering that to bolt straight forward is not always the way to get out of the bog,—it is quite reasonable and to be expected that the assertion that the miseries of the agricultural labourers come by the Corn Laws, should present considerable difficulties ; and they may even pronounce it at first sight ridiculous and absurd, in which opinion they will be encouraged by the horse-laughs of those among their betters who are driving them upon destruction. On the credit therefore of some good-will shown towards the suffering classes here and elsewhere, the agricultural labourers in the dis turbed districts—the men who are marching under the banner of ' Swing,' if he *has* a banner—are invited to sit down under the first convenient hedge, and engage the best reader in their company to explain to them the following case. Suppose then a farmer,—or a farmer's labourer, for they are both in the same plight,—has two sons and two daughters, which it is well known is about the number that, taking one with another, a married couple has. And suppose, as is evidently the fact, that there are a number of other people in the same circumstances in the neighbourhood, and the hope and wish of the parents is, that the sons of one shall marry the daughters of another, and sit down in some honest calling to maintain themselves in godliness and decency as their fathers did. Now let us see, what chance they have for it. Fifteen years ago came the Corn Laws ; in other words, an Act to prevent the manufacturers from exchanging their work for corn with foreigners. And the farmers and farmer's labourers crowed loud, and thought it was a fine thing for *them* ;—that is, fifteen years ago they crowed, but do they crow now ? It shall be granted that when this unjust restriction on the manufacturers began, it was an advantage to the man whose trade it was to hold the plough. The quantity of land which was to grow corn in England was artificially increased ; and this made more farms to let, and more farmer's labourers wanted to work upon them ; and therefore it was easier for the farmer and the farmer's man to find employment for himself, and for his two sons and two daughters as they grew up upon his hands. There was increased room made for them to spread, at other people's expense ; and therefore they went on merrily, and spread accordingly. But this could not last for ever. Allow the fact to be, that one fourth more land in England was brought into cultivation by the Corn Laws. It is plain that it will be merry times for ploughmen while they are breeding up to this mark ; but why are they to be merry when they *have* bred up to it ? Is it the slightest consolation, comfort, or advantage to them, that they are now *five* hundred thousand poor starving devils, instead of being *four?* Or is it any comfort to the higher farmer who sees himself crushed out of all possibility of livelihood by the competition of men for farms, that there are ten of them to bid against each other instead of eight? Impress therefore on yourselves, you whole regiment of Swing, that if the Corn Laws were a fraud upon other people, they were, like all other frauds, of short-lived advantage to the owner ; and that you are now come to the time when, unless you can live upon the meat and drink of fifteen years ago, the roguery that directed the plan has at all events done *you* no good, whatever it may have done to any body else.

But you will say,—and it's all right,—that this has only proved, that you are where you would have been before ; and therefore you have only to be thankful for what you have had already. But hear more ; there is a ' bit to follow.' See how the case would have stood with you, if there had never been Corn Laws at all. It may be quite true, that instead of *five* hundred thousand farmers and farmer's labourers, there would only have been *four;*—that is to say, there would only have been four hundred thousand of you that would have been farmers and farmer's labourers ; and the rest would have been somewhere else. And what is more, they would have been living merrily somewhere else, and every body would have been merry, and you would have been merry too ; for it is nothing but the impossibility of finding employment for your two sons and two daughters, either in farming business *or in any thing else,* which drives you up in heaps to starve one another. If two thirds of the farmers sons could get comfortable situations although not farmers, it needs no extraordinary wisdom to see that the pressure of competition among farmers would speedily diminish, and farming become a good trade again for the remainder ; and the same with farmer's labourers. None of you have ever taken an oath that your two sons and two daughters shall be nothing but what their parents were. The labourer never had any objection to see one of his boys set up in a little shop, or another go creditably to sea in the employment of the merchant that buys his pork at Christmas ; or to have his daughters married to his neighbours sons as soon as they had succeeded in any of those callings. The farmer used to exult, when his landlord's influence established one son upon the high stool in a merchant's counting-house ;

for there *were* merchants in those days,—it was before the land-lords had spoilt all by their selfish tyranny. All these trades and callings,—that is to say, every branch of manufactures and commerce,—would have been brisk and flourishing. Our sailors would have been 'rampaging' over the world; and now they are dying in the streets, because the merchants have nothing to carry or bring home, and Indiamen flog them beyond endurance. An industrious man might have lived by his industry, though not perhaps in one given calling that should be fixed upon. It used to be so; and would have been so still, if England could have held her own against the invasion of the squirearchy. And to this we must come back; or else go on in the present miserable state of things to the end of time.

The question then is, how we are to come back. And here it may be agreed, that the change must not be all at once, for then it would create pressure on the agricultural labourers faster than the openings made in other ways could take it off. And heaven knows that the agricultural labourers, like all other labourers, are miserable enough. Nobody wants to diminish the sufferings of others by increasing theirs; but to get rid of the whole burthen of misery, which is breaking every body's back for the use and benefit of those who never work at all. There-fore, as said before, it must be done gently. Nobody, for instance, could complain, if the mischief was as long in taking off as it was in laying on; and this, or something like it, would be done by taking off a shilling a year from all the rates on foreign corn till they were gone. But it would not be difficult to show, that a quicker course than this would be for the general good; though this would be better than nothing, and is the very least that men in their senses should think of agreeing to accept. Get the mischief into a way of being ended some time, and then take all other methods in aid that ingenuity can devise; but do not let the man lie perishing with his broken leg without thinking of having it set, and cry "O lord! O lord! why that would be a six weeks business at the least."

Once more then, the 'deluded followers of Swing' as the newspapers call them, are begged to sit down and give their serious attention to the assurance here given them, that however unlikely it may at first appear, the Corn Laws are the origin, cause, and maintenance, of their present suffer-ings, and that they have only to chuse between going on as they are for ever, or joining with the rest of their countrymen in a demand for the total removal by the quickest method that prudence shall direct. It is not expected that they should find this out at once; any more than men who have vastly greater opportunities of gaining knowledge have found things out at once. But what is requested of them is, that they will think of it, that they will attend to it, that they will turn it over in their minds, and see if it may not after all come under the proverb, that what looks the longest way about, is sometimes the nearest way home. Let them take it to the schoolmaster, let them discuss it at the blacksmith's shop, let it be inquired into on Sundays at the bakehouse and in the church porch. And above all things get it to the little farmers and the great; let nobody fall into the error of believing it is a question in which only the paupers are concerned. A trial has been made of robbery, and it has only brought the farmers and farmer's labourers into a state of indescribable misery; would it not be wise to try honesty, and see if it may not lead to better things? Was there ever a piece of dishonesty yet, that by God's just judgment did not in some way fall on the heads of the inventors in the end? Make up your minds upon this point. See your way clearly through the wretched deception by which the land-lords have attempted to raise their own rents and send *you* to the poor-house. Burn no more haystacks, but join heartily with your countrymen of the manufacturing districts in a legal demand for the removal of the Corn Laws, which have ground you all to the dust together; and you will be astonished to see what sort of people will be ready to take your part. Foreign trade has been prohibited; call for its being opened. You are starving as it is; try whether you will be starved twice over, by the country's having foreign trade. Make some inquiry too, into the sort of men who recommend this to you. Ask if they have any interest in deceiving you; or if they ever tried to deceive any body, whether they had an interest or not. Inquire too, whether they are inferior in education, or in the habit of finding out the reason of one thing from another thing, to those who take the other side. And if they are not, then let them have at least a hearing, and such confidence afterwards as you shall think that they deserve.

This is what may be said to the suffering classes. If there is any need to defend the saying it, the defence will not be far to seek. When men from some cause, no matter what, find themselves at sea in the same bottom, and some urgent peril begins to press on the floating community; there are two courses for every man to take, who has ever pretended to addict himself to the study of sea-borne business. One is to go below; and, if the danger be very pressing, to go to bed. The other is, to stand the peril out, quailing before no man's fears, crouching before no man's folly, rising in loudness in support of reason in proportion as others may try to put it down, and braving the risk of being sent to make the land in a whale's belly, sooner than yield an inch to the knavish lubbers that have brought us into the scrape. It is in this spirit, that new allies proceed to join the little company, who having leisure and education, are too proud to turn them against the public interests, and too wise to use them against their own. Not that the coincidence may be perfect ; or the agreement so complete, as not to leave room for friendly dispute in better times. But it is quite sufficient for pulling at the same rope, till at all events the ship's head is laid the right way, and something like a course is steering for bringing her into port.

Suppose now, the peril were, a failure of provisions ; and there the gallant ship was laid,—*hove to*, as the sea monsters call it,—with the crew, that is to say the vulgar hawlers, dying about the decks, and here and there a portly person engaged in calculating how many pieces a biscuit could be broken into, and whether the captain's fowls could be reduced to five quarts of water in the place of six. Imagine such a scene, and estimate the boldness of the individual who should maintain, that all this might be well as an accessory, but the first thing was to turn the head towards some place where provisions grew ; and that no plea of the urgency of earlier relief, could atone for the procrastination of this only final chance of safety. Nor would the case be altered, even though it could be proved that the suffering would be temporarily increased by the efforts necessary for the process of deliverance. It has not pleased heaven to make remedies always luxuries, more particularly where the evils endured have been the consequences of men's own misconduct. When the community has allowed itself so long to drift down the stream of folly, for the sake of the paltry baits held out to individual cupidity, it has no right to expect that the way back should be as easy as the going, and may thank its stars if ever it finds itself on safe ground again, either with or without the salvation of the individuals that led it into the mischief.

There is no use in keeping back the truth. A particular class, the landed interest as they rejoice to style themselves, succeeded in persuading the community that nothing could go well unless they had their way. How much of this was self-deception, heaven only knows ; but if they succeeded in making fools of other people, there is no known reason why to a certain extent they should not have succeeded in the same way with themselves. At all events they had their way ; and the first thing they did, was to prohibit the exchange of the poor man's industry for bread. Whether the manufacturers, if they had haply got the upper hand instead, would have laid a tax on home-grown corn, by way of increasing the quantity that should be bought with their goods from abroad, is what there has not been opportunity to try; but if they had, it would not have been one whit a more outrageous and barefaced wrong, a more wanton and reckless abuse of power, or a fouler and more degrading violence for a civilized society to submit to. If men under such an exertion of tyranny on the part of the manufacturing interest, had risen in masses and been put down by the sword and the executioner, it might be true enough that this evil was an inevitable consequence, and for that very reason there would be two evils instead of one to be reckoned for with the manufacturers whenever the day of justice should arrive. There would be no use in tampering with such a rank oppression. It would be an ill which those who were given to bear, would bear; and those who were not, would not; and the end would be, either the timely retreat of the plunderers of society, or a waiting till public indignation had risen high enough to drive them from their hold.

And it does not follow, that, if humanity was suffering under such an infliction from the manufacturers, the efforts by which it was put down would all be directed by the purest reasoning and the most exact statistics. The buccaneers of the society must make up their minds to take what might befall them. There would be no use in their crying out, that *this* starving wretch was out of the line of political economy, and *that other* was a bad practical philosopher. All these errors would be trifling peccadilloes, compared with the grand stalking wrong, that was at the bottom of the well or ill directed resistance of the community. Nothing can be more eminently typical of passive moderation, joined to considerable powers both of offence and defence, than a drove of oxen under the guidance of humanity and wisdom; but let them be once goaded into madness by the feeling of intolerable suffering, and it is no excuse for the authors of the mischief, that they will stick a peer of parliament as soon as the basest of their persecutors. The ignorant and the poor,—those who are ignorant because they are poor, and poor because they are ignorant, and whom laws have been passed to make both one and the other,—cannot be expected to reason like doctors in divinity, while suffering under evils the smallest of which would fill a gazette if it could by possibility happen to the authors of their pain;—evils as distinctly referable in all their branches to the voluntary and determined acts of those who are the causes of their infliction, as the sounds of a musical instrument are to the striking of the keys;—evils which they have been told over and over, and will be told again tomorrow, and the day after that, exist simply because their betters would have it so, and because the portions of the higher classes who think they gain by wrong are more numerous, united, and active than those of the same classes who set themselves in opposition to it. It is no secret; the members of the existing government avowedly hold office by the confession of the necessity for reform; and never in the history of mankind was reform so necessary, as in a country whose commercial policy is one continuous fraud upon the industrious classes, for the benefit of those whose trade and calling it is to live without working. If the labouring man eats bread, a payment is to be made for the maintenance of one portion of the aristocracy,—there's no mistake, there can be no mistake,—the aristocracy; though the receivers themselves are losing more at one end than they are gaining at the other, with the possible exception of those who are born to the right of providing for their children out of the public purse. If he aspires to tea, he must pay for the support of another portion somewhere else; and if he dreams of sugar, he must keep another; and to crown all, if liberation from any of these abuses is demanded for him, he is told plainly that there shall be no remission of the abuse unless he buys it at full value from the holder. He is the horse, the ass, the mule, who is to be saddled with every 'splendid *lazzarone*' that finds himself too lazy to walk. It is not enough that he is to abstain from his rich neighbour's property, and even to defend it at the hazard of his life when called upon; but this property is to be held imperfect and but half conducive to the enjoyments of the owner, unless it can be employed to double itself out of the basket of the poor. If the world's history were looked through, there would not—with the single exception of negro slavery—be found so glaring and huge an instance of the abuse of power and the general misery consequent on giving one selfish class the right of legislation for the rest, as is presented by the commercial policy of this most ill-used country.

The puritans were fond of speculating, on what a man in their place of torment would do and say, if an offer were made to give him one more trial in the present world. All perdition comes, by not thinking of this in time. If Napoleon could have re-enacted the hundred days, what a different conclusion would certainly have been come to. If the French *ex*-ministers could commence where Napoleon left them, how carefully would they turn their path from leading to the Luxembourg. And when their successors shall have caused revolution, with the cession of twice as much as would have satisfied if given, how willingly would they retrace their steps, if gods or men would give the faculty. So if a whig ministry could begin again where it stands at present, six months after a whelming revolution has been brought on, how carefully would it eschew the debility, the tergiversation, which induced the mischief. All revolutions come by there being nobody who had sense to join the people, and give them half of what was the next day taken by violence. Does the English ministry believe, that the people will not have something in the end ? And does it think that what would have satisfied them in November, will satisfy them in March ? Or, perchance, does it wish to wait for a few more apparitions of the Sibyl with her books ? The inference drawn by the people will only be, that the ministry is lying by to measure forces, and that consequently what they finally obtain, will be in exact proportion to the energy with which they make their feelings known. It is as true under one administration as under another, that ' Never by any other means than the making the ruling few uneasy, can the oppressed many obtain a particle of relief.'* If there was a disposition to make an exception in the present case, it has been much enfeebled by procrastination. The people are intreated every where, to spare no effort, omit no exertion, which may make the Whigs 'uneasy' at the prospect of swerving from their promises.

The conductors of the present work have of necessity a certain number of friends, who will demand to see *their* statement of the points on which the community ought to stand, as the immoveable conditions of any confidence in, or support to, the present ministers. First, then, the immediate removal of the Six Acts ; and, either at once or by a small number of definite gradations, of all the taxes affecting newspapers and advertisements. If any vested interests present themselves in opposition, let them be told to thank heaven for having gone on so long in their iniquity, and to content themselves with at all events the smallest portion of gradation and delay. Let the pitiful amount received by the revenue from the wrong, be laid on any thing that can be seen, or felt, or heard, or tasted, or smelt. Let it be laid on our heads or on our heels, or on any thing that is between. But let us be rid of the gross scandal and open shame, of paying a tax for being blindfolded, in order to be afterwards led by the nose where the bear-leaders may please.

---

* Bentham.

Let it be stated without passion or animosity, but with the decision of men who rest on a geometrical proposition, that an administration which begins by representing the necessity of preventing the communication of men's thoughts and wants, is one that may be submitted to, but never treated with. Secondly, a substantial alteration in the arrangement and extent of the elective franchise, with the protection of the Ballot to its general exercise. Thirdly, the contemporaneous removal of the Corn Laws and of the pretended protections given to manufactures in return, by any gradations that shall assign a period for their entire termination; and the maintaining of the revenue, if necessary, by a tax on property, with a just scale of rates in :as:ng with the magnitude of the amount. In other words, let there be a tax that shall be paid *once*, even though accompanied with some unpleasantnesses in the collection; and not a tax that shall be paid ten times over in its consequences, in order that a certain number of individuals may have the pleasure of thinking they jockey each other in the shares. These points are what the Sibyl is advised to stand on now; and there are as many more, ready to be added, if she is obliged to call again.

Of the publications at the head of this Article, the first is from a quarter in which the science of Political Economy—which is in truth only the science of not being cheated by our betters—is under obligations for an introduction to academical rank in the University of Oxford. It would be affectation, not to own the satisfaction felt at the close accordance between the contents of the Three Lectures, and the conclusions derived from a separate course of study as conducted in great part in the pages of this Review. Of the Lectures themselves, it is not easy to say anything so brief, as that they correspond to the Three Lectures on the Mercantile Theory of Wealth from the same quarter, which have been characterized as ' the ablest and most entertaining publication on a question of political economy, that has appeared since the time of Adam Smith.' References in support of this character may be made to the *cork-screw maker* in page 47,—to the laced coats of our ancestors in page 53,—and to the impossibility of a man's income not being spent, in page 54. This last is interesting, as it bears on the newest plan for the restoration of the late French dynasty, by the refusal of its partisans to spend their incomes. ' Quâcunque viâ datâ, every man must spend his income [*should there not have been added*, or leave it for somebody else to spend?]; and the less he spends on himself, the more remains for the rest of the world.'

On part of Mr. M'Culloch's celebrated examination, it is remarked,

'This reasoning assumes that the landlord, while resident in Ireland, himself personally devours all the cattle produced on his estates; for in no other supposition can there be the very same amount of commodities for the people of Ireland to subsist upon, whether their cattle are retained in Ireland or exported.'—p. 27.

Without inquiring whose arguments might be contradicted by it, is not the real solution, that the cattle are bred because they can be exported, and would not be bred, or not to the same extent, if they could not?

In the last page will be found the exposure of the fallacy, much wrought on at the present moment, that it would be a burthen on the country to disband soldiers, and a relief to take on more.   Just as if the money saved by the disbandment, would not be employed in finding support for as many people somewhere else; and the opposite.

The Preface is the only part on which any serious alteration can be suggested.   It is completely true, that ' *the rate of wages depends on the extent of the fund for the maintenance of labourers, compared with the number of labourers to be maintained.*' The rate, therefore, may manifestly be affected at two different ends ; one by increasing or diminishing ' the extent of the fund,' and the other by increasing or diminishing ' the number of labourers.'   The Corn Laws are the great engine by which ' the fund' is voluntarily and artificially diminished ; and the objection to the Preface is, that, though it does not overlook the Corn Laws altogether, it does not put them into their due place.   For instance, there is room for voting a point-blank amendment on the proposition that

' The principal cause of the calamities that we are witnessing, has been the disturbance which the Poor Laws, as at present administered in the South of England, have created in the most extensive and the most important of all political relations, the relation between the employer and the labourer.'—*p.* vi.

The principal cause is not in the Poor Laws, but the Corn Laws.   If—to borrow from an illustration formerly employed*— a number of rats were caged up and supplied with a limited quantity of food, and encouraged to multiply till they starved each other by the subdivision of the allowance ; a disturbance in the mode of feeding,— in the poor laws of the rat community,— might be the proximate cause of a tremendous uproar; but there would be no doubt that the other, the shutting up, was the primary cause, and the cause on the removal of which the cessation of the evil would entirely depend. The greatest objec-

---

* Art. on Free Trade, No. XXIII.

tion is therefore to be felt to the substitution of any palliatives for the removal of the primary cause. Let the primary cause be removed, or put in a course of gradual but certain extinction, and then palliate by as many ways as can be devised; but till this is done, all palliatives lie under the predicament of tending to the preservation of the leading evil.

The palliative proposed at present, is to colonize; in other words, to force the people of England to breed, as is done by the negroes in some of the West Indian islands, for exportation. To which the direct answer is, that nobody has a right to make laws which shall force the people of England to transport themselves. They love their own country; and will not have it made uninhabitable, to please the aristocracy. The plan of the landed aristocracy is this; that England shall have no more corn than *they* shall sell, and then the competition for it will ensure high prices; but to diminish the danger of resistance that might ensue, the people shall be taxed to pay for sending one another abroad. The transportation is to be the landlords *valve;* which shall prevent the machine from blowing up, but leave the owners as much pressure as without danger can be enjoyed. They will be content without *all* the pressure, because it is too dangerous; but they will have as much as with safety can be left. They have taken all they dare from the people by the Corn Laws; and now they come forward to say they want *twelve millions more,* to pay for carrying them into transportation. They have made the country untenable; and now they want to tax the inhabitants, to carry them away. The English might be happy and increasing at home; but it suits an overbearing order that they shall neither be happy nor increasing, and therefore they must pay twelve millions for being carried abroad. This plan of Emigration, so long as it is not preceded by an arrangement for the extinction of the Corn Laws, is a thing to be resisted *à l'outrance,*—which means with tooth and nail. If once the people of England submit to it, they will be the landlords breeding cattle for ever and for ever. The manufacturing and commercial classes may give up all hope of breaking their chains; and the country at large will settle down into one mass of slavery under the owners of the soil, hopeless because modified, and interminable because the oppressors have had the cunning to provide for the escape of what they would be unable to control.

In this state of things it is impossible not to impress upon the manufacturing and commercial interests, the importance of seizing the opportunity when their oppressors are embarrassed with the consequences of their oppression in the South, to come forward with united voices for the removal of the great

national wrong. No man of common sense says, Because my
enemy has his hands full, therefore I will wait till they are
empty. No man in the common concerns of life, attends to
the puling representations of a plunderer, that it would be un-
pleasant to him to be pressed just now, and therefore he hopes
his pursuers will stay till it is more convenient to him. The
master manufacturers are perfectly able to distinguish between
the rights of property, and maintaining men in the power of
taking other people's property. The operatives also, instead
of squabbling, like the rats, for wages which the masters are
prevented by law from being able to give, will join the universal
cry of 'We will not keep the landed aristocracy.' How is a
master to pay wages, if the landed aristocracy make a law
against the goods being exchanged for what is wanted in
return? The landlords are aware of their danger, and will
undoubtedly push the Emigration scheme with all their might.
And if they succeed, they will have

> ' Slipt the slave's collar on, and snapt the lock.'

The Correspondence and letters connected with the London
Mechanics Institution, are open to the same objection of sub-
stituting the proximate cause of the evil for the primary. They
all dwell upon the means of diminishing the numbers in the
cage, without adverting to the simple Act of Parliament by
which the rats are caged at all. Thus when the President
states that 'Excess of population, absolute and relative, is
the occasion of our recent and immediate oppression,' he states
what is irresistible and true. But when he proceeds to say
' an excess the result of *peace*,' he should have said ' of the
Corn Laws which followed upon the peace.' The multitude,
the rank and file, of the London Mechanics Institution are
begged to sift this difference. It certainly is to be lamented,
that a mass of well-meaning Mechanics in Southampton Buildings should have unanimously come to a determination ' that
there do not appear to be any natural and unforced means of
profitably increasing the demand for labour in the United Kingdom to such an extent as to absorb the existing redundancy of
the supply of labour,'—and have overlooked the fact, that the
landlords have prohibited labour from being exchanged for the
only things for which there is a demand.

Taxes, as they affect the labouring classes, may be divided
into those which will be ultimately shifted upon the employers,
and which therefore produce only a temporary operation on the
labourers, viz. during the time in which the shift is taking place,
—and those which act, and are intended to act, as a pro-

hibition upon the exchange of labour in certain quarters where it would otherwise be effected. An instance of the first may be the tax on malt; which will be a good to the labourers, only till their employers can find opportunity to screw them out of the amount by the reduction of their wages. It is not affirmed that this is not a good,—but that it is a fleeting good, and one of which the whole amount is never great. To represent it therefore as a *great* good to the labouring classes, would be a fraud; and if the labouring classes have been led to accept it as a *great* good, they have been deceived. Two years might perhaps be stated as the limit during which its operation may be sensible;—on the principle that in the variations consequent on one revolution of the seasons, the greatest part of the advantage to the labourers will be in some shape or other screwed out of their wages, and that any thing that may be left the first year will be clean swept away in another. Of the other kind of taxes, the Corn Laws and other restrictions upon foreign trade are instances; and these fall on the labouring classes in the same way that the cage falls on the rats, and produce on them an effect whose magnitude exceeds beyond all proportion the positive amount of the taxation. The Resolutions therefore of the Mechanics are true of one species of taxation, and not the other.

Last in the course of examination, comes the History of ' Swing ;' an ominous name at this moment, though there was a time, the auto-biographer declares, when the Miss and Master Swings went to church with their hair pleasingly combed, like the family of any prime minister. The Life and History of Swing is a novel in the manner of Mrs. Hannah Moore's Cheap Repository; and like its predecessors, it is sometimes deficient in attention to probabilities, and accumulates on the head of the hero a greater number of remarkable events than ordinarily fall to the share of an individual. But something of this kind appears to be inseparable from the character of a hero; for he could hardly be a hero, of whom nothing could be told but what was common to mankind. The present hero was born of a small farmer, on the day on which Mr. Pitt became minister of England; which makes his age about forty-seven. He was intended for college, but his elder brother dying, he took to his father's business instead; and, on the strength probably of his academical prepossessions, married the curate's daughter. His landlord dies; and is succeeded by an heir who has no care for Swing, and turns his farm into a fox-cover. On being re-monstrated with, the landlord replies, that every man can do what he pleases with his own. Upon which it may be ob-

served, that though landlords may do what they please with
their own, it is extremely hard that they should do what they
please with what is not their own ; and particularly that they
should prohibit other men from selling the produce of their
labour, and thereby bring on the state of things which con-
demns a discharged tenant to starve. Swing, however, starves
as he needs must. He makes various efforts to escape, as the
caged rats do in like circumstances ; and after selling his stock
and cattle at a loss, to support his family, he tries to maintain
himself by working as a gardener.

' Up to this period I had never attended a political meeting in my
life, nor took any part whatever in politics ; I thought our laws and
legislators too good to require alteration or change; and if I hated one
thing more than another, it was Radicalism, the abettors of which I
considered no better than rebels and revolutionists, who wanted to
destroy our glorious constitution, and cause anarchy in the country. I
began, however, now to think otherwise. I had seen all around me,
my neighbours reduced from comfort to poverty, and from poverty to
the poor-rates ; and as, in the greater number of cases, it had arisen
from no fault of their own, it occurred to me that some change was
necessary; as had England been governed as it ought, those things
could never have taken place. Reflections of this sort determined me
to attend the great meeting at Manchester, then about to be held, and
I accordingly went there. Every thing passed quietly off until noon,
when, to my horror and surprise, a charge was made by the military
and yeomanry on the peaceable and unarmed multitude that were
assembled, and I, amongst others, was wounded by a sabre-cut in the
arm. Bleeding profusely, and with my arm hanging useless by my
side, I went into Manchester and got it dressed ; I was kept awake the
entire night by the pain of my wound, but consoled myself with the reflection that immediate and condign punishment would be inflicted on
the lawless soldiery who had dared to massacre a peaceable multitude
assembled to petition Parliament. " The King," said I, " will certainly
send down a commission to have the monsters tried for their blood-
thirsty outrage." What was my astonishment and indignation, in
ten days after, when I saw a letter from the Secretary of State, thank-
ing in the King's name, the military and magistrates, for massacring
the people at Manchester.'

' I no longer wanted a proof that our country was sadly mis-
governed,—that a great change was necessary,—and that the Reformers were the only real friends of the people.'—*p.* 4.

There are parts of this, that would do no discredit to De Foe.
The unfortunate ex-collegian (if he can be called *ex* who was
never *in*) gets well of his arm, but unhappily employs it in
picking up a partridge, and finds himself once more at issue
with his enemies. He goes the ordinary course, which all
mankind must do who pick up partridges. He gets free after

six months, and is just in time to meet a demand upon his garden for two years tithes. The tithes devour his cow ; and new claims of the same kind send him to be harnessed to the parish cart, that last scene where " the envy of surrounding nations" are ground down into increased rents for the framers of the Corn Laws. In his wrath he writes a threatening letter, and signs it ' Swing.' The curate's daughter dies, as she had better have done before. His children crawl under a stack for shelter, and set it on fire by accident; and the next morning finds the neighbourhood filled with charges against ' Swing.'

A publication of this kind must have vast effect in carrying through a country the sense of wrong, and the eager desire to get rid of it. And the government must be of extraordinary mould, which at such a period engages itself in contests with the press at the instigation of political rivals, instead of applying itself to the reduction of the causes of complaint. A Bourbon government made an aide-de-camp wait twenty minutes, while Paris was filled with strife; the rule of three will give the policy of waiting for three months. From the landlords there is little to expect. They will sacrifice all and every body, for the smallest chance of putting off the evil day. At present, they seem to look on the church as the first victim ; and there are only the fundholders to come next. If the revenues of the church are attacked to save the landlords, the man who holds funded property afterwards, deserves what he will get. Either this Polyphemus of the landed interest must be got the better of, or the only consolation left for any body will be to be eaten last.

Art. III.—1. *Statutes at large. 5th Geo. IV. c. 95. An Act to
Repeal the Laws relative to the Combination of Workmen, and for
other purposes. A. D. 1824. 6th Geo. IV. c. 129. An Act to
Repeal the Laws relating to the Combination of Workmen, and to
make other provisions in lieu thereof. A.D. 1825.*

2. *A Manual of the Law with regard to Public Meetings and Political Societies.* By Thomas James Arnold, Esq. of Lincoln's Inn,
Barrister-at-law.—London ; A. Maxwell. 1833. pp. 82.

WHAT the Whigs out of power vehemently reprobated, the
Whigs in power suffer to exist. What faith, then, can be
had in Whiggism? If there were not some ground for confidence, that the people of England are on the middle passage to
an Administration consonant with the public spirit, a Tory
Government might be better borne. Not that any relish is felt for
their doctrines or practices, but that then the field is open, and
the fight is with a declared enemy.

The Whigs are neither for us nor against us ; and like all
Protean personages of the sort, they look to their own advantage in turning the scale against the combatants on either
side, just as it may suit to make the successful party a tool for
their own purposes.

True, they boast of sundry reforms,—and these must be
admitted. But except the grand reform of all, their Alpha,
they have given none which fully recognizes and adopts any
great principle. They seem disposed to travel regularly through
their alphabet, and beginning with their Alpha, calculate on
retaining office till they have reached, in their crooked course,
and after a long day, their Omega. What have they done for
political liberty ? They have reduced taxes, and amended the
condition of the slave, which they could not help. They have

opened the East-India trade, and kept the Bank Charter from growing worse, and they have done many more small things; but what have they done for political liberty ? Have they repealed the Six Acts? Have they amended and improved the trial by Jury ? Have they amended the Libel-law ? Have they repealed the Corn-laws ? Have they not passed the Coercion Bill ? Have they not abolished flogging abroad and preserved it at home, exhibiting the pusillanimity wherewith they charged the planter ? Have they not justified and struggled for the prerogative of enslaving the sailor by impressment ?

The people of England want not now the pettinesses, the half-doings of these men ; they demand first, the charter of their liberties, the grand principles on which good government must rest, to be conceded in some great measures. All the details will follow as the early fruit of such concessions.

This course of reflection has been suggested by the conduct of the Government in relation to the conviction of the labourers, at the last Dorsetshire assizes.

What Whigs are and may be, was there announced,—though not for the first time. The Irish Coercion Bill, and the prosecution of Mr. Barrett, as well as sundry other dallyings with Irish politicians, had shown their nature ; but this was not made clear to the people of England,—it was not brought home to them.

This case is an instance of the tyrannies that may exist in a free country—the laying hold of an old, nearly obsolete, and no wise applicable Statute,—to bring parties to punishment for an offence they knew not to be within the prohibitions of the law.

The case of the Dorsetshire labourers cannot be better set forth than in the words of the Morning Chronicle, now and for some time past a professed moderate.—

' The real crime ' says the editor ' was, the participating in the aggressive tactics of the Trades' Unions....It has been asked, what would be said were any of the peers or magistrates, who have taken Orange oaths, to be sentenced to transportation. The legal crime is the same as that of Loveless, but then the real crime is not the same. The only thing to be said is, that in England a man is never punished for that on which he is convicted. What influences the jury, is hardly ever that which is given in evidence. The judge is little guided by the verdict in his sentence, and in the subsequent trial by the Home Secretary, which is the final one, the first trial has little to do with the matter. Whether it be possible to order the matter otherwise we know not ; but we conclude with repeating, that a man is never punished for that of which he is found guilty.'

This able statement contains the very kernel of the matter; but for present edification on the shape and nature of this tyranny, it is necessary to dwell somewhile on the state of the law on the subject,—the circumstances under which the law was made, — and the reasons for supposing it not to be applicable to the case in question. There are besides sundry moralities to be illustrated by means of the instance, which it would not be right to pass over.

For the present object it will be sufficient to use as the authority, the able manual of Mr. Arnold. Even this book, well as it is arranged, does not present the law in so clear a shape as it might be put in one Act of the Legislature. The necessity of recurring to Hawkins's Pleas of the Crown, or Judge Foster's work, or any other, is sufficiently ludicrous. The statutes and bits of statutes at the end, only add to the confusion, not of Mr. Arnold's method, but of the subject. This little book contains some eighty-two pages. The whole law, as appears from his excellent digest of it, might be contained in a third of that space. Small as the book is, it costs 2s. 6d. The Useful Knowledge Society should have circulated it for 6d., and thus afforded to the poor Dorsetshire labourers the bitter fruit of knowledge at a cheaper rate than banishment. But such a publication would be too little recommendatory of the Government, and of contentment and reconciliation with things as they are. It might however have had the effect of diverting the members of the Trades' Unions from a useless struggling for impossibilities, to a determined outcry against the continuance of such tyrannies as the Corn-laws, or laws like this, which are suffered to press against the poor man, leaving the rich and the powerful free.

The Acts, in fine, relating to this subject are the following, passed in the years which are cited with them. It is important to observe these epochs, for they tell at sight, in most of the cases, the motive and occasion of the law.

During all this period the legislation on government was motived in fear. Every demonstration of public feeling was carefully repressed by the severest measures, which had usually for their proximate cause some rabble-outrage, unconnected with political feeling,—a mere momentary ebullition, which in quieter times would be but an ordinary police affair.

Anybody unacquainted with the character of English law, would have been puzzled, in perusing these statutes coupled with the Combination Law, to divine whether the Dorsetshire men were guilty or not of any infraction of the law.

In 1797, when the people of England were seized with panic

on account of the French Revolution, an Act was passed to prevent the seduction of persons in the army and navy from their allegiance, which in the preamble to the Bill (37 Geo. III. c. 123) was alleged to have been attempted by means of oaths unlawfully administered to them.

This Act determined that—

Any person proceeding 'to administer, or cause to be administered, or be aiding or assisting at, or present at, and consenting to, the administering or taking of any oath or engagement purporting or intended to bind the person taking the same to engage in any mutinous or seditious purpose; or to disturb the public peace; or to be of any association, society, or confederacy, formed for any such purpose; or to obey the orders or commands of any committee or body of men not lawfully constituted, or of any leader or commander, or other person not having authority by law for that purpose; or not to inform or give evidence against any associate, confederate, or other person; or not to reveal or discover any unlawful combination or confederacy; or not to reveal or discover any illegal act done or to be done; or not to reveal or discover any illegal oath or engagement which may have been administered or tendered to, or taken by such person or persons, or to or by any other person or persons, or the import of any such oath or engagement; shall, on conviction thereof by due course of law, be adjudged guilty of felony, and may be transported for any term of years not exceeding seven years; and every person who shall take any such oath or engagement, not being compelled thereto, shall, on conviction thereof by due course of law, be adjudged guilty of felony, and may be transported for any term of years not exceeding seven years.'

Is this the Act? Under what category of offence were the men charged? Surely not for mutiny or sedition. Are the bare words ' to disturb the peace,' coupled with the preamble, to be construed in our specialty scheme of legislation, as descriptive of a substantial offence? Is that the object of the Trades' Unions?

In the 39th year of the same reign (1799) another Act (39 Geo. III. c. 79.) was passed to put down the societies of United Englishmen, United Scotsmen, United Britons, United Irishmen, and the London Corresponding Society, on an allegation that a traitorous conspiracy had been long carried on against the Government; and that they used unlawful oaths, and engagements, and secret signs, and committees, and secretaries, and other officers, in a secret manner   and that many of these societies were composed of different divisions, branches, or parts, which communicated with each other by secretaries, delegates, or otherwise ; and by means thereof maintained an influence over large bodies of men, and deluded many ignorant and unwary persons into the commission of acts highly criminal.

It then abolishes all these societies by name ; and declares that every society the members whereof shall, according to the rules thereof, or to any provision or agreement for that purpose, be required or admitted to take any oath or engagement which shall be an unlawful oath or engagement, within the intent and meaning of the Act, &c. (37 Geo. III. c. 123), or to take any oath not required or authorized by law ; and every society the members whereof, or any of them, shall take, or in any manner bind themselves by any such oath or engagement on becoming or in consequence of being members of such society ; and every the members whereof, or any of them, shall take, subscribe, or assent to any test or declaration not required by law, or not authorised in manner hereinafter mentioned ; and every society of which the names of the members, or of any of them, shall be kept secret from the society at large, or which shall have any committee or select body so chosen or appointed that the members constituting the same shall not be known by the society at large to be members of such committee or select body, or which shall have any president, treasurer, secretary, delegate, or other officer, so chosen or appointed that the election of such persons to such offices shall not be known to the society at large, or of which the names of all the members, and of all the committees or select bodies of members, and of all presidents, treasurers, secretaries, delegates, and other officers, shall not be entered in a book or books to be kept for that purpose, and to be open to the inspection of all the members of such society, and every society which shall be composed of different divisions or branches, or of different parts, acting in any manner separately or distinct from each other, or of which any part shall have any separate or distinct president, secretary, treasurer, delegate, or other officer, elected or appointed by or for such part, shall be deemed and taken to be unlawful combinations and confederacies.

It then goes on to enact, that every person who shall become a member, and every person who shall directly or indirectly maintain correspondence or intercourse with any such society, or with any division, branch, committee, or other select body, president, treasurer, secretary, delegate, or other officer or member thereof, as such; or who shall by contribution of money, or otherwise, aid, abet, or support such society, or any members or officers thereof as such, shall be deemed guilty of an unlawful combination and confederacy.

Then follows the 52nd. Geo. III. c. 104. (1812), An Act to render more effectual the first-mentioned statute ; by which it is made felony, and punishable with death without benefit of clergy, to administer any oath or engagement intending to bind the person taking it to commit any treason or murder, or any felony punishable by law with death ; and any person taking such oath or engagement, not being compelled thereto, is made liable to transportation for life, or for such term of years as the court shall adjudge.

Does this Act more clearly denounce the offence ? Was this aimed at Trades Unions ?

The 57th Geo. III. c. 19. is the next of the train of this species of legislation. It passed in 1817, and is an Act for the more effectually preventing seditious meetings and assemblies. Its preamble tells, that—

' Assemblies of divers persons collected for the purpose or under the pretext of deliberating on public grievances, and of agreeing on petitions, complaints, remonstrances, declarations, and other addresses to his Royal Highness the Prince Regent, or to both Houses or either House of Parliament, have of late been made use of to serve the end of factious and seditious persons, to the great danger and disturbance of the public peace, and had produced acts of riot, tumult, and disorder, and might become the means of producing confusion and calamities in the nation.'

It then enacts that no meeting of any description of persons exceeding the number of fifty, other than a county or local meeting called by the Lord Lieutenant or Sheriff, &c. &c. should be held without notice given by seven householders ; and sundry other conditions of a Tory tendency.

This Act forbids the meeting of more than fifty persons within a mile of Westminster Hall, (except such parts of the parish of St. Paul's, Covent Garden, as are within that distance), and it repeats sundry provisions as to unlawful oaths, adding a new condition, that the appointment of persons by a society, to induce or persuade any person or persons to become members of that society, shall render it an unlawful confederacy and combination.

Finally, there is 60th Geo. III. c. 6. ' An Act for more effectually preventing seditious meetings and assemblies, to continue in force for five years.' This was one of the Six Acts. It expired in 1824 : but it is more than doubtful, whether its provisions do not stand alive in the last-mentioned Act which has not been repealed, though superseded pending the existence of this Act. The common notion is, that it is repealed ; but he would be a rash man who should act as if it were, for nothing but the event of a decision on his case could prove it, and who could prophesy of that? This Act of 60th Geo. III. also proscribed all meetings of which notice had not been given by seven householders, and inserted in a public newspaper, with sundry vexatious provisions such as should characterise one of the Six Acts; unless the meeting was called by a Lord Lieutenant, Sheriff, Mayor, and sundry other functionaries. The provisions are in other respects similar to those of its predecessor.

Besides these Acts might be enumerated several others, as 1st Geo. I. st. 2. c. 5, or the Riot Act; in which twelve persons unlawfully, riotously, and tumultuously assembled, may be dispersed by a Justice on proclamation; and if they do not go about their business in an hour afterwards, they are felons without benefit of clergy, and must suffer death. This was passed in 1715, just after the accession of the first George, when fears of the Pretender occupied all minds loyally inclined. The 60th Geo. III. c. 1, or Castlereagh's Military Training Act; under which half-a-dozen persons at play with wooden swords may be seized and transported for seven years, or imprisoned for two.

The 13th Car. II. st. 1, c. 5, against tumultuous petitioning; which prohibits the soliciting of more than twenty signatures to a petition for alteration of matters established by law in church or state, unless the same has been consented to by three Justices, or the major part of a Grand Jury. Penalty 100*l.* and three months' imprisonment.

Then there is 2nd Ed. III. c. 3, commonly called the Statute of Northampton, which forbids anybody to go armed to market. And the 17th Ric. II. c. 8; and 13th Hen. IV. c. 7, which makes any assembly illegal; and there are dicta to show that an assembly means any two or three gathered together for any purpose.

And there may be many more statutes which no one knows of; and so there may be safety as to them till they are known. But no lawyer's opinion is worth a fig as to those that are known; their meaning must depend on the circumstances that may happen to arise.

But for the present object it may be urged, that the later statutes which are supposed to be the present operating law, (the 37th, 39th, 52nd, 57th, and 60th Geo. III) relate to unlawful oaths and unlawful societies, and are sufficiently marked with the impress of their age;—matched together, arising out of the same causes, and placed on different foundations from those of the Trades' Unions. Until 1824, the last-mentioned

bodies were illegal, and might have come under some points of
the descriptions of illegality contained in the abovementioned
Acts relating to political societies ; but in that year they were
relieved of their illegality.   More than this, among the Acts
repealed with the old Combination Laws, were several relating
to the oaths which such bodies had been accustomed to take
for their purposes, and in their place there were no provisions
to prevent the taking of such oaths.   Yet the specific acts of
offence of which such bodies were supposed to be capable,
violence and intimidation, &c., were met with a specific provision, and the punishment declared was three months imprisonment ; and by these Acts it was declared, that offences should
be tried, not under the old common or statute law, but by the
new law.

This is a short statement, and the upshot of the whole is that
Trades' Unions are not, and never were intended to be comprehended in the terms of the Acts above-mentioned, forbidding
unlawful societies and unlawful oaths ; and if they were, that
they were taken out of the operation of them by the statutes
of 1824 and 1825 ; such Acts being directed against illegal
societies, and these being then made legal ; and that therefore
the punishment of the Dorstshire labourers should have been
imprisonment for three months, instead of transportation for
seven years.

Such is the complexity of the law, that anybody may be
forgiven for not knowing what it is.   Men are not to be
punished because they act in violation of a rumour of a law
which can be traced to no source ; at least none but Whigs or
Tories would punish them for it.   There is not, however, proof
that the men knew even of a rumour forbidding their doings.
Secresy does not always imply knowledge of wrong-doing,—
but feebleness, from any cause, and the desire not to be
thwarted before the strength to meet the enemy has been
acquired.   Else all Cabinet Meetings, and Secret Councils, in
other quarters, were sinful ; which may be so, though not so
deemed by Whigs or Tories.

There is a healthful principle illustrated in this matter, which
all governors would do well to regard ;—not to employ instruments which they would not that others should employ against
them.   The forced oaths of allegiance and submission,—the
superstitious and false honour fostered by themselves,—are
made the means of their undoing.   The sanction by themselves
invigorated, is made strong for the work of their enemies.

Abolish oaths of all sorts, and the sanction will become feeble
and inefficient for the support of others.   But further, do right

and fear not, and all the enlightened and the patriotic, without oath or engagement, will give prompt and energetic support. Mete out to all equal justice. Unbind the bonds of industry. Connive not at the robbery of the food of the industrious classes. Give them honest bread, honest law, and honest government. But can such moral daring be expected from the men who abolished slavery and established impressment; who freed the black back of the negro from the whip, and reserved it for the white backs of the soldier and the sailor ? They have no right conception of their vocation and their power ; no confidence in the strengthfulness of honesty and right dealing. It is not thus that the reformers of a free people should act.

What lessons of wisdom might not the Whigs have learnt, in the recollection of their own opposition to these tyrannical measures. But they know they have deserted their principles, and have not the strength which would come from the faith of the people even in their intentions; and therefore, with precipitation that was scarcely decent, did they hurry away these victims of an ignorant policy. But such is always the cowardly fear of the wrong-doer. They could not appeal to their acts, saying ' Have we ever swerved from a straight-forward, disinterested, and patriotic course ? The Reform Bill which we began, is it not the means, full and complete, of a perfect representation of the people ? Can the rejection of a call for justice in the distribution of political power, in the rights of industry, be imputed to us ? Why are you then so ungrateful ? Can you not wait a little for the accomplishment of what is still your due ? Is there aught of reason to doubt that, disregarding the interests of individuals or classes, we shall push on with might and main for the greatest happiness of you all ?'

Facts did not serve for such professions, and the appeal to reason must make way for the appeal to force. An example was wanted ; and the benefit of the doubt could not be spared, lest an enemy should gain a momentary triumph. The acts of the Unions were wrong. It might be so—but that was not reason enough to strain the law contrary to its purport and spirit, to punish them in a case not comprehended in the law. If a Sheen is suffered to go free for a slip in his name when clear proof of murder was made, there seems better reason for pardoning men who were ignorant of Acts of Parliament, which were not known to very many better-informed persons who may pretend to some knowledge of such things.

But it is the practice of the English law to teach by example. A man is hanged, or banished from his home, or sent to the treadmill, that people may ask where he is gone, and wherefore.

But no thought is taken of the expense of all this to the poor culprit, and whether the people might not have been made to know that such and such a penalty would be inflicted if they did such and such a thing, and the culprit have also had the benefit of the teaching. This is nobody's business ; and the olden method of hanging by the neck for the sake of warning others, is still held by, to the extent that modern feelings will endure.

And well might they be ignorant. The English laws are not promulgated except to the magistrates who put them in force; and are so overlaid with verbiage,—the meaning is so carefully concealed, and the principle, if there be one, is so narrow, so circumstantial, and technical,—that it requires a patient collation and comparison, of text and circumstance and common law and judicial decision, to descry the object in its precise application. Add to all this, that there are old, nay, ancient Statutes,— dicta of ancient writers,—all originating in and applicable to an ancient and by-gone state of things ; so that a man needs not only the Statutes at Large, but the advice and assistance of sundry legal Mentors each learned in his own department of the manifold English law, to suggest all precautions against the doing wrong ; and *then* it is a chance, if he escape out of one mesh, that he does not fall into another.

Is this liberty ? Twenty of us may not sign a petition,—ten of us may not go down to the gallery of the House to look after it,—three of us may not assemble,—we know not what we may *not* do, through the kindly interference of past legislation ; and yet all this, which was the work of the old Parliament—the curse and rottenness of the nation—now happily removed, if the people would but know it, and act as if they did,—is lovingly acted upon and cherished by the Whigs, who cried out against it in their day of weakness.

And now again, the Government have resisted the repeal of the taxes upon the means of making the laws known ; on the higgling ground of probable loss to the revenue. They could not comprehend the force and virtue of moral power. But there was dishonesty plain and palpable in not meeting the question fairly. Their evident tactics were to suffer the Radicals to speak to exhaustion, and answer no more than the courtesies of the House demanded. If it was really felt that the matter was a pounds, shillings, and pence question ; then why not submit it to the scrutiny to which figures may be put ? The *calculations* of the mover were met by the *opinions* of the financial minister ; and that not upon a secondary or merely incidental ground of resistance, but on the main and substantial one. This might have been a seeming, but was it an honest observance of the truth? But it is of the nature of the Whig and Whiggism, to admit the justice of the claim, and find reasons of detail for not granting it. Just men in words, in actions not to be trusted.

This indirect fostering of tyranny is more to be guarded against than the bold uncompromising adherence to it by Tories. They avowed their motive; the others act upon it and profess differently. Is it wonderful that the people are irritated, when the men who for forty years clamoured against these things suffer them to continue? It is too bad to last, and may get worse instead of better, if all popular constituencies do not, whenever the opportunity comes, get rid of the worst parts of the present House of Commons, and chuse men better, if possible, than the best.

It is of no use to war against the truths that are demonstrated. It is proved by all recent experience, that bold and reliable statesmen do not exist. Such as there are, can be depended on only as they are driven; and that which the people can control, is the House of Commons. What that is, the ministry must be; neither better nor worse. Perhaps the people have not Archimedes's point whereon to rest their full power to wield matters as they will; but let them use wisely what they have, and the end is in their keeping.

THE REPEAL OF THE COMBINATION LAWS.

We do not know of anything that has been more calculated to excite uneasiness and apprehension, than the tampering which has been for some time carried on with the working classes of this nation. Upon the industry, subordination, and general good conduct of these classes, the peace, prosperity, and even existence of the empire, mainly depend. This will admit of no difference of opinion, and surely it must be alike indisputable, that nothing could be more deserving of universal reprobation, than measures tending to injure them.

It is, in our eyes, one of the great recommendations of our laws and institutions, that, generally speaking, they did not emanate from the reveries of speculation—that they were not formed to supply wants which were not felt, or to correct theoretic faults which were not proved by experience to be injurious. They only received being when the necessity was distinctly apparent, and when the evil called aloud for remedy. Their origin was thus legitimate, and their fruits upon the whole have been of the most beneficial character. The Laws against Combinations thus originated. They were formed to remedy evils which existed, and which demanded remedy. We are not called upon to say that these Laws were faultless, or that they

did not, like all other laws, occasionally mingle injury with benefit. They were repealed on the ground, that the principle on which they stood was a false and pernicious one. Time had not rendered them a dead letter, or reversed their nature and operation. They were, when they were repealed, precisely what they were when they were framed, relatively, as well as otherwise. Their fruits, after abundant trial, had been thought exceedingly beneficial. The primary authors of their repeal were a knot of men who were strangers to business, to the working orders, and to human nature. They avowedly acted upon abstract reasoning, and not upon actual fact. By these men—people whom the Combination Laws had never touched—the petitions were chiefly got up ; and the Laws were repealed, not to remove a proved evil, but to carry the excellent to perfection. The repeal was sanctioned both by the Ministry and the Opposition.

It was, we remember, loudly trumpetted forth at the time, that an article in the Edinburgh Review had great influence in promoting the repeal. It seems to be the fate of that unhappy Work, that experience is ever upon the watch to knock its reasonings to pieces as soon as it may utter them. The argumentation of the article in question seemed to us to be of the most vicious character ; and we took occasion to intimate this to our readers immediately after the repeal. A new mode of managing public interests, is, however, now the fashion. Men, who have gone from the nursery to the school, and from the school to the lawyer's chambers, or the newspaper-office—men living apart from, and having no acquaintance with, the world—having little knowledge of human nature, and none of the mechanism and working of trade and public interests generally—these are now regarded as the only men who know anything of the science of government. Things are only thought to be true, in proportion as they are paradoxical in their appearance. It is first assumed that all men are alike, and that all nations are in similar circumstances, and have similar and common interests ; it is then assumed that men are always actuated by interest only, and that if left to themselves they will never take a wrong step in prosecuting their interests ; it is next assumed that everything which takes money out of, or does not bring money into, the public exchequer, is pernicious ; and that the lowest point of universal cheapness will carry us to the highest point of national prosperity. It is then assumed that regulations—the great characteristic of civilized society, are injurious—and that the farther we retrograde towards the condition of a horde of savages, the more beneficial it will be for us. The jargon is easily acquired, and a schoolboy may chatter it with as much volubility as the oldest philosopher. Under such a system, a youth of fifteen is as competent to stand at the helm, as such a man as the Earl of Liverpool.

The following, perhaps, will give our readers some idea of what a thorough-bred Political Economist of the present day is. He goes to examine a steam-engine, and the machinery to which it gives operation. He looks first at the fire.—" Good Heaven !" he exclaims, " what a consumption of coals !—The fire is ruinous, and must be quenched." He then glances at the pump for supplying the water for condensation. " The fools," he groans, " what a loss of power !—The pump must be destroyed." Then he turns to the fly-wheel. " Worse and worse," he cries ; " half the power of the engine is lost on these useless things." He knocks off the fly-wheel, and then looks at the connecting-rod. " Ah !" he sighs, " what an enormous waste of iron is here ! It is five times too long, and too thick." He cannot discover the connexion which one wheel has with another, therefore he destroys half of them. He cannot see that friction ought to be allowed for, or that strength and nature of materials ought to be matters of calculation. He can only find utility in those things which seem more immediately to finish the work ; and to benefit them, he demolishes that which renders them useful.—He lays the whole in ruins.

Setting aside competency, the honesty of those who took the lead in the repeal of the Combination Laws, was very far from being free from suspicion. Some of the principal of them had long been leading political agitators. They had in hand various schemes of sweeping innovation ; they were unable to obtain the favour of the higher classes, and they were anxious to enjoy that of the lower ones at almost any price, to enable them to carry their schemes into effect. The latter were forsaking them, and the repeal seemed to be a most promising project for winning them back, for freeing them from other influence, and for gaining a complete ascendency over them. Mr Hume was the great man in the business—the ostensible parent of the repeal. Perhaps no man in Europe was worse qualified than he was for undertaking a measure so important and complex—which bore so powerfully and comprehensively upon the relations of society, and the general interests of the nation. Notwithstanding all this, the repeal, as we have already said, was sanctioned by both sides of Parliament.

The Combination Laws were repealed ; immediately afterwards the working classes proved that the reasoning which had procured the repeal, was, in the main, a tissue of falsehoods and absurdities ; when Parliament met again, it was called upon to re-enact practically, these very laws, as a matter of absolute necessity. There are two or three points in this, which, we think, deserve serious consideration.

We imagine, in the first place, that, in this repeal, the general principles upon which this nation has always been governed, were altogether departed from. We have, as a people, always hitherto been taught to venerate our laws and institutions, and to regard, with extreme suspicion and dislike, all attempts to alter or abolish them. We have been instructed to look less at the theory of things, than at their working. This has been uniformly inculcated by our general government, and blind must he be who cannot perceive that it forms the principal bulwark of our national possessions. Our Parliaments and Ministries have always professed to make it their grand ruling principle. An existing law of large operation, could only be altered or abolished on these grounds : theoretic objections were to be disregarded ; smallness of utility was to have but little weight ; and distinct, abundant, and conclusive evidence of the existence of injurious defect and real evil, was to be produced. If, upon such evidence, the alteration or abolition were undertaken, it was proceeded in with the utmost caution and circumspection ; it was gradually carried into effect, step by step, that it might give no shock to the habits of the country, and occasion no derangement in our complicated system. This may have appeared to retard our progress, but we believe it has accelerated it. Our pace has been regular; we have made no false steps ; we have taken no wrong paths ; we have kept in the high road, and thereby have avoided all the stoppages which wild attempts to strike across the fields, and to leap hedges and ditches, would have made in our journey. That we have travelled by the wisest route, and at the quickest speed practicable, seems to be proved by the distance at which all other nations are behind us.

This sound and constitutional mode of conducting the affairs of England, was, we say, departed from in the repeal of the Combination Laws. The real question was this—Had these laws operated to sink, below the proper point, the wages of our labourers? The history of the country, and the experience of every one, replied in the negative. In good times, many of the working men of manufacturing and trading places, could earn as much in five of the working days of the week, as would both support their families, and enable them to spend the sixth in idleness and dissipation. If, in bad times, wages were too low, this was,

in general, evidently owing to the inability of masters to pay more, and not to the Combination Laws. Wages had, upon the whole, advanced, and the working classes of the time were enjoying a greater share of the necessaries and comforts of life, than had been enjoyed by those of former generations. This was not a matter of doubt—it required no Parliamentary Committee and witnesses to bring it to light—it was before the eyes of the nation at large. The real question was, however, put aside—theory was the great thing looked at—it was not because the Combination Laws produced proved evils, but it was because they were condemned by the Political Economists, that sentence was pronounced against them. Of course, no attempts were made to expunge their pernicious parts, and remedy their defects ; they were, in effect, torn out of the Statute-Book.

In the second place, it was one of the leading doctrines of the Economists, that these Laws ought not to exist. They proclaimed them to be a great national evil, and declared that the greatest public benefits would flow from their abolition. Sheet upon sheet of argument was employed to establish this, and to prove that the working classes would, after such abolition, do exactly the reverse of what they have done. If a portion of that which is called Political Economy, have been thus decisively refuted, does it not throw very heavy discredit on the remainder ? Does it not prove that the Economists are a very unfit race of men to be taken as guides in legislation ?

In the third place, the repeal of the Combination Laws was not an insulated measure. It formed part and parcel of what is called the new system of Free Trade. It was the first great step towards establishing Free Trade—it was to release the market for labour from the restrictive system. The Ministry and the Legislature were in favour of it, and yet experience has proved that it was a very pernicious measure ; that it stood upon false theory. Does not this prove that it is possible for the remainder of the new system of Free Trade to be equally erroneous—for the mighty changes which our commercial laws are undergoing, to be pregnant with calamities, rather than benefits ? Does it not prove that these changes are proceeded in at too rapid a pace, and with too little of caution and examination? We hate this new method of rooting up laws and systems by wholesale; it savours too much of the maxims of revolutionary governments for us. Its fruits in other countries where it has been tried, convince us that it will not produce much benefit here. It is at variance with our national character and habits, and it is at variance with the principles on which this nation has always, except in ruinous times, been governed.

In the fourth place, although every one now knows that the repeal in question was a pernicious measure, and was carried into effect on mistaken principles, no one in the House of Commons has been heard to say—"We erred grievously in the last session, and we must now be more wary." On the contrary, this house has seemed to regard the consequences of the repeal as so many reasons for plunging still deeper into Political Economy—into change and abolition. The whole blame is most unworthily cast upon poor Mr Hume, who, to do him justice, bears it in a manner worthy of a stoic. The very men who nominally assisted him to prepare his bill, point their fingers at him, and cry—" It was you who did it !" If we did not know the contrary, we should suppose that Mr Hume, single-handed, had carried the repeal in despite of every other Member of the Legislature.

It has long been well known, that political freedom depends for existence upon restrictive laws; it has been established in the last twelve months that there can be no Free Trade in labour without restrictive laws; and we suspect it will soon be proved that there can be no real freedom of general trade in this country without a restrictive system. We think the people of England will soon be prohibited from following various trades and occupations which they now follow; and that they will be thus prohibited, not by restrictive laws, but by the want of them—not by the statutes of the realm, but by the interference of other nations. We think it the most monstrous of all monstrous things, to suppose that the trade and industry of this country can thrive without laws for their regulation and protection.

In the fifth place, the New Marriage Act, and the repeal of the Combination Laws, appear to us to have supplied conclusive evidence that it is much more easy to alter than to amend the laws of England.

In all this, we are not arguing that laws and systems should never be altered or abolished. It would be preposterous in us to do so. The whole that we contend for is—adherence to the old and constitutional mode of altering and abolishing. If defects, errors, abuses, and evils, really exist, it can always be established by other evidence than abstract reasoning, the dreams of speculation, and the assumptions of untested theory; it can be established by direct proof, by complete demonstration. Let such proof and demonstration be produced, and then alter and abolish.

In all probability, the new Law against combinations will be known to our readers before these pages will reach them; but when we write, it is only in preparation, therefore we can give no opinion respecting it. We, however, fear from what has been said in the House of Commons, that it will be only a milk-and-water measure. It has been said, that it is not to revive the old laws, it is only to amend Mr Hume's bill. This seems odd and absurd enough, when the object of this bill was to destroy the laws against combinations, when it was supported by the doctrine that combinations were laudable and beneficial, and when it has been asserted that it indirectly promulgated such doctrine. The new bill must be intended to undo that which the one of Mr Hume was intended to do, and did do; and if it be not very strong and comprehensive in its enactments, it will yield very little benefit. The repeal has produced prodigious mischief; it has given maturity to a spirit and a system, which feeble efforts, and a short period of time, will not render innoxious.

It is scarcely necessary for us to say that there is not a finer race of people in the universe than the working classes of Britain. All know this who have had opportunities for studying their character; and every one may know it who will take the trouble of ascertaining what rank this nation holds among other nations. That man would never be respected by us who could look at the wealth, glory, and greatness of this empire, and yet feel no admiration for the industry, bravery, and other good qualities of those to whom they are, in so large a degree, owing. But then it does not follow from this, that these classes ought to be exempted from proper control. Several of their best qualities of heart render it the more essential for them to be under due restrictions. With the idle, phlegmatic ass, we have scarcely anything to do, save to dig at his flanks to urge him forward ; but the mettlesome, high-spirited horse requires a different mode of management. With the latter, we have but little need of the spur, but we cannot possibly do without the bridle.

The language employed by the Economists was, of itself, sufficient to produce combinations of the worst character. These people represented that combinations were even laudable, and that they could scarcely ever produce evil ; they asserted masters to be tyrants, and they led the labourers to believe that it was impossible for them to demand too high wages. According to them, the Combination Laws only existed to gratify the cupidity of the masters, and to enable them to enslave and hunger their workmen. They led the servants to place themselves on an equality with the masters, and to think that there was as much dependence on the one side as on the other ; they said almost everything that could breed animosity between the two classes. Their anxiety to destroy the obedience of the one, and the authority of the other, was most remarkable. In Mr Brougham's pamphlet on the Education of the People, we think the terms, servants and masters, are never used ; it is constantly—the working classes and their employers. We conceive the idea of this to be an importation from America, and we are very sure that it is a useless one. Why are the good old English words—servant and master, to be struck out of our language ? What have they done ? Whose ox have they stolen, and whom have they defrauded ? They can show as honest, unstained, and respectable a face, as any words in the dictionary, and we will not part with them for any American trumpery whatever. We will have no such innovations.

None of this was lost upon the labouring orders, and no sooner were the Laws repealed, than combinations, filled with the worst spirit, sprung up in all quarters. These combinations soon thought that it was their interest to do much more than to exact the highest wages possible ; they thought it was their interest to place the mas-

ters under the most grinding tyranny. It was now for the servant to command, and the master to obey. As the former might be pleased to dictate, the latter was to discharge or retain his workmen, to send his goods to market, and to conduct his business generally. This was not sufficient, and the combinations thought it their interest to place such labourers as did not belong to them, under the same tyranny ; no man was to be suffered to work and eat, when it was their pleasure that he should be idle and starve. As the authorities of the realm could not well be employed to enforce all this, the combinations became the administrators of their own laws. They murdered and maimed without mercy ; the masters were deprived of the control of their property ; various trades were stopped and grievously injured, and a loss was occasioned of many millions. Perhaps Mr Brougham remarked this inverted state of things, and thought the terms—masters and servants, could not be used with any propriety ; he ought, however, to have called the labourers, the employers.

The figure which Mr Hume and the host of economic writers cut upon this, was irresistibly ludicrous. They were spinning round upon their knees from one combination to another, and imploring them, with tears, to act differently. " Now, do, good, sweet, dear people, behave better.—You are destroying our characters—you are disgracing us—you are knocking up Political Economy. Remember what we said for you, and do not make storytellers of us. Parliament will be after you with a rod—you will be switched —you will be sent to bed supperless, and we protest we will turn our backs on you !" It was unavailing ; the combinations were now masters, and were not to be dictated to, even by Mr Hume. It is due to this individual to say, that the business seems to have given him a slight surfeit of legislation ; he has blushed divers times, and has shown much modesty during the session. The other people who insisted, in their speeches and reviews, so strenuously on the repeal, have gone on as usual ; they have gone on dictating upon public affairs, and calling for innovation upon innovation, just as though the repeal had not covered them with shame, and proved them to be unworthy of being listened to.

That these combinations should be

wholly dissolved, if possible, is proved by various most important considerations.

It was alleged that the great object of the repeal was to make the trade in labour perfectly free—to give full and equal freedom to both servants and masters. Well, the first great step in Free Trade—in the overthrow of monopolies—has been to place labour under a close and gigantic monopoly. It matters not what the masters may be able to give—what servants, who do not belong to the combinations, may be willing to take—what the price of provisions and the needs of workmen may be—what labour there may be in the market—the will of the combinations is to be the only thing to fix the wages. All the things by which these ought alone to be fixed, are to be wholly deprived of operation. When wages form the main ingredient in the price of most articles, it may easily be conceived how this will affect general prices—when the manufacturer is exposed to the competition of foreigners, and is bound to manufacture at a certain price, or not at all, it may easily be conceived how it will operate on trade.

The master is not, in effect, at liberty to choose his servant; and the latter is to be chosen, not for his character and qualifications as a workman, but for his character and qualifications as a member of the combinations: he is to study to please these combinations, and not his employer. Our readers need not be told how perniciously this must operate upon the industry, skill, good workmanship, and general character of the servants. Under such a system, the very best servants are in the greatest danger of wanting bread, and the very worst have the greatest certainty of always having it in abundance.

The masters and servants are converted into hostile bodies. The old feelings of reciprocal good-will and regard for each other's interests, are destroyed, and replaced by strife and animosity. The servants care not what injury they may do their masters; they are struggling for their ruin. This goads the latter into the same spirit; it makes them refuse to give anything beyond the amount of the bond; it makes them afraid to give good wages, lest part of the money should go to the combination fund; it dries up their benevolence and ge-

nerosity, and renders them callous to the sufferings of the servants, when these really do suffer.

The combinations have the effect of raising wages far above the proper figure. They not only enable the servant to fix any value he may think fit on his labour, but they compel him to demand considerably more than the sum which he judges to be necessary for his maintenance. He must contribute constantly and largely to the funds of the combination, and his contribution must, of course, be taken from his wages. The masters are therefore compelled to pay large sums in wages, which are not needed for feeding and clothing their workmen, and which are to be employed only in working their own injury and ruin. They are constrained to furnish every farthing of those funds which are only employed to rob them of the control of their property, and to destroy their trade: they are compelled not only to pay their servants for the time in which they employ them, but for the weeks and months in which these think proper to do nothing. When the master is, in most cases, bound to a certain price for his articles, the exorbitant rate of wages must operate powerfully to narrow the quantity of employment, and the demand for labour.

These combinations destroy all equality in sacrifices for the public weal. The masters have little or no power in fixing the rate of wages; they must give whatever the servants declare to be necessary for supplying themselves with bread. As they cannot declaim against high wages, they declaim against the high price of provisions. The servants compel them to pay much more than is necessary for the purchase of food, and then they cry out that corn is too dear. Of course, those sacrifices which the manufacturer's competition with foreigners may call for, are not to touch his workmen; they are to be thrown principally upon the agriculturists. These workmen are to live plentifully, and to have large wages for weeks and months of idleness, whatever the master's prices may be; if he cannot make his customers pay for this, he must make the farmers and the agricultural labourers pay for it. From the farmers and the husbandry-labourers is to be sponged, in the long run, the money which forms the funds of these

D

combinations, and which enables the town-labourers to spend weeks and months in idleness, turbulence, and, too often, crime.

In a political light, these combinations are calculated to yield the greatest evils to the empire. The town working-classes of the three kingdoms are, to a very great extent, organized into a gigantic confederacy. However numerous the combinations may be, they still, in reality, form only one body : the army may be divided into regiments, but, nevertheless, these form but one army. This confederacy exists to promote the private and personal interests of its members only ; and, like most other bodies which exist on the same principle, it cares not what interest it injures or ruins, provided it benefits its own. It tramples upon law, and the rights of the rest of the nation, to the utmost point possible. It not only places the masters under a ruinous tyranny, destroys competition in the market for labour, and stifles emulation among the workmen in respect of industry, skill, and sobriety; but it emancipates the working classes from all authority and influence touching moral and political conduct. The labourer's bread is made to depend in no degree on his good morals ; however vile a profligate he may be, and however pestilentially his conduct and principles may operate upon his younger and less experienced associates, the master has no power to discharge him. He must be placed on a level with a man of the best character ; he must be protected from everything that might reform him ; he must be kept to corrupt all the innocent youth that come in his way. We need not point out how this must operate on the morals of the working classes generally. Many of the workmen possess the elective franchise, and, generally speaking, they are incapable of exercising it properly without advice. The masters are the proper men to give such advice, but they are now the last people in the world who would be listened to. Their influence is gone; they are now the obliged party. The working classes are thus left without proper leaders—they are placed in opposition to all above them, and they will follow any demagogue who may address them.

In addition to all this, the combinations, from their perpetual efforts to violate the laws—their invasions of the rights of the masters and the labourers who do not belong to them —the brutal punishments which they inflict—and the spirit of enmity and vengeance which they keep in action, must operate powerfully to fill the working classes with contempt for the laws, with disregard for the rights of others, and with the worst principles.

We care not for what Mr Brougham may say against the working classes being dependent on their masters; we care not for the new schemes of education which are now bewildering the country ; we are very sure that the working classes of this nation are not, at present, in a state to be independent of their masters; and we are, moreover, quite sure that they never will be in such a state. Woe to England, when its labourers shall be so far independent as to be only governed by laws ! It is essential for the good of the labourer, as well as for the good of the state, that he should be under the authority of his master in respect of general conduct as well as labour ; that his master should instruct him in what constitutes a good member of society, as well as in the mysteries of his calling; and that his master should coerce his bad morals, as well as his idleness and bad workmanship.

The magnificent edifice which society forms in this country, can only stand so long as the different classes which compose it shall be properly cemented together, and shall duly bind each other to the proper place and the proper duty. The lower orders must be cemented to the class next them— they must form its basis, and must have sufficient weight to bind them to act their part in the support of the structure. The foundations are, however, now tearing themselves asunder from the rest of the building, and if this be suffered to reach its completion, it will not need a prophet to foretel the consequences. The working orders are, in regard to connexion and control, separating themselves from the rest of the community, and establishing a state of things the most unnatural and portentous. This must be speedily remedied, or it will be beyond remedy. If they be not under the moral government of their masters, they cannot be governed at all ; and if they be not duly governed, they will plunge the nation into ruin.

In times of distress our working orders generally become furious politicians. It would be the most easy thing imaginable for this immense confederacy to assume a political character, and it would be pretty sure to do this, were trade to receive any serious injury. We need not say what the consequences would be, were it to become fiercely actuated by the spirit of Radicalism. Were these combinations to proceed as they have done, they would soon look for other slaves in addition to the masters: they would soon find tyrannizing over the latter very insufficient for protecting what they call their rights and interests. They are already attempting to rivet their chains on the farmers and husbandry-labourers; they would next place commerce under their despotism; they would regulate our imports and exports, and give us another new system of trade. It is the nature of such vicious bodies to keep continually thirsting for additional spoils and authority, and to be satisfied with nothing.

Setting aside all other matters, if they continue to exist, trade must perish. Hemmed in by them on the one side, and rival foreigners on the other, the masters must either emigrate to other countries, or submit to ruin.

It is therefore the duty of every friend of his country to do his utmost towards the dissolution of these combinations. The servant has an undoubted right to take his labour to the best market, and to be perfectly free in making his bargain; but the master has an equally undoubted right to the same liberty. If it be impossible to frame laws that will give the exact degree of liberty to both—that will make the market in labour perfectly free to both seller and buyer—laws must be framed that will make the nearest approaches to it. If it be impossible to avoid giving a little advantage to one of the parties—to avoid leaving something to the discretion and generosity of one of the parties—on every principle of reason, experience, and interest, the masters ought to be the favoured party. The servants have just given decisive evidence that they cannot form it without bringing the most grievous ills upon the state; and the masters long did form it, without in any way abusing the privilege. The masters of this country may laugh at the fashionable slang touching tyrants

which is employed against them; their conscience is pure, their hands are unstained. As a body, they have always exercised their authority over their servants in a manner becoming Englishmen and Christians. Had they endeavoured to tyrannize as their servants are now tyrannizing, the country would soon have been made too hot to hold them.

We exhort the masters to bestir themselves to the utmost against the combinations, and to trust less to laws than to their own efforts. It occurs to us that the adoption of the following plan would be far more efficacious than any law that could be framed.

Let them change their mode of hiring; let them hire their workmen no longer by the week, or for an unfixed period, terminable on short notice. Let them follow the farmer's plan, and hire for twelve, six, or three months certain. If at the first they be compelled to hire the whole of their men at the same moment, they must not hire them all for the same period, for this would set them all at liberty together, again to combine. They must engage some for twelve months, some for nine, some for six, &c. By this plan, only a small portion of the workmen would be able to strike at the same moment. When those engaged for the shortest period should be at liberty, and should want to form a new contract, all the rest would be firmly bound, and could not join them in combining to suspend trade and tyrannize over the master. If the master could not agree with them for a new engagement, he could still keep his other hands at their work, and engage new ones in the room of those who might leave him. He would likewise be able to get rid of such men as might not suit him. The grand principle to be kept in sight, should be, to guard vigilantly against more than a small number of the workmen being at liberty at the same moment for the renewal of contracts.

To illustrate this, we will assume a master to employ regularly forty workmen. All these have left him, and it is necessary for him at present to re-engage the whole on the same day. Let him bind ten to him for a year, ten for nine months, ten for six months, and the remaining ten for three months. When three months shall expire, ten of the men will be at liberty, but all the rest will be bound; the ten free ones must wait three months before they can get ten more to join them. Let him then hire the whole, as their terms may expire, for a year certain. By this mode, no more than one-fourth of his men could ever strike at once, and their striking could do him but little injury.

Under this system, the wages could be paid in weekly sums as usual : it is as applicable to labourers who work by the piece, as to those who work otherwise. It will apply to those trades which only employ workmen a part of the year, for the men could be bound for the season. The masters must be far better judges of its practicability than ourselves, but we certainly think it a very practicable one. It would, no doubt, clash with old customs and habits, but these are such as might be changed without difficulty. We cannot see why the mechanics, &c. should not be hired as the clerks, shopmen, and husbandry-labourers are hired : if the weekly system were universally adopted, we are pretty sure that the combination system would rage as furiously among the clerks, shopmen, &c. as it does among Mr Brougham's pupils. That the working classes would set their faces against such a system, is abundantly certain, but they might be conquered. The present state of things must be remedied, whatever efforts and sacrifices the remedy may call for. These combinations are, in reality, most pernicious, odious, and oppressive monopolies, and they must be dissolved. It is idle to say that they will, under regulations, produce good. Their principle is vicious ; they exist not for public, but for private benefit, they seek to benefit associations of individuals by injuring the rest of the community. They give to these individuals a vast portion of unconstitutional and dangerous power, which is sure to be generally employed to the detriment of the weal of the state.

We entreat the masters in this nation to reflect deeply upon the doctrines which certain political men are putting forth in favour of what they are pleased to call, the independence of the working classes. Although these doctrines emanate from faction, and have for their grand object the profit of faction, they are still capable of working incalculable mischief. Their glaring falsehood is, alas ! in these

days, no security against their being believed in. They strike, no doubt, at the vital interests of the empire, but they strike more immediately at those of the masters ; and it is the masters principally who must render them innoxious. We conjure the latter, by what they owe to themselves and their country, to make a determined stand in defence of their just rights, and in resistance to these fearful innovations. We call upon them to insist boldly upon possessing that authority over their servants which they have always hitherto possessed, which the servant has always hitherto surrendered to them in his contract, and upon which the wellbeing of themselves, the working classes, and society, so largely depends.

It is the authority of the master over the general conduct of the servant, which compels the latter not only to labour for a certain number of hours, but to do a sufficiency of work, and to do it in a proper manner. It is this authority which compels the servant not only to do his duty as a workman, but to do his duty as a member of society. It is this authority which educates the servant—which makes him industrious, active, skilful, sober, and honest. To this authority, the working classes of Britain mainly owe their high character. Let it be destroyed—render these classes independent—give to the latter the power to bind the masters from interfering with them in anything beyond a stipulated period and quantity of labour —and you will strip the workman of all his valuable qualities. The twelve hours per day of labour will soon dwindle down to seven or eight: the industry and activity will soon degenerate into sloth and carelessness : the skill will soon sink into ignorance : the sobriety and honesty will soon change into dissipation and knavery : and the good morals will soon become general depravity.

The masters are the main agents in maintaining public tranquillity and order : so far as regards these, they have a more powerful influence in governing the nation than the laws and the government. The uninformed and the wilful—the vast overwhelming majority of the population—are distributed in small portions among them, and each master instructs and governs his portion. What makes the Irish peasantry so depraved and ungovernable? They have no masters. What has recently made our working classes of various large places imitate, as far as possible, the conduct of the Irish Rockites?—They have been emancipated from the control of masters. If the authority of the masters be destroyed, we must have laws to keep us in order which will scarcely leave us the shadow of liberty: there will be no possible alternative between this and the insupportable tyranny of the multitude. Liberty may fall in this country—perhaps it will fall—but if it do, it will be overthrown by those canting, bragging, selfish, hollow-hearted hypocrites, who call themselves its exclusive worshippers.

And what, in good sooth, is to be the substitute for the authority of the masters? What is to render the independence of the working classes harmless? Education—lectures, and mechanics' institutes. Do then none need discipline and control but the uneducated? Are those who have received costly educations the most industrious and moral part of the community? Are our men of *science* the best friends of peace and order? Alas! Alas! that there should be a single man in this nation so simple as to mistake doctrines like these for wisdom! If these mechanics' institutions are to be sub-

sidiary to the education given by, and the authority of, the masters, let them prosper; if they are to destroy these, let us at once have an Act of Parliament for their suppression.

What political benefits are to flow from the independence of the working classes? Do these form the only part of the community which has a stake in the public weal, and which is capable of displaying integrity, wisdom, and patriotism, in the discharge of political duties? Why are we to be so greatly terrified by the political influence of the masters? Have they no interest in public order and prosperity? Are they without honesty and intelligence—are they sycophants, parasites—the tools of power, and the slaves of party and faction? Every one can answer the questions.

Let the friends of the country set their faces against the new doctrines, and adhere steadfastly to the old maxims, which have brought us to our proud elevation—let our national industry be protected from the tremendous evils which are arraying themselves on every side against it—let it be kept in employment—let no foreign workman be resorted to, so long as an English one can be found to do the work, even though the charge of the latter be somewhat higher; * and, above all, let that authority be jea-

---

* We believe the "restrictive system" never reached the importation of French milliners and dress-makers. We think these precious foreign commodities are not even subject to a protecting duty on being imported. They, therefore, naturally enough, are very plentiful in the metropolis. We cannot, do what we will, entirely close our ears to scandal; and we absolutely have been assured, that there are British ladies of high rank, who, when they order their dresses, give strict injunctions that these shall only be touched by the outlandish people. We have been further assured, that these British ladies of high rank are constrained to act towards the French women as the nurse acts towards the spoiled child, when she wishes to keep it from an outrageous fit of squalling: We have been even further assured, that these British ladies of high rank endure insulting impertinence and insolence from the Gallic damsels, almost as though they were matters to be proud of.

It is quite impossible for us to believe this of our lovely countrywomen. That a British Peeress, or the lady of one of our country gentlemen, should thus lavish her favours on a foreign ingrate, and studiously withhold employment and bread from the humble, obliging, and industrious daughter of her own country, is a thing that can be believed by no one. It is the more incredible, because no earthly cause can be assigned for it. If our English girls were devoid of taste, and could only stitch with pack-thread, and needles six inches long, the case would be different; but a man has only to look at the females of the middle classes, to be convinced that English hands can make dresses capable of giving the utmost effect to the charms of any female whatever. We, however, think, that when the English dress-makers are so fully employed that not one can be obtained, a lady of rank will then reluctantly employ a French one. We think this, because we have occasionally seen ladies of rank garbed in dresses, so grotesque and unbecoming, and having such a

lously preserved, from which the working classes draw the greater part of their best characteristics. Do what we will, we cannot reach perfection. Every system must have its evils, and the best one is that which has the fewest and the lightest. After all our changes and legislation, we must at last leave a great deal to the discretion and honesty of some part or other of the community ; and the best plan must be, to confide this to those who may have the best security to offer in respect of character and circumstances, against the trust being abused. To make the working orders the favoured portion in regard to power and authority, is to do what madness alone could sanction.

There is one important topic connected with this question, on which we must not be silent. The combinations have generally asserted, that the high price of provisions compelled them to demand advanced wages. A clamour has therefore been got up for the admission of foreign corn, and Parliament is pledged to make some alteration in the Corn Laws in the next Session. Now, we beseech our Country Gentlemen to insist upon having the most full and correct information laid before them on the following points, before they consent to anything whatever that may depress the corn-market :—

1st, The exact wages paid by every trade and manufacture to the workmen employed in them.

2d, The exact sum which these workmen really require for procuring a sufficiency of the necessaries of life.

3d, Whether these workmen are not receiving wages far higher than are necessary for procuring them such a sufficiency of necessaries.

4th, Whether these workmen are not receiving wages, which not only support them in a plentiful manner, but enable them to contribute largely to the funds of the combinations, which not only support them thus when they deign to labour, but which enable them to spend weeks and months in idleness, to the grievous injury of the empire.

5th, Whether these workmen are not receiving—making every proper allowance—double the wages received by the husbandry labourers.

6th, Whether these workmen—taking all things into calculation—do not possess much greater incomes than the mass of our counting-house clerks, naval and military officers, officiating clergymen, and shopmen.

The most full and correct information, we say, must be demanded on all these points. It is alleged, that the sums paid for the labour of these workmen render it necessary for the price of corn to be lowered ; and certainly this ought not to be listened to, until it is satisfactorily proved that these sums are not greater than they ought to be.

When we write, some of these workmen are earning in London three pounds a-week, others fifty shillings, and others forty-five and forty shillings. Some of those who have lately struck, were hired at the rate of five shillings per day before they struck ; and, if they thought proper to make what is called seven days in the week, they earned thirty-five shillings weekly. Most of those workmen earned before their strikes twenty-five, twenty-eight, and thirty shillings per week. In London, the mass of the clerks, shopmen, curates, half-pay officers, &c.—men who have been educated as gentlemen, who are compelled to appear as gentlemen, and who are

---

murderous effect upon their beauty, that we have been quite convinced these dresses never could have been made by English fingers.

As to the calumny, that a British lady of rank will submit to the impertinence and insolence of the outlandish women, it is really shocking. The wives and daughters of our high-minded nobility—the females born on the soil of England, and filled with that blood, in which pride and lofty spirit luxuriate to the last—submit to disgrace like this ? No, no—it cannot be. It would be just as possible for them to fall in love with apes and monkeys.

We hear, too, that among our females, the partiality for foreign silks, laces, and gloves, is as great as ever. This we are compelled to believe. We lament it, and are ashamed of it. It will, however, in due time, greatly benefit trade, and this must satisfy us.

constrained to live at far greater expense than the workmen in question—have not, perhaps, more than from seventy to one hundred pounds per annum.

In all this we are saying nothing against high wages, if they can be with propriety demanded. We should rejoice if our labourers could earn ten pounds per week, even though ten shillings might supply them with necessaries, if they could do this without producing injustice and public evil. But the question is not, whether general high wages be, or be not, beneficial—it is, whether one part of the working-classes shall be doomed to penury and want, that the other part may receive far higher than necessary wages? It is declared, that the present wages of the workmen in question cannot be paid without a reduction in the moderate rents of the landholders, the scanty profits of the farmers, and the bread-and-water earnings of the husbandry-labourers. It is declared, in effect, that our country population must be condemned to distress and privation, that our town population may riot in profusion and extravagance. We protest against such outrageous injustice and oppression. If trade ought to injure one part of the community more than another, it certainly ought to injure those who are engaged in, and not those who have nothing to do with, it. If trade cannot be maintained without sacrifices—if, in reality, a grinding tax must be imposed upon us to make it flourish—in the name of common justice let us all suffer equally. Bring down the profits of the merchants, manufacturers, and tradesmen, to the level of those of the farmer—reduce the wages of the town workman, until, all things considered, they only equal those of the husbandry-labourer—and then, whatever sacrifices may be necessary for the prosperity of trade, we will answer for it, that agriculture will bear its part without a murmur. But this abominable attempt to sacrifice, not only one great interest to another, but one part of the population to another, must be fairly resisted, whoever may countenance it. This has always been a land of justice and equi-

ty, and we trust it will remain so. In spite of all that Political Economy has invented, or may invent, we maintain that the government has a right to give, not only the most full, but the most equal, protection to the property and industry of the nation; and that it cannot favour one interest, or one part of the people, to the cost and injury of another, without grossly violating its duty.

Let these misguided workmen who are agitating the country, and preparing for it the most serious evils, be assured that, in the upshot, they will be the greatest sufferers from their madness. The cup of bitterness will not be long in reaching them. Their turbulence and outrages—their sickening cant, touching their right to inflict the most grievous wrongs on all but themselves, have already stripped them of all respect and sympathy on the part of the rest of the nation. They stand the objects of general indignation—they are regarded as men who disgrace their country—who are acting the part of enemies to their country. Do they suppose that the masters, and the rest of the community, are men to be robbed of the control of their property and of their sacred rights by them, or any other people in the universe? If they do, they will soon be better informed. They may rely upon it, that if one law fail to curb them, another will be framed that will; and that if nothing else will do, the rest of the nation will unanimously place them bound hand and foot at the mercy of the masters.

We entreat the more moderate and honest members of the combinations to withdraw from them immediately, and we call upon those of the working classes who are unconnected with them to remain so. The working-orders ought to be the last to prepare public evils, for such evils always fall upon them the most heavily. Calamity cannot visit the empire without pouring its worst ills upon them. They can only prosper through the prosperity of the masters; and they will ever benefit far more from gaining the respect and good-will of the masters, than from exciting their animosity.

THE COMBINATIONS.

In an article on the Repeal of the Combination Laws we intimated our fear, that the law then in preparation would be a milk-and-water measure. This law has since come into operation, and our readers have not now to learn from us its character. Mr Wallace stated, on its being brought before Parliament, that it probably would not go far enough for some people, who were guided by their *prejudices*. This adoption of the slang of the revolutionary school by a member of the Ministry, was not, we think, a very seemly matter ; the more especially, as it was done to stigmatize those whose friendship has not been wholly useless to the Ministry. Mr Wallace has, however, we suspect, discovered by this time that he has prejudices as well as other people. We are strongly tempted to imagine, that before long, he, and certain of his colleagues, will be laboriously employed, not in smiling at the prejudices of others, but in endeavours to remedy the evils produced by their own.

The new law has been brought into action—the fatal error of Mr Hume in repealing the common law touching masters and servants, and involving such repeal in impenetrable mystery, has been rectified—the defects of that sage statesman's bill have been remedied—and what is the fruit ? The mildest answer that can be given is —Nothing. Combinations have gone on increasing, the system has been rendered more comprehensive and pernicious, the demands of the workmen have been more unreasonable, outrages have been as frequent, more atrocious murders have been committed, trade has suffered still greater injuries, and the community at large has been still more heavily taxed by the combiners. Parliament might just as well have not wasted a single moment of the Session on combinations.

It would be idle in us to repeat in detail what has appeared in most of the newspapers; we will therefore content ourselves with noticing a few of the fruits which combinations have produced *since* the new law obtained being. In Ireland, a number of murders of the most horrible description have been committed ; the Irish papers state that trade in some parts has been brought into a state of ruin, and that various masters are preparing to withdraw from it altogether. The ship-wrights in the Thames have, as they have told the world,[*] refused to work for any master who employed men who had been traitors to them—that is, men who had seceded from their combination, and been willing to work on terms which they did not dictate. In consequence the trade has been long stopped, and, as it is stated, a licence has been obtained for sending a vessel up the Baltic for repairs. The combiners, or, to speak more properly, the conspirators, have pointed out Mr Young as

---

[*] We give this from a letter which appeared in the Times on behalf of the ship-wrights. The papers, however, state that their great object was that they might work by the piece, and not by the day. The masters have been compelled to submit.

the individual who has shown the greatest firmness in resisting them, and we hope that gentleman values the honour they have done him as he ought. We thank him in the name of his country for his spirited conduct—for his manly opposition to their detestable tyranny. We need not dilate on what has taken place at Sunderland—on the attempt to stop the ships and cargoes of others, and to drive crews of seamen by force from employment, merely because they disposed of their labour according to law and right. In Scotland, according to the papers, the collier combination has compelled some hundreds of workmen to strike against their inclinations,* when they were able to earn what would be equal to fifty shillings per week in London. This wise and patriotic body, it seems, regulates other matters beside wages; it regulates the supply and price of coals; not a coal must be sent to market without its permission. Its members are represented to labour only four or five days in the week, and how they employ the rest of their time may be easily conjectured. Of course, about one-third more labourers are employed in preparing the coals for market than are necessary, and the price of coals to the consumer is greater, by about half the wages paid for digging them, than it ought to be. This grievous addition is made to the cost of coals, even when the market is sufficiently supplied; but it does not satisfy the combination. The papers state that the supply is inadequate, and that there is every reason to believe the combiners mean to push the price to an enormous height on the approach of winter, by keeping coals from the market. It cannot be needful for us to say, that coals in this country rank among the necessaries of life, and that it is as essential for them, as for corn and animal food, to be kept at a moderate remunerating price. The various combinations have proceeded vigorously in adding to their numbers and perfecting their organization, and they now tell us that they are regularly connected with each other, and form a gigantic whole. They have set up

their own newspapers, which, as is very natural, inculcate the worst doctrines and feed the worst spirit. The system is creeping upwards as well as in other directions, and in London and various other places, the shopmen of drapers, &c. have formed themselves into combinations. As soon as the workmen of one calling obtain their exactions, those of another strike; and there are constantly three or four important trades stopped in some part or other. The continual maintenance of the workmen of three or four trades is a matter of no consequence to the purse of the body of combinations; the money necessary can be at any time extorted from the masters; the taxes levied by the combiners need neither the sanction of Parliament nor the aid of the law to enforce payment.

When the laws permit all this, it is of some importance to inquire into its nature, and into the promises which it gives touching the future.

There are persons—even legislators—even official men, who stated, some time since, that they foresaw before the Combination Laws were repealed, that the repeal would be followed by what they called a re-action. They represented the excesses of the combinations to spring from temporary causes, and that the natural operation of things would speedily end them. There are Political Economists who very recently protested that if the combinations were not molested they would soon become harmless, and wages would find their proper level. If they could be trusted, it would be very useless in us to say another word on the subject; but unhappily everything in reason and experience proclaims that they are not to be trusted.

The working classes called for the repeal of the Combination Laws that they might combine; they combined that they might promote, as far as possible, their own interests, not for a moment, but *constantly.* Their objects were offensive more than defensive; and they were principally to raise wages, shorten the hours of labour, and curtail the authority of the masters as much as possible. Every man

---

* Since we wrote this, the master of these workmen has been constrained to agree to their demands, and their example has been followed in other collieries.

who keeps a servant knows, that this servant, without combinations, is always in effect struggling in favour of these things. The servants formed themselves into bodies, they met regularly for the purpose of discovering grievances to redress, and advantages to obtain ; they subjected themselves to a heavy permanent tax, and they kept constantly accumulating funds which could only be employed in making war on the masters for their own benefit. It is astonishing that any one could be so marvellously ignorant of human nature as to imagine that bodies like these would only be mischievous for a moment, and would become, of their own accord, harmless. Were we to concede that the Combinations would always act honestly in respect of intention, still nothing would be more certain than that they could continually follow the most injurious conduct. Man is never satisfied. It is impossible for workmen to meet weekly to deliberate on their conditions, without working themselves into the belief that their wages are too small, their time of labour is too long, their masters are too arbitrary, or that something requires alteration in their circumstances. They may conscientiously believe this, and still they may be altogether in error. It is not in the nature of things that men should tax themselves to form a fund, and then suffer it to lie idle when it might procure them benefits. The combination-fund is in a great measure to the workman, what his capital is to the tradesman ; it is formed that it may be employed to bring in as much permanent gain as possible. But it would be preposterous to suppose that the combinations would always be actuated by honest motives : their leaders are, many of them, men of very bad principles, and they must often be largely influenced by avarice, sensuality, idleness, stubbornness, and other bad feelings of human nature. The principles and objects of the combinations, and the character of those who composed them, made it morally certain, when they were first formed, that nothing but the want of means could prevent them from *continually* producing the most grievous evils.

The combinations have rapidly increased in numbers and power ever since they were suffered to exist. This has not been a matter of chance—the

reverse of what might have been reasonably expected. Nothing else could be looked for—nothing but some miraculous change in the laws of nature could have prevented it. The working classes had permission given them to combine, when they confidently expected that combining would yield them great benefits ; trial amply realized their expectations. Interest and feeling led the workmen of a trade to combine ; this gave them a monopoly of the labour of that trade : they demanded an increase of wages, withheld the supply of labour until their demand was complied with, and they could not be resisted. One trade was stimulated by the success of another. The workmen who did not combine perceived that those who did greatly improved their circumstances by it ; they perceived that to combine, was, in effect, to raise wages, enlarge privileges, and become, in a great degree, the masters of their employers ; they perceived that this was to be achieved only by combining. The risk diminished as the system strengthened, until, at last, there was scarcely any risk at all. However combination may injure the working classes as a whole, it demonstrably yields great profit to those who engage in it : it gives to the latter double and treble the wages and immunities enjoyed by those who cannot resort to it. It was not in human nature to resist the temptations which combination spreads around it, and of course the working orders combined to the farthest point possible. The workmen of almost every trade are now united in combinations ; they are sufficiently powerful to do nearly anything they please. Look what way we will, we can discover nothing in the shape of law, counterpoising body, or anything else, that is capable of preventing them from continually abusing their tremendous power.

If we look at the masters, what can they do ? They have made the most desperate resistance, they have made the most gigantic sacrifices, and still they have been defeated in almost every contest. In the two or three instances in which they have conquered, they have owed their victory chiefly to the mismanagement of their opponents. The servants can choose their time and ground, keep their places from being filled by others, prepare funds, and rely upon being maintained for a term of almost any duration. Almost the only thing that they risk is the being compelled to live more economically during the strike ; but then they have nearly a certainty of being successful, and of being able to fare the more luxuriously afterwards. At the time when the master has the most orders on hand, and the greatest need of workmen, the latter leave him if he will not submit to such terms as they please to impose upon him. He cannot get other workmen, he can find no other masters to execute his orders and let him receive the profits, his customers take their business elsewhere, and he perhaps loses them altogether. The masters cannot combine to assist each other as the workmen can. If the latter only supply each other with money to subsist on, they suffer scarcely anything from striking, and they may remain out of employment for any length of time : but the former cannot enable each other to retain even a portion of their profits and connexions, they must endure a tremendous loss, they can only suspend their business for a short period, and then they have scarcely anything before them but unconditional submission. The workmen have so many advantages, that they are irresistible. If the combinations be only true to each other, they may do as they please. To do this, they have only to lend to each other a trifling part of what they extort from the masters. The money furnished by one that is in employment, to another that has struck, is, in truth, but a debt which is discharged by the borrower when the lender needs it. Reasoning on the point is, indeed, very unnecessary. The fact which we have cited, that in almost every contest the masters have been defeated, and have been compelled to submit to the most humiliating, as well as injurious, conditions, decisively proves that they are perfectly incapable of acting as a check upon the combinations.

While this is the case, it has been likewise abundantly proved, that it is impossible to oppose and restrain the combinations by means of uncombined workmen. To combine is a matter of party feeling, as well as personal profit, and the enthusiasm of the mass of the working classes is in its favour; of course almost all the workmen of every calling join the combinations who are able. Those who do not combine, are com-

paratively a few scattered, unconnected individuals, who are exposed to the scorn and hostility of the mass ; they must work for under-wages, they cannot be adequately protected, they have no common fund to look to if they lose their employment, and they are commonly the worst workmen. If a number of them can be gathered together to supply the places of those who strike, what is the consequence ? they meet the hatred, not only of the members of that combination which they injure, but of the members of every combination : they move only amidst bitter and unprincipled enemies ; they are daily exposed to insults and mortifications, against which the laws can provide no protection. They may be told that the laws will punish those who may maim or murder them, but then they know that this will not prevent men from attempting to maim or murder them. They are aware that their lives are continually in danger.

As to the laws, they now sanction the existence of the combinations, and they are totally inadequate to restrain them from evil. They suffer men to combine in any numbers—to form laws of their own—to create funds—and to demand any wages, no matter how unreasonable. They say, indeed, that the men shall not prevent others from being employed in their stead, and they might almost as well say nothing. In most cases, particularly in the more important trades, men cannot be found to replace the combiners. If such man can be found, they not only prevent the combiners from attaining their objects, but they deprive them of employment altogether. When this is the case, it is not to be expected that the latter will respect the laws, the more especially as their obedience will subject them to a heavier punishment than their disobedience, provided they abstain from assault and murder. When men whose passions are excited to the utmost pitch are placed in such a situation, that they must either lose what they are contending for, and their bread into the bargain, or commit violence upon those who are bringing the loss upon them, they will generally prefer the latter, in spite of laws. Depraved and desperate spirits will always be found in every combination to perpetrate any atrocities towards their rivals. Those are not wise laws which suffer bodies of men to place themselves in such a situation, and they will never be effective ones. That which forbids the combiners to "molest" such workmen as would take their employment from men, can be evaded in numberless ways, and it is almost daily violated: it yields very little benefit.

People—and people too, who are very high in influence, if not very wise in action—still speak of education as a thing that would keep the working orders from improper conduct. Mechanics' Institutes are still to form the nostrum for the combination-madness. We doubt that anything could be conceived more false and absurd. What is the constant language of these people—of the Political Economists, the Liberal systemmen, the Whigs, and the Benthamites? It is, that all men, and bodies of men, will abuse power if they possess the means. They eternally declare that Ministers, Legislators, Judges, Public Companies, and bodies of all descriptions, although the individuals, and those who guide the bodies, may be men who have had the best education, in respect of sentiment as well as science, and who are sensitively alive to the principles of honour, are nevertheless sure to abuse their power for their own profit and gratification, if they are not effectually restrained from it by laws or other things. They never speak of trusting wholly, or in part, to education; but they insist upon having all the restrictions that could be framed if no such thing was known. This is very wise. Yet the very same people, when they speak of the combinations of mechanics—bodies which exist only to promote their own interests—they speak of them as needing only education to keep them from abusing their power. We will waste no comment upon this monstrous absurdity. Education, with regard to this point, will have no better effect upon the mechanic and labourer, than upon the Secretary of State, Member of Parliament, and East India Director. We believe that the Mechanics' Institutes will make no perceptible improvement in the character of the working classes as a whole—we believe that in spite of them, and perhaps in some cases by means of them, these classes are sinking in character, are becoming more vicious and disorderly; but if we knew that they would

give a good education to every working man, we should still know likewise that the combinations of working men would as certainly tyrannize and trample upon the rights of others if they could, as bodies of gentlemen. Education will not do—the combiners can no more be placed under sufficient internal restraints than other people—they must be prevented from possessing the power to tyrannize and injure, by laws, or the power of other bodies, or they will use such power as any other description of men would use it. Nothing could be more indisputable, and that must be a most unaccountable delusion which keeps any thinking man in ignorance of it.

Nothing, therefore, exists which is capable of duly controlling the combinations; it follows, as a matter of course, that they possess a vast portion of arbitrary and unconstitutional power, and that they continually abuse this power. Strikes are now about as numerous as ever; and they most of them take place for the most abominable and injurious objects. Wages have been advanced, avarice has had its meal, and now idleness must be gorged. The workmen of one calling strike, that they may be idle half of their time, and starve the surrounding population; those of another strike, that other men may be employed to do a part of their work, while they stand with their arms folded looking on; those of a third strike, that they may emancipate themselves from the control of the masters, and work when, and as, they please. These strikes, notwithstanding their objects, are generally successful. When we look at all the characteristics of the combinations, at human nature, at other bodies of men, and at the lessons of experience, we can arrive at no other conclusion, than that, so far as regards themselves, these combinations will become more and more powerful and fruitful of evils.

These things, therefore, appear to us to be very undeniable.

1. That these combinations are precisely what might have been expected to follow the repeal of the Combination Laws.

2. That the crimes and evils which they have produced, are precisely the fruits which the system is calculated to produce.

3. That if the wish for increase of

income, indulgence, and power, can
operate permanently on the human
mind, and if the complete success of a
system can strengthen and perpetuate
it, the combinations must exist permanently, and keep increasing in power
and evil consequences.

4. That the combinations have kept
rapidly increasing in numbers and
power from the first; that they are exactly calculated to gratify the prevailing wishes of the working classes; that
such of these classes as can combine
derive great advantages from them;
that they now comprehend the mass
of the workmen of large places; that
they keep increasing in strength, and
the means for resisting them keep diminishing; that they now possess a
most dangerous share of arbitrary and
unconstitutional power; and that by
the abuse of this power they continually produce the most serious individual and public evils.

5. That nothing whatever at present exists which is capable of controlling them; and that, according to
every principle of reason and experience, they are sure to become more
potent, tyrannical, and mischievous,
until they are crushed, either by law,
or the ruin of trade.

It now behoves us to inquire why
the existence of these combinations is
tolerated?

It is said, that the labour of the
workman is his property, his capital,
and that he has a right to make the
best of it. If this mean that he has
a right to do what he pleases with it,
it is false. No man has a right to use
his property to injure his brethren and
the community. The use of all descriptions of property is, and ought to
be, regulated by law. He who has
land, is prohibited from raising upon
it certain articles, and he is under
other regulations in regard to the use
of it. He who has money is prohibited from employing it in various
ways, and he is bound from taking
above a certain rate of interest for it.
The author has his literary property
taken from him after a certain period,
without an equivalent. The artist is
not suffered to employ himself in for-
ging bank-notes and coining. The
labourer is not suffered to work on the
Sabbath, or to employ himself in various ways that might yield him great
profit. It is imperiously necessary for
the weal of both the individual and

the community that the use of all
kinds of property whatever should be
under the regulation of the law.

We willingly admit that the workman has a right to obtain the highest
wages in any lawful employment that
he can, by his individual efforts; but
we protest against his having any
right to associate with others to place
the market for labour under a monopoly. Whatever may be the case with
the individual, a corporate body has
no rights, save what the laws may
please to give it. To argue that the
body ought to have the same rights as
the individual, would be to argue for
public ruin. The workmen of a trade
form themselves into an actual corporation—they obtain the complete control over labour in that trade—they
put upon it any price they please—
they prohibit all individuals from being employed who are obnoxious to
them—they take property from the
command of its owners—they will not
suffer the masters to send more goods
to market than they think proper—
they subject the poor to severe privations—they do immense injury to
trade—and they bring the most grievous evils upon innumerable individuals and the empire. Look at the
colliers of Scotland, the shipwrights
of London, and the seamen of Sunderland. If men have a right to associate to do what these men have done,
to employ their property as these men
have employed theirs, then they have
a right to rob, commit treason, or do
anything. Where is the difference
in effect between taking a thousand
pounds from a master in the highway,
and preventing him from gaining the
same sum by fair and lawful trade—
between making open war on the country, and imposing upon it heavy taxes,
and destroying its trade, revenue, and
power?

It is perfectly clear to the whole nation—it has been again and again established by the most decisive proofs
—that these corporations of workmen
violate, in the most outrageous manner, the rights of innumerable individual workmen, and of the masters. It
ought not to be necessary for us to
say, that this is directly at variance
with all the principles of right, with
reason, equity, and the whole spirit of
the constitution. To argue that the
workmen have a right to form themselves into such corporations, is to ar-

gue that these corporations have a right to do this; for it has been proved that they cannot exist without doing it.

A great deal of misapprehension prevails, touching the effects of these corporations. Many people affect to place them and the masters on the same level; they seem to imagine that the contests between them affect principally themselves, and are for things which must be exclusively enjoyed either by one side or the other. We will, therefore, detail these effects a little farther.

The workmen of a trade all leave work at the same moment; and, in most cases, it is utterly impossible to procure others in their stead; however unjust and unreasonable their demands may be, the masters have scarcely anything before them but compliance. To attempt to starve them out has become a hopeless matter. If the different combinations comprehend only forty thousand members, and if every member subscribe only a shilling per week, this will raise two thousand pounds weekly—a sum sufficient to maintain four thousand men *constantly* at ten shillings per week each. If the combinations act with common prudence, they may, with no greater a sum than this, enable the workmen of almost any trade to stand out, not only for months, but for years, and to impose any terms they please on their masters. They may cause trade after trade to be stopped, until they place every trade under their own regulations. The masters, in reality, pay the subscriptions, and almost any sum can be extorted from them. The combinations often enough support more than four thousand idle men.

Labour is thus, in most trades, placed under a close monopoly; its price is regulated by nothing but the will of those who have it to dispose of; it is a thing which must be had. The master knows no business but his own—he cannot perhaps leave it, without sustaining a tremendous loss in buildings, fixtures, &c.—his want of knowledge would perhaps ruin him were he to embark in any other; and, in addition, he can scarcely find any other that is not equally under the despotism of the combinations—he cannot do without labour, and therefore he must give whatever his servants may demand, provided it will leave him a subsistence.

The having to buy labour at a monopoly price, must no doubt operate differently on different masters. Those who are not exposed to the competition of foreigners, may increase the price of their articles as wages are increased. This has already been done in various trades. These masters, however, do not escape without injury; they are compelled to employ a much greater capital to do the same business; and the advance of price injures consumption, and, of course, their trade.

The case is wholly different with those masters who are exposed to the competition of foreigners. They can make no increase of charge to their customers, whatever increase of wages may be demanded by their workmen. We at present barely possess a superiority over foreign manufacturers, and they are rapidly gaining upon us. In some branches of our boasted cotton trade, they can equal, if not surpass us. Mr Huskisson, as far as we remember, stated in Parliament, that, before the advance of wool on the continent, the continental manufacturers could successfully compete with us even in the South American market; and that this advance enabled us to regain our superiority. We are now undersold on the continent in some descriptions of woollen cloth. Our manufacturers can only stand their ground by being content with very low profits; they can obtain no exclusive advantages in the purchase of the raw material; and if the price of labour be raised to them, they must either resign their trade, or carry it on to be ruined.

By and by, most trades will be exposed to the competition of foreigners in one way or another.

These masters, at the best, will never be suffered to obtain fair and necessary profits; they will, at the best, be kept in such a state, that any unfavourable turn in the market will plunge them into bankruptcy. If their trade be not immediately taken from them, it will be gradually diminished; and if they be not at once ruined, they must be so in the upshot if they continue in business.

We have spoken of the masters, and we must now speak of another party, which is even more interested in the question than they are. This is the community.

The first description of masters, in effect, purchase labour for the community; the latter, in reality, buys the labour of the workmen, and the masters are but its agents. The extortions practised upon the masters, are, in truth, practised upon the community. The combinations make monopolies of almost every trade; and they impose grievous taxes upon the nation. If a man in London wear four suits of clothes in the year, he pays a tax of at least three pounds per annum to the learned and masculine company of journeymen tailors. He pays this more than he would have to pay, if these creatures would be content with reasonable wages. By means of it they have, according to report, accumulated a fund of enormous magnitude; and they heroically drive women out of the trade—levy what contributions they think fit upon the metropolis—and commit all kinds of tyranny. The colliers of Scotland are not even content with levying a grievous tax upon coals; they will not suffer people to have them in sufficient quantities. In all the trades carried on by this description of masters, the advance of wages has been at once, and of necessity, thrown upon the community.

With regard to the other description of masters, the community suffers still more from the combinations. They strike at its commerce, revenue, maritime superiority, power, wealth, and prosperity as a nation. They threaten it with almost every ill that could befall a people.

It is astonishing to us that this should be debated as a question that affects chiefly masters and servants—that it is not taken up as one between the empire and the combinations. It is notorious, that in almost every contest, the combinations have demanded more than was sufficient for supplying the workmen with necessaries; and that there was even a superabundance of workmen in the trade. It is notorious, that in almost every strike, the workmen had sufficient, and often more than sufficient, for supplying themselves with necessaries before they struck; and that, in many cases, the object was less an advance of wages, than the curtailment of the just con-

trol of the masters, or the proper hours of labour. Every man may see, if he pleases, that, however the combinations may injure the masters, still the real struggle is between them and the country. He may see, if he be not wilfully blind, that the triumph of a combination is at the best a tax imposed upon the country, and that it is often a great injury done to the trade, &c. of the country; while the triumph of the masters protects the country from these. The masters are obviously fighting the battles of the public; and yet they are spoken of as though they were contending only for their own benefit. If our trade be worthy the cry which is kept up in its favour; if it ought to be preserved, we must protect its sources—we must protect those who carry it on, and their capital. That is a strange kind of wisdom which boasts of the vast importance of trade, and then resigns it to annihilation.

We must now say a word on the fruits which the combinations yield to the working classes.

Those who combine, no doubt, reap from it very high wages and great privileges. Their curtailment of the hours of labour operates as a heavy advance of wages to the masters and the public, while it puts nothing into their own pockets. Thus, their comparative emancipation from control, the combination-fund, and their frequent strikes, cause them to derive not much real benefit from their additional wages. They drink more; they expend more in pleasure; they have more idle time; but their families have very little more to subsist on than they would have if no combinations existed. Their character, in all respects, is rapidly sinking, and this must in the end cause them to lose much more than they are now gaining. As to the mass of them becoming readers, nothing but raving madness could expect it. Nature most wisely has positively disqualified the mass of mankind for being regular lovers of reading; human quacks cannot yet conquer her, and no superhuman ones have arrived among us that we have heard of.

These men form only a very contemptible part of the whole of the working classes. The husbandry labourers, the greater part of the seamen, the labouring men of large places, the surplus hands of the different trades, &c. &c. cannot well combine. This contemptible part inflicts on the vast majority of the working classes the most serious injuries.

The combiners represent, very truly, that theirs is a war of labour against capital. The egregious dolts! it is the same as a war of the belly against victuals. Our land is fully occupied; it will not support any additional inhabitants; and, in consequence, the increase of population is constantly thrown upon trade, or, in other words, upon trading capital, for subsistence. This capital is, to a very great degree, in this country, what land is in America to the increase of population; and it is just as wise in our working orders to war against it, as it would be in those of America to war against land. The combiners, by reducing profits to the lowest point, prevent the accumulation of capital and the extension of trade; of course, they prevent the rising labourers from procuring employment. By diminishing capital, they diminish trade; and they thereby deprive, not only a portion of themselves, but many labourers who do not belong to them, of the means of subsistence. The working classes have as much interest in the accumulation of capital as any other class; if it do not accumulate in proportion as they increase, the mass of them must always be distressed.

The combiners, by raising wages so much, have no doubt injured consumption; by their turbulent conduct, they have prevented much capital from being employed in trade. Had it not been for them, very many workmen, who are unemployed and in distress, would have been earning comfortable wages.

The combiners prevent very many workmen from disposing of their labour on any terms save those which they may dictate, and, in truth, from disposing of it at all. This has been so much dwelt upon, in and out of Parliament, that we will not enlarge upon it.

They have obtained a monopoly in various trades against the rest of the working classes; by it they force the surplus hands and the increase of population upon those callings in which combinations cannot be formed, and thereby sink wages in these callings below what they ought to be.

The different kinds of workmen are so much dependent on each other, that if those of one kind strike, they throw many of other kinds out of employment. Thus when, in Scotland, Mr Dunlop's colliers struck, it compelled some hundreds of men employed in his iron-works to cease working. They must, likewise, have rendered numbers of men employed in conveying and delivering coals, &c. idle. The strike of the London shipwrights must have deprived many hands belonging to different callings of work. The strike of the Bradford weavers must have done prodigious injury to innumerable workmen who do not belong to them. The members of the combinations have funds to subsist on, but the greater part of those whom they force out of work cannot belong to combinations, they are deprived of employment against their wishes, and left without bread. If the combiners do any serious injury to the export trade, they will reduce numbers of seamen, sloopmen, labourers, &c. to starvation.

The different kinds of labour are so connected with each other, that, if one kind be overpaid, it generally causes some other kinds to be proportionally underpaid. Thus the woollen manufacturers are bound to price in the foreign market; they cannot expend above a certain sum in producing their goods. If the wages of their weavers, &c. be advanced to them, they must sink the price of wool; and this must in part depress the value of husbandry labour—they must reduce freights, and this must in some degree reduce the seaman's wages. They must, in reality, take a large part of the advance of wages made to their own workmen from the wages of other workmen, if they continue their trade.

The combiners sink wages in those callings in which combinations cannot be formed; and, by raising them in their own, they advance the price of many necessaries. They thus prevent husbandry labourers, the labourers of towns, and all workmen who cannot combine, from obtaining a fair price for their labour; in many cases, they deprive them of employment altogether, and they impose upon them a heavy tax at the same moment. The poor man in Scotland has perhaps to delve every day for what will barely keep his family from starving; and still he is compelled to pay a tax weekly to the colliers, that they may riot in extravagance, and be idle half their time.

The combinations have in their hands, more or less, almost all the necessaries of life. Bread is under the control of the bakers ; the quartern loaf in London is generally twopence more than it ought to be, according to the price of wheat. Coals are under the control of the colliers. The shipwrights, coopers, &c. lay their fingers upon colonial produce. The various kinds of manufacturing combinations have in their hands articles of clothing. There is scarcely a single article consumed in the dwelling of the poor man, as well as of the rich one, which is not considerably and unnecessarily enhanced in price by the combinations.

Our limits will not allow us to dwell on this point any longer ; we have, however, we trust, said sufficient to show that the combinations are bringing the most grievous evils on the great majority of the working classes—that they exist to benefit the few at the cost of the many.

There is another point of view in which these combinations must be looked at with regard to their influence on the interests of the nation.

Nothing, we think, could well be more dangerous than for a government to suffer immense classes of its subjects to form themselves into an organized body, for purposes of private gain—the more especially if they be composed chiefly of ignorant, passionate men, and their objects be to be gained at the expense of the rest of the community. What injuries and troubles have not the Irish Catholics caused to the empire from their forming only in part such a body ? Now, into such a body, great numbers of the working classes have formed themselves. The different combinations are connected together, they act together, they form a whole, and this whole is the more mighty from being composed of a number of parts. This body controls vast numbers more of the working classes, and the passions of the mass are in its favour. It is looked upon as fighting the battles of servants against masters—of the poor against the rich generally.

The combinations, therefore, of the three kingdoms, and their friends among the working classes, form a gigantic confederacy, which is daily increasing in magnitude, which possesses abundant funds, which is tremendously powerful, and which is under the guidance of unprincipled men, who are quite above the influence of the government and the better classes : Its avowed object is to sponge as much as possible from the rest of the community in money and privilege. It endeavours to crush trade with one foot, and agriculture with the other. No man, we hope, is so simple as to suppose that this body will keep apart from politics. It cannot. Every public measure must affect it in some degree ; it is already deeply tainted with ruinous politics ; its objects are in their nature political, and they must inevitably drive it into political opinions, and conduct of the most dangerous description. It is perfectly impossible for a body to pursue such objects as it pursues, without becoming a revolutionary one. In addition, it is surrounded by revolutionary teachers, and all kinds of means are employed to fill it with revolutionary principles.

Let trade be flat and distressed for a season—we are not sure that such a season is not on the eve of commencing ; —let the members of the combinations be subjected to privations, and then what will be their conduct ? Unable any longer to raise wages and shorten the hours of labour, to war against the masters and the public, they will direct their hostility against our laws and institutions. The old cry will be raised against corruption, taxes, the government, &c. &c. The body which the combinations form must, under privations and suffering, be turbulent, disaffected, and guilty ; it must convulse the empire, and shake the constitution to its centre. This is the more certain because the combinations are doing the most deplorable injury to morals.

That is not political economy, but politital idiotcy, which endeavours to increase trade by things which injure morals, disorganize society, banish industry, destroy peace and order, weaken the government, array one part of the community against another, and generate sedition and convulsion. He who practises the principles of political economy without making them subordinate to the general science of government, will only produce public ruin. Trade is threatened with destruction by the combinations—by the things which have been hatched for its benefit by those who call themselves its sole friends, and the only people who know how to make it flourish.

Thinking as we have stated, we have naturally been curious to know the opinion of public men touching the combinations. Mr Huskisson, who, of course, must be looked upon as the organ of the Ministry, called them odious and the like ; but he stated that he was decidedly hostile to the reenactment of the old laws against them. All sides called these laws cruel, tyrannical, &c., and manifested towards them bitter enmity. Now, these laws were simply intended to prevent such combinations from existing. They left the workman, *as an individual,* free as air, free as he is at present. They suffered him to demand what wages he pleased, to make what stipulations he pleased, and to pass from master to master as he pleased. He could only bring himself under their operation by combining. They never touched the vast body of the working classes. Now, if the questions were put to us, Which ought to exist, such laws, or such combinations ? Which are cruel and tyrannical—such laws, or such combinations ?—we should decide at once in favour of the laws. If we were asked whether laws would be cruel and tyrannical, which should prevent the Irish combinations from committing murder, and destroying trade—the Scotch one from withholding coals from, and robbing, the community—the Sunderland one from endangering the lives of, and taking bread from, innocent men — the London Shipwrights from tyrannizing over their masters, and driving the carrying trade to other countries—one part of the working classes from plundering and oppressing another part, and bringing grievous evils on the nation at large—we should say No !—we should say again, No ! and we should challenge every member of the Ministry and the Opposition to gainsay us.

If, as Mr Huskisson admits, these combinations be robbing and oppressing a large part of the working classes—be outraging the rights of the masters—and be doing the most serious injuries to trade, it is certainly most unaccountable that they should be suffered to exist, and that laws intended to

prevent them from existing should be called cruel and tyrannical. We are very sure that the Constitution never intended things yielding such fruits, to be found in the nation ; and that the tolerating of them is decidedly at variance with its spirit. The Constitution wishes to give equal liberty and protection to all ; yet the masters—almost the most valuable class of men in the country—and the workmen who do not combine of almost all trades, have infinitely less of liberty and protection than they would have under any despotism in Europe. Our greatest statesmen have thought that the Constitution goes almost too far in its wish to favour the individual ; but now the individual is nothing, and the body—the self-constituted, irresponsible body, is only to be favoured. Our friends of liberty have always affected to look upon bodies with jealousy and dislike, and yet they are the furious champions of the stupendous body which is formed by these combinations. Now, compared with it, what are the East India Company, and the Bank Company, either as trading monopolists, or as political bodies ? They are powerless and contemptible. The combinations produce grievous robberies and oppression, they do the most serious injury to morals and trade,—they threaten the Constitution with destruction, and the empire at large with the most terrible evils :—this is abundantly manifest, and it convinces us that laws for their annihilation are called for by liberty, right, justice, reason, and the constitution. Mr Wallace may call this prejudice if he pleases ; it is not for him to change our opinion.

If the combinations were essential for preventing the price of labour from falling below what it ought to be, we should say less against them ; but they are not. On the contrary, they, as we have shown, lower wages and raise the price of necessaries to the majority of the labouring population. We will never admit that the ploughman and the labouring man ought to be starved for the benefit of the coal-digger and the shipwright. If labour be not superabundant, no combination of masters can prevent it from obtaining its proper price. The master is always anxious to increase his trade as far as possible, and he will ever give the highest wages in his power, rather than throw away trade and profit. While the Combination Laws were in full operation, wages in many callings were often enormously high. Before these laws were repealed, the masters, in some important trades, raised wages without a strike, and they have scarcely in a single instance stood out for a week, or a day, against reasonable demands. It is a matter of general notoriety, that in almost every contest, the demands of the combinations have been most unreasonable and unjust.

Nearly all, we presume, was done in the last Session that could be done to prevent the combinations from being mischievous, without putting an end to their existence; and it has yielded no benefit whatever. The power to demand what wages they please, to choose whether they will work by the day or the piece, and to regulate their hours of labour, cannot be taken from them; it would be gross tyranny to take it from them; and they need only this power to produce what they are producing. It is chiefly by the exercise of this power that they oppress and injure as they do. They must either be put down altogether, or be as mischievous as they are: the art of man cannot render them harmless by anything but their annihilation, without grossly violating the principles of liberty and right.

Mr Huskisson, however, who seems to be about as far gone in political economy, as Mr Brougham is in party politics, has in view a different remedy, and this is, the admission of foreign manufactures. It was made law in the last Session that ships might be sent to other countries for repairs, if the trade of the shipbuilders should be stopped by contests between the shipbuilders and their servants. This passed both Houses unanimously, if we except the dissenting voice of Mr Robertson—a gentleman who deserves the thanks of the country for his honest and manly conduct on this and other occasions. It constituted such a grievous insult to the majesty and impartiality of the Law of England, as we never expected to witness.

Has it indeed come to this, that the Government of this great empire is so powerless and spiritless that it cannot bring back a handful of shipwrights to their duty without the aid of foreigners —without giving that to other countries which belongs to the trade and

revenue of our own? Has this Government so far lost its understanding, that it cannot distinguish between the right and the wrong—the innocent and the guilty? Have our statutes become so impotent, blind, and vicious, that they can only remove evils, by committing wrongs—that they cannot coerce the culpable without robbing and punishing the meritorious? If all this have happened, it has certainly happened without cause—it has happened from choice, and when all imaginable means existed for its prevention.

This new law has been tried, and the result shows very clearly its character. The shipwrights of London, not their masters, stopped the trade. Why? Their great object, according to the papers, was not an increase of wages, or a diminution of the hours of labour, but that they should work by the piece, and not by the day, as they had previously done. This was evidently to render themselves as far as possible independent, and to force workmen not belonging to their combination out of employment. Now, when a workman receives from a master all that he requires for his labour, he certainly ought to be satisfied; he can have no right to control the master in the management of his business, and to prevent him from employing such other servants as he may wish. The servants stopped the trade for what were obviously indefensible objects; the masters resisted them evidently in defence of their just rights. Well, how did the new law operate in such a case? It made no inquiry as to which were in the right and which in the wrong—it treated both sides as though they were alike guilty; nay, it inflicted a much heavier punishment upon the masters than the servants, and, in effect, compelled the former to submit to the latter. Because the masters could not prevail on the servants to abandon unjust demands, the law took their business from them, and constrained them to accede to these demands. It became their enemy and the champion of the combination.—Permission for ships to be repaired abroad must injure the masters more than the servants, and it must even enable the latter to triumph, if their terms be not perfectly ruinous.

This was bad enough, but it was not all. The growers, importers, and carriers of timber, the shipsmiths, the long train of people who depend upon

the shipbuilder in addition to his regular servants, had their trade and
employment taken from them by the
law, because the shipwrights were refractory, although they had nothing
upon earth to do with the strike, and
although they had previously suffered
grievously from it. The framers of
this law ought to have been aware,
that, if the stoppage of the trade injured shipowners and others greatly,
still the trade could not be transferred
to other countries without injuring,
quite as much, other equally innocent
persons. The law coerced and punished all save those whom it ought to
have coerced and punished ; to the latter it gave licence and reward.

This may be law, it no doubt is law,
although it introduces a new principle
into English legislation. It is not,
however, justice. Ministers and Parliaments may alter and make laws at
pleasure, but they cannot change the
principles of justice and right.

According to what was said in the
House of Commons, the extension of
this law is to be the next panacea for
the combination-malady. If the combinations do not conduct themselves
better, foreign manufactures are to be
poured into the market to restrain them.
Would, then, the admission of foreign
manufactures affect none but the workmen ? Would it have no other effect
than to keep these workmen from improper conduct ? Would it reach no
trades save those which should strike ?
Would it correct the misdeeds of all
combinations ? Is nothing necessary
to warrant it save the turbulence and
guilt of a part of the working classes ?
Alas ! alas ! that we should have to
ask questions like these.

Suppose a combination of workmen
should strike, should make the most
unreasonable and unjust demands, and
should be resisted by the masters,
what would be the effect of the admission of foreign goods ? It could only
reach the servants through the masters. The latter, although they might
be acting in defence of their just rights
and the best interests of the community, would have the alternative placed
before them of submitting to the combination, or seeing the market glutted
and their trade taken from them by
foreigners. They would accede at
once to the demands of the workmen.
The admission of foreign goods, if it
were regulated by the disputes between

masters and servants, would be the
most powerful auxiliary that could be
formed for the latter. Nothing could
possibly be more unjust in principle :
it would act on the assumption, that
both sides were alike wrong, and that
it would affect both sides alike ; it
would in almost all cases give the triumph to the guilty ; and to do this, it
would sacrifice the interests of the nation.

It would reach far beyond the contending parties. The growers or importers of the raw article, and their
servants, a multitude of persons totally unconnected with the strike, would
be as much affected by it, as those who
should be so connected.

If foreign manufactures were constantly admitted to prevent strikes
from taking place, it would have but
a poor effect in keeping the combinations in order. The cotton, woollen,
and some other trades, are now largely exposed to the competition of foreigners ; but this does not prevent the
workmen engaged in them from combining, and from acting as unjustifia-
bly as other workmen. The combinations would always keep the masters bound hand and foot ; they would
tyrannize over them and over such
workmen as might not combine, as
they do at present ; they would still
have their strikes, and they would be
about as mischievous as they now are.

But the admission of foreign goods
could not affect many of the worst of
the combinations. How could it reach
those trades which undersell all the
rest of the world ? How could it reach
the shipwrights, unless we got our
ships built in other countries ? How
could it reach the coopers, when they
should suspend trade in the West India docks ? How could it reach the
colliers of Scotland ? How could it
reach the seamen of Sunderland ? If
foreign goods were admitted to the utmost extent possible, it would leave
the worst part of the evil perfectly un-
touched.

While the admission of foreign
goods would have very little effect upon combinations in such trades as it
could reach, it would do the most deplorable injury to the workmen belonging to these trades who cannot join the
combinations. Although labour is at
a monopoly price in various trades, it
is in most of them in reality superabundant. There are workmen in al-

most every trade who can scarcely procure employment; the admission of foreign goods would add greatly to their number, and it would consign them to starvation. It would render labour still more superabundant, and lower wages still more, in such callings as cannot combine.

Those must be statesmen of an unaccountable stamp, who conceive that the admission of foreign manufactures would have no other effect than to correct the misdoings of the combinations;—who imagine that such misdoings would justify them for admitting such manufactures, without calculating what effect it would have upon the industry, trade, and prosperity of the empire.

There are people who protest, that the opening of the corn-market would render the combinations harmless. These persons rave, as though flour and butcher's-meat were almost the only things that cost the workman anything; they overlook tea, sugar, candles, soap, clothes, coals, house-rent, and the combination-tax. In very many cases only one-third of his expenditure is caused by the purchase of flour and butcher's-meat. We will venture to say, that many workmen in London who have combination-wages, expend nearly as much in porter, gin, and tobacco, as in bread and animal food. Now, if the ports were opened, and the price of wheat were reduced one-third, how would it operate? It might reduce the quartern-loaf to sixpence: On butcher's-meat and butter it would have very little effect, unless it plunged the country into great distress—it might reduce them, perhaps, a penny per pound. Single workmen might gain by this about a shilling per week, and married ones something more than two. Now, is there any man who, after looking at the proceedings of the combinations, can believe that this would induce any one of them to lower its wages and change its conduct? * They have ceased to plead the high price of provisions in justification of what they do. It was not because their wages would not supply them

with bread, that the combinations of Ireland, the colliers of Scotland, the shipwrights of London, and the seamen of Sunderland, refused to work. The combinations will prevent the price of other articles from falling with that of corn.

While this measure would produce no benefit with respect to the combinations, it would, putting the farmer out of sight, injure most grievously the husbandry-labourers. Their wages are already in many parts much too low, and it would depress them very greatly. The outcry for "cheap bread" is preposterous. Bread never can be cheap to a whole community; if it be cheap to the town, it is dear to the village. A vast part of the inhabitants of this country never had so much difficulty in procuring bread, as they had when it was at the lowest price they ever knew it fall to. It is as unjust to starve the producers of bread, as to starve those of ships, coals, and manufactures. Shipwrights, colliers, &c. have as much right to work for inadequate wages as ploughmen.

Some wiseacres argue, that laws for putting down the combinations would be useless, because some secret combinations existed when the late laws were in operation. They should argue likewise, that as there are always thieves and murderers, the laws against theft and murder are of no value. The abolished laws were in existence during very prosperous as well as unprosperous times; and in no period during their existence did combinations produce one-fiftieth part of the evils which they have produced since the repeal. This is sufficient to decide the question. Common sense may convince any man, that if it were unlawful to combine, the combinations could not do what they are now doing; if they could exist at all, they would be infinitely less powerful and mischievous.

That Parliament will be compelled to do something with regard to these combinations, in the next session, is abundantly manifest; what it will do, is a matter on which we shall offer no conjecture. Time was, when, if a great

---

* Corn is now falling, and appearances seem to indicate that the fall will be considerable, yet labour amidst the combinations is rising. If the Economists had been listened to, and the ports had been opened in the last Session, what would have been the present state of the corn-market?

evil existed, it might have been very safely predicted, that Parliament would take natural and effectual measures for removing it, but that time has passed away. He would be a rash man, indeed, who, after looking at the principles which our legislators have embraced, would venture to speculate favourably on their future conduct. If Mr Hume's fatal bill had been like the New Marriage Act, unconnected with new creeds, and new systems, and merely intended to improve what seemed to be capable of improvement; all that it destroyed—when it came into being, would, likely enough, have been restored in the last session. But unhappily it emanated from the new creeds and systems which are so much the rage, and what it did cannot be undone, without confessing them to be erroneous.

To re-enact the Combination Laws would be to say that Political Economy is false, and that certain great political bubble-blowers are not infallible; it would shake the new creeds and systems to their centre, therefore the abolition of these Laws must doubtlessly be still called a most wise measure. Projectors and innovators are never the men to recant and go back again; to them no such thing can exist as refutation. The French revolutionists could only be stopped by the guillotine; and death alone could take from Joanna Southcote the belief that she was pregnant.

Ever since the beginning of the world, it has been looked upon as a thing above all question, that the servant should be obedient to his master. The Scriptures have made such obedience a religious duty; human laws have made it a civil duty; philosophers and statesmen have insisted, that not only the weal, but the very existence of society depends upon it. Lawgivers have always made its protection one of their leading objects. It has been guarded as a thing that benefitted, not merely the master and the community, but the servant himself even more than either;—as a thing essential for keeping the latter from crime and ruin, for making him moral, industrious, and skilful, for enabling him to rise from his servitude and acquire property and elevation.

Has this been demonstrated to be erroneous? Have the speeches of Mr Hume and his coadjutors proved it to be false and pernicious? Have intellectual giants risen among us, and shown, by overwhelming evidence, that what has been regarded for six thousand years as unerring wisdom, is only folly and prejudice? No! It has been denied, scoffed at, trampled upon, and cast aside; but it has not been refuted. It has been abandoned for the reverse, but argument and evidence, eloquence and wisdom, have had no share in producing the change.

It is now admitted, even by legislators and rulers, that servants ought to be suffered to throw off their obedience to their masters—that they ought to be equally independent—that they ought to be controlled in nothing save such work as they may deign to undertake—that they have a right to be idle two or three days in the week, if they think proper—that they have a right to organize themselves into immense bodies, and bind down the masters to any terms they please, in respect of obedience, wages, and hours of labour—this, we say, is admitted even by rulers and legislators. Has the admission been produced by reasoning and experiment —by the fascination of eloquence, and the irresistible potency of surpassing talent? No!—these have had nothing to do with it; its justification is yet hid in darkness.

Mr Hume's bill was the most fatal and ruinous measure that has been sanctioned by Parliament during a very long series of years. It has caused the loss of a large number of lives —it has occasioned the commission of a mass of atrocious crime—it has ruined a multitude of individuals, and grievously injured a multitude more —it has occasioned the loss of millions of property—it has given a tremendous shock to the industry and trade of the empire—it has done the most terrible injury to the character of the working classes—it has arrayed servants against masters through a large part of the country—it has nearly destroyed one of the best supports of good government—it has generated strife, animosity, and turbulence— and it has sown the seeds of almost every ill that can visit a nation. If the parent of such a bill were not insensible to shame, he would never dare to show his face again in the community. Yet this bill was sanctioned by all the wisdom of Parliament! it is still cried up as a just and wise one, in respect of its leading object.

So much for the *new* wisdom of this *enlightened* age—wisdom, in comparison of which, as we are told, the wisdom of former ages was but childish folly. So much for the great men—the giants—of the present day—great men, in comparison of whom, if we are to believe themselves, the great men of former times were but brainless pigmies. Time will put all this to the test, although, in doing it, it may involve the nation in horrors.

It is not for us to say, in contradiction to some of our first authorities, that a nation has its birth, youth, manhood, old age, and death, like an individual. But we may say, that however long the life of a nation may endure, it must, like that of an individual, consist of alternations of prosperity and adversity, gain and loss, happiness and affliction, enjoyment and suffering. In both cases, the sun and the cloud, the calm and the tempest, will keep continually replacing each other. According to the history of this and other countries, a period of prosperity has always been followed by one of adversity; and, in proportion as the one has been resplendent, the other has been terrible. Europe was in a more flourishing and happy condition than it had perhaps ever previously been in, just before the French Revolution; we need not describe what followed. This country enjoyed unexampled prosperity just before the Revolution in the time of the first Charles; all know what succeeded. That the sunshine in which we are now basking will have to give place to the storm, is a matter which the nature of things renders abundantly certain; and that the storm will be of a very awful character, is a matter which a variety of circumstances renders almost equally certain. One part of the community sighs for a complete change in our form of government; another part sighs for the destruction of our church establishment; the existence of almost every component part of the constitution is made matter of question in one way or another. The shape and proportions of society escape not, and a wish is largely prevalent to make in them the most sweeping alterations. Our laws and systems are undergoing a course of hazardous experiments. One great interest is placed in opposition to another. The town working classes, those whose character for the last ten years may be found in the history of Radicalism, the Queen Caroline madness, and the Combinations, have formed themselves into a stupendous confederacy for objects which can fail only by miracle, in plunging the country into distress, and in making them the enemies of our laws and institutions. The most powerful engines are at work to provide them with the worst teachers, to fill them with the worst principles, and to make them scorn and hate the upper classes. To look at all this, and not to expect a fearful future, is an impossibility. History shows that the fiend of revolution will walk the earth till the end of time; what country this fiend will next ravage, is not to be revealed by us; but we fear that the things necessary for tempting it, and enabling it to triumph, will soon be far more abundant in our own, than in any other.

PROGRESS OF SOCIAL DISORGANIZATION,

No. II.

THE TRADES' UNIONS.

EVERY man of common observation must now see to what the headstrong passion for innovation is rapidly leading. It is in vain to conceal, it would be folly to attempt to deny, that, under the influence of the prodigious changes of recent times, a spirit has been nurtured, which at length threatens the very elements of society with dissolution. As long as the lower orders were deluded by the cry for Reform; as long as they were infatuated enough to believe that, by supporting the Whigs in office, they would convert the age of iron into that of gold; as long as they were deceived by the assurance, that, by obtaining the command of the Legislature, they would readily find a remedy for all their sufferings, they were kept tolerably quiet, as against their rulers, and their fury turned exclusively upon their devoted opponents of the Conservative party. Now, however, that device will no longer answer its purpose. The battle has been fought; the victory has been gained; Tory misrule is at end; Whig wisdom and liberality have been for three years and a half in full operation; and the people naturally ask, what is the end of these things? What have we gained by all the efforts we have made? Where are the fields, the wages, the plenty, which were promised us? Finding that they have gained nothing by all they have done, that wages are as low, taxes as burdensome, employment as scarce, suffering as general, as before the arrival of the promised millennium, they return in gloomy discontent to their firesides, and, throwing aside all confidence in public men, and all hope of relief derived from the Legislature, sternly resolve to take the matter into their own hands, and,

by the force of numbers, and the terror of combination, obtain that instant and practical relief, which they have sought in vain in the delusive theories of their deceivers.

The TRADES' UNIONS, therefore, which have now spread with such portentous rapidity through the whole country; which have arrayed millions of Englishmen in combination against the authority of law, and the order of society; which threaten to overwhelm industry by the accumulation of numbers, and extinguish opposition by the terrors of self-authorized punishment; * which lay the axe to the root of the national resources, by suspending the labour by which it is created, and lock up the fountains of prosperity, by paralysing the capital which must maintain its producers, are a natural and inevitable, but not uninstructive step in the progress of revolution. They indicate, and that, too, in a voice of thunder, the arrival of the period when the vanity of hope has been felt, and the falsehood of promises experienced; when the hollowness of professions has become apparent, and the selfishness of ambition manifested itself; when Whig aristocracy can no longer employ the multitude as the instruments of its will, and democratic flattery can no longer supply the want of real relief. The manufacturing classes seem now resolved to take the matter into their own hands; they disdain to make any appeal to their own Legislature, or give any instructions to their darling representatives; but boldly fixing a rate of wages, a period of labour, and a set of regulations for themselves, they bid open defiance to all the constituted authorities in the state, and invite Government and

---

* We are aware that all the respectable organs of the Trades' Unions disclaim acts of violence; but experience has proved, that while they exist, they cannot be prevented, and that, practically, whatever they may say, they amount to a tyranny of numbers over helpless industry.

their masters into an open contest with millions of desperate men, upon whose labour great part of the national resources is dependent.

This fearful revolutionary system, therefore, need excite no surprise in any thinking mind; we have long foreseen it, and foretold it, in this Magazine, an hundred times over. It is the reaction of experience and suffering against the delusive hopes nursed by the predictions and changes of former times; the proclamation, in the hundred-mouthed trumpet of the national voice, of the vanity of all former innovations; the public admission, that, from the regenerated Legislature, the people have nothing to hope; and that, for any real alleviation of their sufferings, they must look to their own right arms and their own firm resolution. It is to be regarded as a natural and necessary step in the progress of the disease under which we are labouring; as the painful, but inevitable and well-foretold result of the insane innovations of which we have so long been the victims; and as indicating that step to amendment at least which arises from a perception of the deadly tendency of the remedies which have hitherto been administered.

The people, indeed, are not, for the most part, aware of this; they would not admit, if it was put to them, that their present distresses, which have prompted them to form these formidable combinations, are the natural result of the bitter disappointment experienced from the contrast between the promises which were held out to them, and the results which have attended the measures which were pursued; they would perhaps answer, if such a thing was seriously stated in their presence, that it was not because their rulers are, but because they are not democratic, that their confidence in them is gone; and that the substantial benefits which they were told would follow the Reform Bill can never now be hoped for, until the nest of Whig rotten boroughs is as thoroughly exterminated as that of Tory has been, and Annual Parliaments, Universal Suffrage, and Vote by Ballot, have completely and finally admitted the people to the full powers and blessings of self-government. All this, we have no doubt, they would say; and all this, we have no doubt, they sincerely believe. It is not the vanity of democratic principles and self-government which is as yet felt and demonstrated by the existence of the Trades' Unions; it is the vanity of the Reform Bill, and the ruinous tendency of Whig measures, which is proved to have been experienced; it is the loud voice of the manufacturing classes, at whose instigation, and, professedly,' for whose behoof, all the changes were made, which is heard, announcing that they have been cheated and deceived, and that direct self-government can alone admit them to the social benefits to which they are entitled.

That the true friends of the working classes are the Conservatives,— that their worst enemies are the demagogues who lure them by the voice of flattery to perdition, must be obvious from the consideration, that labour and industry of every sort can only flourish during the sunshine of tranquillity and ease, and that they necessarily wither and die amidst the storms and the agitation of Revolution. If a tree is cut down, the leaves and distant branches are the first to wither; and they languish and die long before any symptoms of decay appear in the stem and larger branches, because the sap which vivifies the whole is first stopped in its ascent to the farthest extremities. It is the same with the circulation of capital through the not less extensive and curiously constructed filaments of society. If any shock is given to the heart, the working classes are the first to suffer, because they are the last whom the life-blood reaches, they receive it in the smallest quantities, and have the least stock to enable them to subsist during its interruption. The rich, by a cessation of credit, or a suspension of industry, may be abridged of their luxuries; the middling ranks straitened in their comforts; but the labouring poor are instantly deprived of bread, and thrown without employment upon the world, disabled, by the same cause which has prostrated them, from administering any effectual relief.

The stage in the progress of innovation, which the simultaneous growth of the Trades' Unions in all parts of the country proves to have arisen, is observable in every other convulsion of a similar kind which has yet desolated the world. It corresponds to the revolt of the 10th August in the first French Revolution ; the effort, as Mignet tells us, of the working-classes to shake off the burgher aristocracy who had got possession of the legislature, and who were determined to obtain for themselves those benefits which had so long been held out to them by the demagogues to whom they had lent ear. It corresponds to the revolt of Lyons in November, 1831, when the starving weavers of that great manufacturing city rose in open revolt against the revolutionary authorities of Louis Philippe, and were only subdued by Marshal Soult and the Duke of Orleans, at the head of a greater force than fought the Duke of Wellington at Toulouse ; or the great revolt of the Parisian operatives at the Cloister of St Merri in June, 1832, which was only crushed by a mightier military array than glittered on the field of Jena or Austerlitz. The pacific habits and more orderly character of our working-classes will, it is to be hoped, give a very different character to this stage of the disease in the British Isles from what obtained amidst the fiercer passions and military ideas of their southern neighbours : but the crisis is the same ; it has arisen from the same deep-rooted disappointment at the deceit and delusions of which they have been the victims, and will be attended in the end, if not firmly coerced, with effects not one whit less disastrous.

Few of our readers are acquainted with the real objects of these formidable Associations, or the manner in which they are levelled, not merely against the rights of their masters, and the general authority of law, but the whole principles of religion and morality by which society is held together—by which the strong are prevented from tyrannising over the weak—and civilisation is prevented from relapsing into the anarchy and bloodshed of savage life. We shall give, therefore, a few quotations to illustrate the extent of the danger which now threatens society, and the perilous and seducing nature of the principles which these regenerators of society are pouring into the minds of our manufacturing population.

Cobbett tells us, in one of his recent numbers, that

" *Their intention is to take the government of the country entirely into their own hands.* The view which they take of our present political situation is something like this : both Houses of Parliament, they say, have been most actively engaged in doing whatever they could to bring down the old fabric of society, and they have succeeded so well, that none of the political parties can much longer support it. Were the producing classes not prepared with effective conservative measures, Tories, Whigs, and Radicals would soon be in inextricable confusion. The producing classes, viewing matters in this light, state their object to be to take their own affairs into their own hands ; and by taking their own affairs, they are perfectly aware that they cannot avoid at the same time taking the affairs of the non-producers also into their own hands ; the management of which latter will depend on the particular arrangements which the producers may determine to adopt. These are no trivial objects to have in view, namely, to reverse the state machine so far that the producer may govern the capitalist, and to make the capitalist minister to the wants and pleasures of the producers, instead of the producers to the capitalists ! In this state of things, and with a body of men in the community holding these doctrines, it becomes a matter of serious consideration for both the Government and the public to ascertain their probable result if the course marked out be followed up. There have been Trades' Unions in existence for some length of time ; many of them rich, and partaking of the nature of benefit societies. But the Trades' Union, which is now attracting so much attention, is a thing of very recent origin, arising, in some degree, out of the Political Unions. But the former being dissatisfied with the conduct of the latter, and looking upon them as the creature of the middle classes, *they have followed the steps of the working classes in France, who soon came to view the Girondists as a class who aimed at monopolizing all the benefits of the Revolution,* and keeping the working class in the same state in which they found them. The General Congress of the Union has already twice assembled, once at Birmingham, and once in London, and it is said that another meeting is to be convened early in 1834, at Barnsley, *with the de-*

sign of a general strike throughout the whole country."

If further proof be required, take the following extract from the declaration of one of those societies :—

"SOCIAL REFORMERS. All human beings are good by nature. Ignorance is the only Devil that exists, or ever did exist. Vice is nothing else but ignorance. Truth leads to virtue and happiness. The character of every human being is formed for him, and not by him. If the above be true, all those that examine for themselves will find *every religion taught in the world by the different Priests, is founded on error and in direct opposition to truth and nature;* hence have followed priestcraft, war, law or injustice, aristocracy, and every drone that exists on the labour of the industrious many," &c. &c.

The design then is evident; and as a specimen of the extent to which it has already been adopted, we will quote one or two of the resolutions of a combination formed in Manchester, and called " The Society for Promoting National Regeneration."

" 1. That it is desirable that all who wish to see society improved, and confusion avoided, should endeavour to assist the working classes to obtain ' for eight hours' work the present full day's wages,' such eight hours to be performed between the hours of six in the morning and six in the evening; and that this new regulation should commence on the first day of March next. 3. That persons be immediately appointed from among the workmen to *visit their fellow-workmen in each trade, manufacture, and employment, in every district of the kingdom,* for the purpose of communicating with them on the subject of the above resolutions, and of inducing them to determine upon their adoption. 9. That the workmen and their friends use their utmost efforts to obtain further subscriptions, and that all well-disposed females be respectfully requested cordially to co-operate in this undertaking."

These men are fully aware of their own power. In illustration of this, we subjoin the following quotation from the Trades' Union Gazette of Glasgow, Feb. 1, 1834.

" POWER OF THE TRADES' UNIONS.

" Their's will not be insurrection; it will be simply passive resistance. The men may remain at leisure; there is, and can be, no law to compel them to work against their will. They may walk the streets or fields with their arms folded, they will wear no swords, carry no muskets, assemble no train of artillery, seize upon no fortified places. They will present no column for an army to attack, no multitude for the riot-ac to disperse. They merely abstain, when their funds are sufficient, from going to work for one week, or one month, through the three kingdoms; and what happens in consequence? Bills are dishonoured, the Gazette teems with bankruptcies—capital is destroyed—the revenue fails—the system of government falls into confusion, and *every link in the chain which binds society together is broken in a moment by this inert conspiracy of the poor against the rich.*"

What their religious principles are may be judged of from the following passages in the Prospectus of a new Paper about to be set up in Glasgow, to be entitled " THE FREETHINKER."

" The objects which the projectors have in view, are, chiefly, the establishment of an organ for the expression of free, unfettered opinions—opinions *ranging to the utmost latitude of thought;* the vindication of such of the opinions referred to as are founded in Reason and Philosophy, from the false charges and aspersions of bigotry and self-interest; and the application of an unerring test to the most approved and *vaunted arguments in favour of Theology.*

" Discussions and disquisitions, however, are not to preclude less weighty matters. The lighter arms of satire and ridicule must not be allowed to remain inactive, while follies and absurdities call for their employment, although the shafts should occasionally be borrowed from the quiver of a Taylor, a Byron, or a Voltaire.

" *Shares, Five Shillings each. Price of each Number, 1½d.*"

Let no one be so deluded as to suppose that these resolutions are likely to prove a dead letter, or that the utmost danger is not to be anticipated from the combinations in furtherance of these objects which have now sprung up in all the manufacturing districts of the country. Their organization is complete; their numbers are prodigious; the talent which directs them is considerable; the devotion which generally prevails to the cause is unbounded. It is well observed, in a recent number of an able and intelligent provincial paper, the Stirling Journal—

" Not only is the machinery well adapted, but its effects are fearfully powerful.

In Manchester, Liverpool, Glasgow, Paisley, Bolton, and almost every other manufacturing town, there is hardly a manufacturer who is allowed to say what he will pay for the work done for him; and there is hardly a manufactory to be found into which a workman can dare enter, who has not previously become a member of the Combination. The state of things is a frightful one, and it is rendered doubly hideous from the fact, that it has arisen out of the vile misconduct of the faction now nominally holding the reins of Government. Lord Grey, Lord Althorp, and Lord Brougham, the correspondents of the Birmingham Political Unions, can have no right to find fault with *Regenerators of their Country.* John *Fielden* and *Robert Owen,* and their colleagues, are only acting precisely upon the plan laid down by Lord Brougham and the *Society for the Diffusion of Useful Knowledge.* The *Crisis* and *Penny Magazine* are of a family; and the London University, as originally conceived, destitute of Christianity, is a fit precursor of the doctrines of the *Social Reformers.*"— *Stirling Journal, Jan.* 17, 1834.

The enormous danger and perilous consequences of these Trades' Unions, have now attracted the attention of the steadiest advocates of the Movement; of those who were loudest in their outcry against the former system of government, and the most vehement supporters of the Reform Bill. Sir Daniel Sandford, whose eloquent declamations in favour of the Bill are still ringing in our ears—whose name is indelibly associated in our minds with the words "Oligarchy—Oligarchy—Oligarchy," which he so liberally poured forth to an admiring operative audience two years ago, has addressed the following admirable observations to the Liberator Journal of Glasgow, the great organ of the Trades' Unions in the West of Scotland; and thus illustrates the effect of the Constitutional Revolution which he so warmly advocated.

" I do not presume to condemn the general principle of combinations among workmen for the sake of mutual protection. No liberal man will assert that they should not, on the contrary, be encouraged to consult together for their own interest, and to maintain associations for the promotion of their common welfare. I approved of the repeal of the law formerly directed against such combinations, and would oppose its re-enactment. But,

conceding this wise and wholesome principle, the Unions must not be surprised if disinterested persons should see *much to blame in some of their avowed objects, and in the means of attaining them, which they openly or tacitly countenance.* I esteem it, for example, a most unreasonable object to propose a universal reduction of the time of labour to eight hours a-day. This is a portion of time decidedly below the physical powers of man, and the period of his daily toil in the freest regions of the earth; it is below the average of the exhausting labours of the learned professions; and it is inadequate to maintain the manufactures and commerce of the country. I call it an attempt equally illegal and immoral, when force or insult is employed to swell the ranks of the Unions, by the coercion of those who do not already belong to them. The *Liberator* will not deny, that in some quarters frightful acts of violence have been committed; and I have looked in vain for any strong mark of disapprobation of these acts on the part of the united workmen. Far from perceiving such evidence of true manly feeling, I find in the *Liberator* itself, (a great organ of the Unions,) bitter expressions of scorn and resentment levelled at those who, in the exercise of an undoubted privilege, have abstained from joining them, or have thought fit to leave them. This I cannot avoid designating *as the tyranny of the multitude;* and that man is ill versed in history and in morals, who does not hold *the tyranny of the many to be equally hateful with the tyranny of the few.*"

Let us not deceive ourselves; the great contest between the working classes and their employers, between capital and numbers, which Sir Daniel now so eloquently deplores, is approaching, and cannot be averted. His darling Reform Bill has rendered it inevitable. The operative workmen feel that they have been deceived; that the Whigs have merely used them as a ladder to raise themselves, and that, having gained, by their aid, the command of the Legislature, they are now quite willing to let their valued associates grovel in the dust. It is the sense, the bitter and universal sense of this deception of which they have been the victims, which has produced the present general spread of Trades' Unions; in other words, of immense associations of working men, to obtain, by a simultaneous strike over all parts of the country, and the terror which the display of physical strength can hardly fail to produce, those extraordinary practical advantages which the general condition of the labour market will not permit them to obtain, but which were falsely held out to them as the immense boon which they would certainly obtain by the change in the Constitution of Parliament.

If any one doubts that this has been the real cause of the present frightful schism which has split society asunder, let him take up any of the newspapers or periodical journals which advocated the cause of Reform three years ago. He will there find, that the whole evils of the country, theoretical and practical, were constantly laid on the shoulders of the Boroughmongers; that it was uniformly and invariably maintained, that the resources of the nation were unbounded, and the career of prosperity which opened before it unlimited, if it could only shake off the monstrous load of the Aristocracy; that Relief from Taxation, Increase of Wages, Fall of Prices, and Diminution of Poor's Rates, were held out as the immediate and necessary effect of a Reform in the Legislature, and that all persons who presumed to doubt these exhilarating prospects were forthwith stigmatized as the tools of the Boroughmongers, as influenced by no other feeling but a desire to fatten on the spoils of the nation, and fit to be dealt with in no other way, but with the brickbat and the bludgeon, to be plastered with mud, or ducked in horseponds. It was this infernal cry, issuing from nine-tenths of the Press, and re-echoed by nineteen-twentieths of the popular orators, which procured the return of the Parliament of May, 1831, which extinguished the British Constitution. It was the same false and delusive cry which roused the labouring classes in such multitudes to overawe the House of Peers, when they nobly clung to the ark of their forefathers, in May, 1832. What else enabled Mr Attwood to assemble 70,000 workmen in the neighbourhood of Birmingham, when the Bill was under deliberation in the House of Peers; and wrought them up to such a pitch of exasperation, that it is now admitted they were ready

to have risen in rebellion against the Duke of Wellington if he had retained the seals of office, after the resignation of Earl Grey, and were on the point of shaking society to atoms by a run, got up for political purposes, on the Bank? Was it to elevate the Whig Aristocracy at the expense of the Tory; to create close boroughs in the North, while it extinguished them in the South; to secure Calne and destroy Old Sarum; to create North Shields, while it gave the death-blow to Gatton; to give an hundred thousand a-year to the Greylings, and take it from the partisans of the former administration, that all this was done? No: it was the prospect of substantial relief from distress; the belief that the hidden cause of the universal suffering, which every one felt, but no one could explain, was now brought to light; the promises everywhere repeated, the assurances constantly given, the prospect invariably held forth of a real and important amelioration of circumstances from the proposed measure, which produced the general, the otherwise inexplicable delusion in its favour.

Now that the experiment has been made, and the reality of the promises uniformly held forth put to the test, it is universally seen how deplorably all classes have been duped by their deceivers. The agriculturists, who were told, that all their distresses were owing to the Boroughmongers, and that high prices, low rents, and plentiful employment would to a certainty follow the passing of the Bill, now find themselves plunged deeper than ever in distress, with wheat down at 50s. the quarter, and the prospect of a speedy Repeal of the Corn Laws, which will retain it permanently on an average even below that ruinously low standard. The manufacturers, who were universally assured that high wages, steady employment, and low prices, would certainly follow the overthrow of the Boroughmongers, now find themselves worse off than ever; with low prices, indeed, but still lower wages, and with a less command of the necessaries and conveniences of life than they had under any former period of their history. Hear what the Editor of the Liberator, and the organ of the Glasgow operatives, says of their present condition, nearly two years after the passing of *Maxima Charta*. We do not vouch for the accuracy of the statement, we merely give it as we find it, to illustrate the sense entertained by the operatives of the working of the great healing measure.

" There are upwards of *fifty thousand families* in the West of Scotland, at this moment, whose average income does not exceed *seven shillings* weekly for each ! Parcel out that miserable pittance into food, clothing, and rent, without any provision for the contingencies of sickness and death ; and such is the fluctuation experienced in the ' majority of trades' —the accidents that many are liable to, and the insecurity of maintaining a place —that there are few at the head of a family who lay their heads on a pillow at night, know whether or not the bread of their little ones will be baken on the morrow. With the *extreme* distress of thousands, and the insecurity of all the working classes, can you, Sir Daniel— *disinterested* as you say you are—lay your hand upon your heart and repeat, that workmen have no plea for taking some decided steps in their own behalf?"— *Answer to Sir Daniel Sandford, Jan. 8, 1834.*

If any farther evidence were wanting, it would be found in the statement of Mr Attwood, as to the condition of the Birmingham iron workers, after they had experienced a full year of the benefits of the Reform Parliament.

" I live in the neighbourhood of perhaps 50,000 honest nailers. I have ascertained from their own mouths, and from their masters' books, that during the war they could gain 16s. per week with the same labour as it now took them to gain 8s. per week. But they still paid 3s. per week rent for their cottage and shop, the same as they did during the war. Now take 3s. from 16s., and it leaves 13s. Take 3s. from 8s., and it leaves 5s. Did any one think that 5s. would go as far in supporting a working man's family now, as 13s. did during the war ? The thing was absurd ; 5s. would perhaps go as far as 6s., or possibly as 7s. But here was a clear injury of one-half in the situation of these honest, poor men."

When results such as these have followed the highly wrought up feelings and extravagant expectations, formed by the delusions universally and artfully spread to procure the passing of the Reform Bill, it is no wonder that the working classes have become generally and alarmingly distrustful of all public men, and that throwing overboard altogether the pilots whom they have placed at the helm, they propose to take the management of the vessel at once into their own hands.*

---

* The following doggrel verses, taken from the Glasgow Trades' Union Gazette of September 14, 1833, will shew how bitterly the people feel the imposition which has been practised on them, and how completely the present approach to anarchy is owing to the false and deceitful promises by which they were deluded into the support of that fatal measure, the Reform in Parliament :

" 'Tis twelve months past, just yesterday, since earth, and sky, and sea,
And rock, and glen, and horse, and men, rang loud the jubilee ;
The beacons blazed—the cannons fired, and war'd each plain and hill,
With the Bill—the glorious Bill, you rogues, and nothing but the Bill.

Our Ministers, so pop'lar then, presided o'er the fray,
On whisky jugs, and cans and mugs, secure sat Earl Grey,
And then as o'er our gladdened throats the stuff we stout did swill,
Our toast was still the Bill, you rogues, and nothing but the Bill.

Lord Brougham the mighty Chancellor, who Eldon's chain did take,
With plans of nice economy, made all the *windows* shake ;
Abuses vile, and such like things, that made our nerves to thrill,
Were all to fly with, ah, you rogues, the Bill, aye, just the Bill.

Lord Althorp high, and Littlejohn, of all the Russels he,
Were then with us—at every fuss—prize gods of liberty ;
Like Sidney grave, or Hampden brave, whom despots dire did kill,
We lauded to the firmament—the drawers of the Bill.

Our taxes, by this glorious Bill, were *all to sink or fade*,
Our shipping was to prosper then, and think, oh, what a trade !
Our agriculture, and our looms, our pockets were to fill,
By, ah, you rogues, the Bill, the Bill, and nought but by the Bill.

But this is not all. Not only do the working classes see that they have gained nothing whatever by the Bill, but the woeful fact is now beginning to open to their eyes, that they have been *made a great deal worse* than they were before; that they have been placed at the mercy of a body of men, who have little or no sympathy with their industry; and that the prevailing interest which now rules the determination of Parliament, is not only *not theirs*, but is actually an *adverse interest*.

With all their professions of patriotism, liberality, and a regard for the poor, there is no Parliament in the memory of man, which has done so little for the interest of the working classes, as that which was borne into St Stephen's on the transports of the Reform Bill. This is a fact, the existence and universal perception of which is completely demonstrated by the votes of the Legislature, and the simultaneous growth of Political Unions in all parts of the country. They have thrown out, by a majority of nearly 200, the proposal of Mr Attwood for an extension of the currency; the only measure which can put a stop to the incessant and increasing distress of the last ten years, and without a speedy adoption of which all attempts to revive industry, or avert ultimate national insolvency, will prove utterly nugatory. They have done nothing towards extending the Poor's Laws to Ireland, a measure imperatively called for, not less by the wide-spread and heart-rending suffering of the working classes in that unhappy and deluded country, but by the privations to which the British house-owners are exposed, by the enormous mass of Irish mendicity thrown upon them for relief. They have resisted and thrown out Mr Sadler's factory bill, and substituted a weak and nu-

gatory act in its stead; thereby perpetuating, without intending it, in the heart of Britain, a system of infantine slavery, and sexual demoralization, a bondage of body and prostitution of mind, unparalleled in the annals of Christian oppression, and unexampled in the history of Mahometan slavery. They have thrown out all attempts to restore protection to British shipowners and manufacturers, adhered steadily to the reciprocity system, and the dogmas of free trade, when every nation on earth is loading with additional duties the import of our manufacturers. They have retained the assessed taxes, the most ruinous tax on the industry of the poor, next to the income-tax, which ever was invented, because it is a direct burden on the funds from which alone labour can be maintained, and a duty, not on the comforts or luxuries of the working classes, but their necessaries; not on their spirits and tobacco, but their bread and their beef. They have adhered to the low duties on beer and spirits, thereby perpetuating the growth of drunkenness and demoralization, multiplying, at a fearful rate, the progress of vice and profligacy, and literally realizing a revenue out of the wages of prostitution, and the brutality of intoxication. They have, at one blow, inflicted an irreparable wound on eight hundred thousand comparatively happy and contented labourers in the West Indies, deluding them by the name of a liberty which they are incapable of enjoying, and depriving them of a protection, and a state of rural comfort, which they have themselves confessed was "unprecedented in any civilized state."[*] They are now strongly urged by the interest in the State which has obtained an ascendency in the Reformed Parliament, to repeal the Corn Laws, thereby giving the finish-

---

But now, ah mark the circumstance, attend, my friends—the mob,
Our jubilee, like Sir John Key, has ended in a job;
Our Ministers, and patriots, have gilded each their pill,
And purged their friends, the Radicals, with nothing but the Bill.

Each one holds up his hands at last, in horror and disgust,
At this same time precious document, once termed the people's trust;
That last and first, was to bring grist to fill the nation's mill,
Ah, curse the Bill, ye rogues, the Bill, and nothing but the Bill."

[*] Reform Ministry and Parliament, p. 6.

ing stroke to the distresses under which the agricultural classes have so long been labouring, and throwing upwards of four millions of rural labourers into penury and want. It is as clear, therefore, as the sun at noonday, that the interest of the producers, of the cultivators, and of the working classes, is not the interest which is predominant in the Reform Parliament; that it is some other and adverse faction which has contrived, amidst the public transports, to possess itself of political power; and that the labouring poor are farther now from obtaining substantial relief than ever.

What, then, is the body which has really succeeded in appropriating to itself the political influence which was once vested in the heads and representatives of the great interests of the State, which was once divided among the agricultural, manufacturing, and commercial classes, and secured to each that due attention to their wants which is essential to any system of good government? We shall give the answer in the words of our bitterest enemy; of one who knew us in many respects better than we did ourselves; who was equal to Alexander in military genius, and second only to Bacon in political sagacity.

"The English," says Napoleon, "are a nation of SHOPKEEPERS." In this single expression is to be found the true secret of the pecuniary difficulties in which all classes have been involved for the last fifteen years, and of the total failure of the Reform Parliament to administer any, even the slightest relief to the real necessities of the nation. It is the undue, the overwhelming ascendency which the class of traders, mo-

neylenders, and shopkeepers, have of late years been constantly acquiring over the cultivators and manufacturers, that is, over the working classes, which has produced all the false measures into which the Tories were seduced in the last ten years of their administration, and has at last precipitated the nation, bound hand and foot, into the bonds of the *shopocracy* and *moneyocracy*, riveted round their necks by the Reform in Parliament.

That this has been the chief cause of all the public distress; that it has been the remote but certain parent of the Free Trade system, the change in the Currency, and the abandonment of the Navigation Laws, the hideous infant factories, and, last of all, of the fatal Reform in Parliament, which has at once prostrated the whole *working and producing classes* at the feet of the *buying and consuming*,—we apprehend to be as clear as any proposition in Euclid. We are preparing and collecting materials for this great subject, which will be fully developed in our next Number, and would have appeared in this, were it not that the instant approach of the great strike on the 1st March, imperatively calls for the consideration of the Trades' Unions, which are in fact only a consequence and corollary from the dreadful political errors into which the people, under the guidance of a political faction, whose interests were adverse to their own, have been led, and the ruinous ascendency given to that faction by the Reform Bill. *

The real interests of the Conservative Party, and of the working-classes, both agricultural and manufacturing, are, and ever must be, the

---

* The above view coincides with what has been recently and powerfully advanced in a most able and original work, entitled Theory of the Constitution, by J. B. Bernard, Esq., Fellow of King's College, Cambridge. With many opinions of that gentleman we by no means concur; and, in particular, his speculations about the approaching discovery of moral evil and regeneration of society, are totally unworthy of an author of so much information. But his book is truly a work of genius: his views of the historical changes of the Constitution, though sometimes exaggerated, are always original, generally just and profound; and his clear insight into the intimate connexion between democracy and monied ascendency, is not only historically true, but in the highest degree important at this time. Mr Bernard and Sir D. Sandford will soon become good Conservatives. Men of original thought, as they are, will never receive the law from Holland and Lansdowne House, as the Whigs do on every subject of politics, literature, philosophy, and taste. We shall take an early opportunity of making Mr Bernard's work known to our readers.

same. The great bulk of the Conservatives live, and ever must live, upon the surplus produce of labour; and it is on the magnitude of this surplus that their prosperity is entirely dependent. What is the rent of land, but the surplus produce of agricultural labour above the expenses of cultivation? The Conservatives, accordingly, are and always have been the strongest advocates for such a protecting duty as shall secure remunerating prices to the farmers, because they know that it is on the existence of such remunerating prices that their own prosperity is entirely dependent; and that this surplus produce was in former times, before the fatal changes in the currency, fairly divided between the landlord and farmer, is proved by the fact that they were both thriving, and in many cases becoming rich; that the produce obtained by the farmer was about equal to that drawn by the landlord; and that the growth and extension of the farm-steadings even outstripped in cost the more splendid edifices constructed by the landlords.

In like manner, and for the same reason, the Conservatives have ever been the steady supporters of manufacturing and operative industry in all its branches. Who but they carried through the Navigation Laws,* which, as Adam Smith observes, were the great bulwark of our shipping interest, and the foundation of our maritime power? Who but they imposed the protecting duties on every branch of manufacture, under the shelter of which they have risen up to their present unexampled height? They have also in every age been the steady friends of the poor. They originally framed, and have since steadily supported the Poor's Laws, amidst all the obloquy thrown on them by the combined influence of liberalism, selfishness, and infidelity; and if that relief is not as yet afforded to the Irish mendicants, it is because the Reform Parliament and the popular party have steadily resisted the extension. They strongly advocated Mr Sadler's factory bill last session, and it was

ultimately thrown out by the democratic party in the Legislature. They steadily uphold the Established Church, the great instrument for the gratuitous instruction of the poor, in the most important of all knowledge, that of their religious duties, and as steadily resist those selfish politicians, the pretended friends of the people, who would lay the maintenance of their religious teachers, not, as at present, on a portion of the landed proprietors, but on the hard-earned wages of the poor. Every county in Great Britain knows and can testify, that the Conservatives are uniformly the most indulgent landlords, the most beneficent patrons of every useful institution, the warmest supporters of every beneficent charity. We are confident we are within the mark when we assert, that nine-tenths of the charity of the kingdom flows from Conservative hands.

On the other hand, what have been the *practical measures* of the liberal or democratic party for the relief or support of those working classes for whose interests they professed such uncommon solicitude? They have abandoned the Navigation Laws, thereby exposing to a ruinous foreign competition the numerous and important classes of shipwrights and carpenters;—they have abandoned or lowered many of the protecting duties on manufactures, and exposed our operatives to a flood of foreign manufactures, which have entirely swamped many important branches of industry;—they have forced upon the Conservative administration, by incessant clamour and delusion, the monetary system of 1819; and the suppression of small notes in 1826, measures which at once doubled the weight of all debts public and private, and inflicted a blow on the industrious classes, greater than all the power of Napoleon had been able to effect;—they have obstinately adhered to the reciprocity system, in the face of the clear evidence afforded by the conduct of other states, that it was all on one side;—they threw out Mr Sadler's Factory Bill;—they resist all extension of the

---

* They were passed by Cromwell, *when Lord Protector* ; that is, by as great a Conservative as Napoleon when Emperor.

Poor's Laws to Ireland;—and they are now preparing, at the bidding of the shopkeepers of London, and the great towns, to overwhelm the cultivators with a deluge of foreign grain, that is, to reduce to beggary and ruin four millions of persons dependent upon rural labour. Enquire in any county of the kingdom, from the Land's End to Caithness, what sort of landlords the democrats are?—how much they contribute to public institutions?—how much they bestow on private charity? You will hear in general that they are the most grasping and niggardly of the community; that they exact every thing from their tenants, and give nothing to the poor; that their names are to be seen at few subscriptions—their assistance felt at few undertakings; that their general characteristic is that of being *alieni appetens*, without the single redeeming point in Catiline's character, *sui profusus*. We speak of the general character of the democratic party. Doubtless there are many honourable exceptions to these remarks.

The manner in which the democratic party who have uniformly advocated these measures, destructive and ruinous though they were to the whole productive industry of the people, have nevertheless contrived to obtain the almost entire management of their thoughts, and succeeded in wielding at pleasure their vast energies, is one of the most startling and extrao linary of the many extraordinary phenomena these times exhibit, and affords a signal instance of the facility with which men may be led, by skilful flattery and alluring expressions, to support the leaders who are really pursuing measures the most destructive to their welfare. They were incessantly told that public happiness was their great object; that the people never could be sufficiently instructed, enlightened, and free; that self-government was the true panacea for all the evils of humanity; and that if political power was only vested to a sufficient extent in the people, all the ills of life would

speedily disappear. Misled by this dazzling phantom, they generally and cordially supported the democratic leaders, and submitted patiently for a tract of years to the most acute suffering, inflicted by the measures of their demagogues, in the firm belief, which was sedulously inculcated, that it was the resistance of the Conservatives which was the cause of all the evil. We have to thank the Reform Bill for having at length put an end to this extraordinary delusion, and by seating the Movement party in complete sovereignty, for the time at least, in the Legislature, brought at once to the test the sincerity of their professions to relieve the people, and their ability to do any thing efficient for the public welfare.

That the evils under which the labouring classes now suffer, and which have produced the formidable organization of the Trades' Unions, are in no respect likely to be removed, but, on the contrary, greatly increased by the greater ascendency of the democratic party, is farther illustrated by the fact, that they exist to fully a greater extent in North America, notwithstanding the drain of the back settlements and a boundless soil, than in the densely peopled realm of Britain.

" The North Americans distinctly admit, that ever since the Revolution which separated them from the mother country, and conferred upon them the blessings of self-government, magisterial and even parental authority has been upon the decline, and that now, at last, combinations exist amongst working men, to such a fearful extent, for overthrowing the institution of property, that a subversion of all authority is apparently at hand, there being absolutely nothing left in that country to preserve its social system from being torn in pieces, but education only."*

What security education is calculated to afford against these enormous evils in an old and corrupted state like Great Britain, has already been fully considered in the former number of this series.†

" There are, in our own country," says the North American Review, " combinations of the employed to procure

---

* North American Review, Jan. 1833, p. 81.
† The Schoolmaster, Feb. 1834, Blackwood's Magazine.

higher wages, political working-men's parties, and fearful signs of resistance to the highest authority in the Federal Union. Nor is this change passing only upon a large scale, where we can survey it, or much of it, at least, as a mere matter of speculation. It is coming home to our cities and villages, and very dwellings. Aristocratical influence, and magisterial power, and parental authority, too, have been declining among us ever since the Revolution. There are abolitions of peerages in our towns ; there are reform bills in our families ; *and our children are educated so freely, as to threaten rebellions, if not combinations, for securing their rights.* There are, indeed, tendencies of this sort, which must be controlled and regulated, or society cannot exist ; tendencies to a radical reform, so radical, indeed, that if not restrained it will tear up every social institution by the roots, and leave nothing behind but disorder, waste, and ruin."

The same truths are forcibly illustrated in Mr Hamilton's recent and admirable work on North America.

" In the city of New York," he observes, " a separation is rapidly taking place between the different orders of society. The operative class have already formed themselves into a society under the name of the *Workies*, in direct opposition to those who, more favoured by nature or fortune, enjoy the luxuries of life without the necessity for manual labour. These people make no secret of their demands, which, to do them justice, are few and emphatic. They are published in the newspapers, and may be read on half the walls of New York. The first postulate is, ' *Equal and Universal Education.*' It is false, they say, to maintain that there is at present no privileged order, no practical Aristocracy, in a country where distinctions of education are permitted. There does exist, they argue, an Aristocracy of the most odious kind,—an Aristocracy of knowledge, education, and refinement, which is inconsistent with the true Democratic principles of absolute equality. They pledge themselves, therefore, to exert every effort, mental and physical, for the abolition of this flagrant injustice. They proclaim it to the world as a nuisance which must be abated, before the freedom of an American be something more than a mere empty boast. They solemnly declare that they will not rest satisfied, till every citizen in the United States shall

receive the same degree of education, and start fair in the competition for the honours and the offices of the State. As it is of course impossible—and these men know it to be so—to educate the labouring class to the standard of the richer, it is their professed object to reduce the latter to the same mental condition with the former : to prohibit all supererogatory knowledge ; to have a maximum of acquirement, beyond which it shall be punishable to go. But those who limit their views to the mental degradation of their country are, in fact, the *moderates* of the party. There are others, who go still further, and boldly advocate the introduction of an *Agrarian Law*, and a periodical division of property. These unquestionably constitute the *extrême gauche* of the Worky Parliament, but still they only follow out the principles of their less violent neighbours, and eloquently dilate on the justice and propriety of every individual being equally supplied with food and clothing."*

We give the operatives due warning ; they have no relief to expect from the democratic party, and as little from the frantic anarchical course they are now pursuing. That their sufferings are great, we lament to hear ; that they neither can, nor will be relieved by the party to whose guidance they have hitherto and blindly surrendered themselves, is capable of demonstration.

The Reform Parliament is governed by an adverse interest to that of the producers. It is entirely ruled by the monied interests and TRADERS. This class has by the bill acquired a monstrous—an irresistible preponderance in the Legislature. We grieve to say this ; but it is self-evident ; and the supporters of the Reform Bill have themselves to thank for having riveted the fetters of an adverse interest about their necks.

To BUY CHEAP is the grand object of all the measures which now emanate from the Legislature, and have emanated for many years past. This is the foundation of the repeal of the Navigation Laws—of the diminution of the protecting duties—of the contraction of the currency—of the Free Trade system — of the incessant and ruinous repeal of indirect taxes—of the threatened repeal of the Corn Laws. For whose behoof is the incessant prosecution of this object undertaken? Is it for the interest of the *producers*, whether agricultural or manufacturing, whether rural or urban? No! It is for the interest of the *buyers*,—of the traders who hope to get their sales augmented by a diminution of the price of their articles, and their profits increased by the reduction of the prime cost of the goods in which they deal,—of the holders of money, and other classes in town who have fixed incomes, derived from the Funds, mortgage, or other unchanging sources, and therefore benefit immensely by every reduction which takes place. But this class have no interest in common with, or sympathy for, the producers of any description,—that is, the great bulk of the labouring classes, rural or urban, in every department; on the contrary, their interest is just the reverse. To sell cheap, and buy still cheaper, is the great object of the monied and trading class; and it is the point, accordingly, to which all their efforts are directed. If they can only get corn cheap, they care not though half the agricultural labourers—that is, two millions of souls—are reduced to beggary; if they can only get cottons cheap, they care not though a million of operative weavers are forced to live in garrets on a shilling a-day; if whisky and gin are cheap, they care not though crime triples under its influence, and millions of human beings are precipitated into profligacy by the spread of the fiery poison. If silks and ribbons are cheap, they care not though the weavers of Spitalfields and Macclesfield are reduced by the free (comparatively) trade in French silks to ruin; if they only get freights cheap, they care not though, by the repeal of the Navigation Laws, the whole class of ship owners and builders are brought to the verge of insolvency, and the "wooden walls of old England" sent to the bottom.

This single observation furnishes the key to the Free Trade system, the change of the Currency, the abandonment of the Navigation Laws, and all the disastrous measures of the last fifteen years. It is the progressive increase of the monied and trading interest, the ascendency of the race of consumers over that of producers, which has gradually obtained for them the dominion of the Legislature, and precipitated the nation into that abandonment of Conservative principles and the protection of producers, and that submission to the dictates of towns, which distinguished the concluding years of the Tory Administration. By an infatuation which has few parallels even in the wide-spread annals of human folly, the manufacturing classes, the urban producers, were led, when the final struggle arose, to join their forces *with those of their worst enemies, the urban consumers,* and under the guidance of the democracy, and the banners of Reform, fought and gained the great battle against the remnant of the producers, reduced, by this unnatural union, and the delusion of republican principles, to a third of their natural forces.

This truth, the real secret of all the distresses and disasters of the present times, and the clear and general perception of which is indispensable towards any thing like a righting of the national vessel, is put in a very clear light by Mr Bernard, to whose able and original work we have already alluded.

Mr Ricardo, a great fundholder and dealer in loans and stockjobbing, was one of the chief authors of the change in the currency in 1819.

" This gentleman," says Mr Bernard, " had obtained considerable celebrity amongst his brethren of the Stock Exchange, as well as amongst all that class of Reformers, whose real object is, not so much to benefit their country, as to enhance the value of money, by various publications on Political Economy; the leading principle of which is to exhibit landowners and farmers in the most odious light possible to their fellow-countrymen, by representing their interests as adverse to those of all other people, in which case their prosperity would alone depend on the degree of injury they could inflict upon others. The doctrine would indeed be true, were all working people, the public as they are called, consumers in a greater degree than they are producers, and were production chiefly confined to landowners and farmers only; but, fortunately for these latter classes, as working people, whether in agriculture or manufactures, all *produce* infinitely more than they *consume,* and are for that reason to be looked upon as producers, who, in company with landowners and farmers, thrive best upon high prices, and not as consumers, who benefit most by low ones; the doctrine is perfectly untrue; or true only, so far as it relates merely to fundholders and stockjobbers, and the several classes of society whose circumstances in life are bettered by raising the value of money, and lowering the rewards of industry.

" Still, Mr Ricardo's plan was a profound one. The idea of sowing dissensions amongst all who happened to be engaged in production, by making a part, and that the most numerous part, believe that they were consumers, rather than producers; and setting them in this way against those who were sailing actually in the same boat with them, the landowner and farmer, in order to weaken the united influence of the entire body; was an admirable contrivance for strengthening the hands of the fundholder, and enabling him to obtain his favourite object of low prices." *

During the struggle on the Reform Bill, the great majority of the producers throughout the country, of whatever class, were seduced by the contagion of democracy and the delusion of a Press, all emanating from, and guided by, the interests of town consumers, to unite against the remnant of the Conservative—that is, the producing interest. Ninety-eight out of the hundred and one county members of England were returned in the reforming interest; and the farmers who brought them in on the shoulders of the populace, are now rewarded for their exertions by the threatened repeal of the Corn Laws—that is, the reduction of grain to forty shillings a-quarter, and wages to ninepence a-day. Almost all the manufacturing towns joined the cry, and by their threatening attitude overawed the House of Peers, when that noble body threw itself almost unsupported into the breach to save the whole producing classes; and they now see the consequences of their conduct in the obstinate adherence to free trade, the reciprocity system, the restricted currency, and all the other measures dictated by the exclusive

interests of the monied classes, and are allowed to cool, after their Reform transports, in garrets, on bread and water, and a shilling a-day to maintain a rising family.

The slightest consideration of the present constitution of Parliament must shew how enormously and unjustly the monied interest and the urban consumers have gained by the Reform Bill, at the expense of the industrious and working classes throughout the state. Out of 500 English members, there are 156 for counties, and 344 for boroughs; that is, the town members are to the county as more than *two to one.* Part, no doubt, of the boroughs are swayed by the landlords in their neighbourhood; but, probably, at least as many county members are returned by the growing influence of city wealth, owing to the increasing embarrassment of the country proprietors. At all events, if it be said that there are 300 English members in the interest of the consumers, and 200 in that of the producers, the fairest allowance is made for the possible efforts of the minority, of all descriptions, who are now attempting to stem the ruinous torrent which has flooded the Legislature. And in the right of voting at elections, how are the different classes of society balanced? A consumer in town, who pays ten pounds of yearly rent, has a vote; a producer in the country requires to pay *five* times that sum to get one. The ten-pound clause virtually excludes the *whole operative manufacturers from any influence,* and vests unlimited power in the spiritdealers, grocers, and shopkeepers—that is, the consumers who live on the fruits of their labour. Thus, both by the places which return members, and the qualification to vote, bestowed with such flagrant inequality on the different classes of society, is that ruinous supremacy secured to the monied classes and consumers, which has been at the root of all the national distresses for the last fifteen years. Now, from the tables quoted below, it appears that the total wealth produced by the agriculturists and manufacturers, amounts to the enormous sum

* Bernard's View of the Constitution, 312.

of above four hundred millions annually, and the population employed in these branches of industry is no less than 10,000,000, while the total wealth earned annually by the trading and monied classes, is L.95,000,000, and their numbers are only 5,600,000. Thus a class producing one-fifth of the national income, and composing one-third of the national numbers, have contrived, by the delusions which they have spread among the working bodies, to usurp a preponderating influence in the Legislature, and to introduce and perpetuate a series of measures, which have precipitated, and are precipitating, the very men whose hands create their income into beggary and ruin.*

In these observations we have classed the agricultural and urban producers together, and considered their joint interests as opposed to that of the money-holders and consumers. We know well the apple of discord which the consumers and the advocates of cheap prices have contrived to throw between these two vast bodies, whose united strength would be irresistible. We are quite aware of the fatal delusion which they have spread, and are spreading,

on the subject of the Corn Laws, and the efforts they are making to detach the whole urban producers from their rural brethren, by the false but specious pretence that dear grain is the interest of the one, and cheap grain the interest of the other. It is therefore of the utmost moment that the working classes of all descriptions should at length acquire just ideas on this subject, and be brought to see that their interests are identical, and cannot be separated; and that it is the fatal disunion which the town consumers and monied classes have contrived to create between them by the phantoms of democratic ascendency, free trade, cheap prices, and political power, which has enabled the adverse interest in society to mount upon their backs, and chain them like captives to their chariot wheels, in defiance of the evidence of their own senses, and the continued suffering experienced in their own persons.

Let the operative workmen and manufacturers, before they give ear to these insidious attempts on the part of their real oppressors, attend to the following consideration: When were they in a prosperous

---

* The following Table illustrates this in the most striking manner. It is taken from Pebrer's and Moreau's Tables, and all compiled from Parliamentary documents,

Annual produce of agriculture in all its branches,	.	L.246,600,000
———— of mines and minerals,	. . .	21,400,000
———— of fisheries,	. . . . .	3,400,000
———— of manufactures,	. . . .	148,000,000
Total Annual Produce of Producers,	. .	L.419,400,000
Annual profits of inland trade,	. . . .	L.48,425,000
———— of coasting trade,	. . .	3,550,000
———— of shipping and foreign commerce,	.	34,398,000
———— of bankers,	. . . .	4,500,000
———— of foreign income,	. . .	4,500,000
Total Annual Produce of Consumers,		L.95,373,000

Producers.		Consumers.		
Number of agricultural persons, and their families,	6,300,000	Shopkeepers,	.	2,100,000
		Tailors, shoemakers, .	.	1,080,000
Miners, . . .	600,000	Soldiers and sailors, .	.	830,000
Manufacturers, . .	2,400,000	Clergy, doctors, &c. .	.	450,000
Artificers, builders, &c. .	650,000	Paupers, . . .	.	110,000
		Annuitants, . .	.	1,116,000
Producers,	L.9,950,000			
		Consumers,		L.5,686,000 *

* Pebrer's Tables 338 and 350.

state? Was it during the war, when prices were high, and, in consequence, a great surplus produce was created throughout the state, or has it been since the peace, when the blessings of cheap produce, cheap prices, and low wages, have been fully experienced? We shall give the answer in their own words.

" The fundamental cause of the Trades' Unions is a want of the necessaries of subsistence. This is certified by the deplorable statements of Messrs Cobbett, Fielden, and Attwood, in the House of Commons, with reference to the manufacturing districts, in many parts of which the average income of an individual was not sufficient to buy bread alone. Mr Cobbett, in reply to Mr Macauley, stated that he would pledge himself to prove that 10,000 persons in Leeds did not get three-pence per day, and he affirmed that his colleague had a statement, which he could verify on oath, and which he obtained by his own personal enquiries, that there were 50,000 persons about Manchester who did not receive each 2½d per day. Mr Fielden's Tables, published last year, exhibit the following facts:—

In 1815, wages per piece to hand-
weavers were   .   . 4s. 6d.
In 1824,   ditto   .   . 2s. 3d.
In 1831,   ditto   .   . 1s. 4d.

Now, add to this appalling fact that eight millions of pounds were last year collected for Poor's rates, and I think, without entering further into dry statistical details, it must be obvious to all but the pampered minions of corruption, that *distress, long, deep, and hopeless distress, is the cause of the organization of the Trades' Union.*"—*Trades' Union Gazette,* Jan. 25, 1834.

The same fact is stated in the same terms in the *Newcastle Press,* Dec. 21, 1833.

" The gigantic organization of the *Trades' Unions* is beginning, and with reason, to attract the attention of the country. These unions are only one amongst the many signs of that great change which is impending over this kingdom: and which it is now impossible either for human cunning or human courage to avert. These unions have sprung out of the long and increasing pressure upon the laborious classes, *whose misery has gone on increasing with their knowledge.* The fruit is perfectly natural. Education will never bring men to believe that they can be half starved to

all eternity under a just or proper government; or that society has any right to call upon men in general to be miserable, for the sake of the continuation of a system. Of this, the productive classes of England are now fully convinced, and they are as fully determined that *they* at all events will suffer no longer."

Now this, be it recollected, is the state to which the operatives have been brought by the adoption of all the principles of the democratic party; by the system of cheap bread, free trade, and the Reform Bill. During the last five years of the war, wheat was at 14s. 6d. per bushel, and all classes, and more especially the operatives, were prosperous and contented; for the last five years wheat has been at an average 8s. a bushel, and they have been, by their own admission, constantly getting worse and worse. At present wheat is at 5s. 4d. a bushel, lower than it has been for the last forty years, and the workmen, as they themselves tell us, are so far from thriving, that they are literally starving by hundreds of thousands on seven shillings a-week. Unless these unhappy men were literally infatuated by the monied demagogues who lure them by democratic flattery to perdition, they would see that cheap prices are immediately followed to them by *still cheaper wages,* and that just in proportion as the price of grain falls, is the quantity of that grain, which they are able to purchase with their wages, lessened also. If by a miracle the price of grain could be lowered to half-a-crown a-bushel, its price in Poland, the only result would be, that their wages would *immediately fall to sixpence a-day,* and the last state of that man would be worse than the first.

The slightest consideration must shew for what reason it is that cheap prices, whether of manufactured or agricultural produce, are immediately followed by great distress to the operatives. The facts, the important facts already noticed, that the produce of agricultural labour in Great Britain is L.246,000,000 annually, and that the home consumption of manufactures is L.88,000,000 annually, while the foreign, even at this time, is only L.60,000,000, alone explain it. The agricultural producers are the chief and best customers of the manufacturers: they consume a half more than all foreign nations put together. Low prices, therefore, which cripple and depress all branches of home purchasers, who are all more or less dependent on this prodigious flood of two hundred and forty six millions annually poured into the state, cripple and diminish, in just a similar degree, the home market—that is, the market which is half greater than all foreign markets put together. Suppose our exports of manufactures were to fall from L.60,000,000 annually to L.40,000,000, in consequence of some general calamity which had befallen their purchasers in foreign states; what prodigious misery would this spread among our operative workmen; and yet the fall of agricultural produce from 60s. to 40s. the quarter, would contract the home market much more powerfully: it would *cut off eighty millions annually* from the funds destined to the purchase of domestic manufactures. These considerations shew decisively that in a nation such as Britain, which rests chiefly on its agricultural produce and manufactures consumed in the home market, the prosperity of the operative classes is mainly dependent on the maintenance of high and remunerating prices to the agriculturists; because it is thus, and thus alone, that their chief customers are provided with funds to buy their goods. In such a state, high prices of rude produce are immediately followed by still higher wages to all classes in general. Prosperity and credit is immediately diffused through all classes of society; whereas, under the wretched paralysis of low prices, the funds for the purchase of the produce of manufactured industry are constantly contracting, the wages of the operative workman fall to a greater degree than the grain which he consumes, and he is starving in the midst of nominal plenty. This doctrine was long ago laid down by Adam Smith.—" High prices," says he, " and plenty, is prosperity : low prices and depression, are misery."

To illustrate the ruinous state of depression to which the operative workmen have been brought by the combined operation of Free Trade, low prices, and democratic principles, we have extracted, in the Table below, the prices of labour, &c., from 1815 to 1832, with the prices of grain, taken from Mr Fielden's Tables, published by the National Regeneration Society. From them it appears, that since 1815 the price of grain has declined, on an average of years, about *twenty-five* per cent, but that the wages of the operatives have declined *above sixty-six* per cent during the same period of their former amount;[*] and that the total returns for " labour, expenses, and profit," under the halcyon days of cheap bread and free trade in 1832, is little more than *a fourth* of what it was under the high prices of the years immediately succeeding the war.[†]

---

[*] Average price of five years, before 1820, 77s. per quarter ; of five years before 1832, 63s. per quarter of wheat.

[†] AN ACCOUNT OF THE COST, &c. OF ONE PIECE OF THIRD 74s. CALICO, from 1815 to 1832 INCLUSIVE,

References to the Columns in the Table.

No. 1. Shows the number of lbs. weight of cotton required to make a piece of third 74s. calico.
2. The average price of the cotton per pound in each year.
3. The average of cotton required to make one piece in each year.
4. The average price of such calico in the Manchester market.
5. The average sum the manufacturer had for labour, expenses, and profit, in every year, from 1815 to 1832, both years inclusive.
6. Average price of a quarter of wheat and a quarter of oats in each year, from official returns.

It is as clear as mathematical demonstration, therefore, that the principles by which the Democratic body are governed, have been proved by experience to be adverse to the interests of the producers of commodities; and that the working classes, seduced and blinded by the flattery of Democratic demagogues, who all resided in, and were actuated by, the interests of towns, have given a fatal ascendency in the Legislature to the very class in the State to whom all their misfortunes have been owing, and whose interests are directly adverse to their own.

The operative workmen feel this; they are aware that they have been misled, deceived, betrayed; that amidst the incessant eulogies of the Democrats, they have been constantly getting poorer; amidst a continual fall of prices, have had daily less to eat, and that, as Cobbett well expresses it, just in "proportion as education has been thrust into their heads, their clothes have been slipping from their backs."

It is in consequence of the strong, the galling, the heartrending sense of their deception,—it is because the utter worthlessness of all the Democratic projects advanced in the interest of the monied and consuming classes in towns to ameliorate the State, has been fully and universally experienced, that Trades' Unions, with all their attendant starvation, perils, and anarchy, have risen up in the land. But are they the way to remedy the evil? Is a complete stoppage of labour on the part of several hundred thousands, perhaps a million of workmen, a way to ameliorate their condition? Is, to use their own haughty expressions, the "snapping asunder every link in the chain which binds society together, by this inert conspiracy of the poor against the rich," the way to augment the resources of *their customers*—the rich, without whose wealth to buy their commodities all their labour must go for nothing? Alas! such a convulsion, if it once becomes general, is calculated to inflict a degree of wide-spread misery upon the operatives, compared with which, all they have hitherto experienced would be regarded as the sunshine of prosperity. On this subject, we cannot do better than quote the eloquent words of that stanch

---

7. Wages paid to the hand-loom weaver for weaving one piece of third 74s. calico.

Year.	1 Number of lbs. of Cotton.	2 Cotton average price. per lb.	3 Price of Cotton. in piece.		4 Price of Calico.		5 Manufacturers' Profit and Wages.		6 Wheat, per qr.		6 Oats, per qr.		7 Hand-loom Weaving, per piece.	
	lbs.	*d.*	*s.*	*d.*	*s.*	*d.*	*s.*	*d.*	*s.*	*d.*	*s.*	*d.*	*s.*	*d.*
1815.	$4\frac{3}{16}$	$19\frac{1}{2}$	7	0	18	0	11	0	63	8	22	11	4	6
1816.	4 do.	$18\frac{1}{2}$	6	$7\frac{1}{2}$	16	0	9	$4\frac{1}{2}$	76	2	22	6		
1817.	4 do.	20	7	2	15	3	8	1	94	0	31	6		
1818.	4 do.	20	7	2	16	0	8	10	83	8	31	6		
1819.	4 do.	13	4	10	13	0	9	2	72	3	27	4		
1820.	4 do.	12	4	3	11	6	7	3	65	10	23	6		
1821.	4 do.	$9\frac{7}{16}$	3	$4\frac{1}{2}$	10	6	7	$1\frac{1}{2}$	54	5	18	11		
1822.	4 do.	$8\frac{1}{8}$	2	11	10	0	7	1	43	3	17	7		
1823.	4 do.	$8\frac{3}{16}$	2	11	9	6	6	7	51	9	22	3		
1824.	4 do.	$8\frac{1}{2}$	3	0	9	0	6	0	62	0	24	1	2	3
1825.	4 do.	$12\frac{1}{4}$	4	$4\frac{1}{2}$	9	9	5	$4\frac{1}{2}$	66	6	24	11		
1826.	4 do.	$6\frac{3}{4}$	2	5	7	2	4	9	56	11	25	11		
1827.	4 do.	$6\frac{1}{4}$	2	3	6	5	4	2	56	9	27	4		
1828.	4 do.	$6\frac{1}{8}$	2	$2\frac{1}{2}$	6	3	4	$0\frac{1}{2}$	60	5	22	6		
1829.	4 do.	$5\frac{5}{8}$	2	0	5	7	3	7	66	3	22	9		
1830.	4 do.	$6\frac{5}{8}$	2	$4\frac{1}{2}$	6	3	3	$10\frac{1}{2}$	64	3	24	5		
1831.	4 do.	$5\frac{5}{8}$	2	0	5	9	3	9	66	0	25	4		
1832.	4 do.	$6\frac{3}{8}$	2	3	5	6	3	$2\frac{1}{2}$	61	0	24	0	1	6

Reformer, Sir D. Sandford, addressed to the Trades' Unions of Glasgow.

" In a contest between capital and labour, taking into account the state of matters in this country, capital must ultimately triumph, at the expense of much confusion and much misery. I can see nothing in this opinion to retract or qualify. It will recommend itself, I think, to the acquiescence of all who examine the question with their eyes open, unblinded by the metaphysical definitions of political economy. The capital by which, in conjunction with labour, our manufactures are carried on, must all be classed under the heads of works and machinery, raw materials, and money. By a unanimous refusal to labour, the workmen may throw the capital of the first description into temporary inactivity; or by an insurrectionary movement, they may destroy both it and the stores of raw material now in the kingdom. Thus may they inflict a heavy loss upon the proprietors; sure, however, in the end to bring want and woe upon themselves. But they cannot at one blow destroy the money already accumulated, or that command of money which credit and connexion give. These potent weapons are in the hands of their employers. Let the workmen meditate upon the inevitable consequence. If one party is to try to starve out the other, the longer purses and wealthier connexions of the masters will carry them through the struggle, and their opponents will gain nothing beyond the suffering attendant on a painful and perilous experiment; or monied capital will take its flight to other lands, where labour assumes a less menacing attitude, and offers the prospect of more secure returns. The labouring classes should remember that capital of this kind, once scared away, is not easily courted back; and they should turn their attention for a moment to certain provinces of Ireland, as a specimen of the condition to which a people may be degraded, chiefly by the absence of capital, arising from the absence of security. Thus I fear that despair at last, if not evil design in the first instance, might drive the working population into the frantic excess of rebellion against law, and attacks on property. But he who holds out hopes of final success to a movement of that character is either a fool or a villain. Even without the aid of a numerous and well-disciplined army, a British insurrection of the labouring classes would assuredly be put down, perhaps with much bloodshed on the field and the scaffold. The holders of property are strong enough to defend themselves, by a general rally of the upper and middle ranks in our cities and our rural districts. I do not apprehend a new edition of the Bristol conflagration. I am pretty confident that on the stage of this country, we shall not behold enacted the dismal scenes of the first French Revolution. And if these tragedies were to be repeated in our days, will any member of the working body point out one result, beneficial to that most important but dependent class, to which they could reasonably be expected to give birth ? "

These observations are deserving of the most serious consideration, and by none more than the wretched, deluded men, who are now tempted by their democratic leaders to attempt what they term an " inert conspiracy" against the whole capital and wealth of the state. Do they really conceive it possible they can succeed in such a design ? Is there any example in the history of mankind of such a conspiracy, how " inert " soever, proving successful ? Have they funds to enable them to hold out against the capital and resources of the masters, the accumulations of centuries, supported, as they will be, by the banks, the monied men, the government ? The Trades' Unions tell, and we grieve to hear the fact, that there are 50,000 families in and around Glasgow, and as many in and around Manchester and Birmingham, who do not know at night that the bread for their little ones will be baked to-morrow. The Liberator boasts that there were 2000 operatives in Glasgow in January last, who had struck work, whose weekly maintenance cost L.500. At this rate, which is evidently the lowest on which a human being can subsist, (5s. a-week,) 200,000 operatives would cost L.50,000 a-week, and a million, L.250,000.* Are they prepared with vast funds of this description to sustain their efforts ? And is 7s. a-week, the amount, as they tell us, of their present earnings, a likely source from which to derive them ?

---

* Liberator and Trades' Union Gazette, Jan. 24, 1834.

But this is not all.—Such vast assemblages of working-men, thrown out of work simultaneously, will, to the end of time, inevitably generate acts of violence and deeds of blood. Oppression towards their fellow-creatures is the necessary and universal result of the congregation of thirty or forty thousand idle, unrestrained men together—t'hing short of military discipline can ever restrain them. Among such vast bodies, there will always be found many daring reckless characters, who will not scruple to perpetrate acts of the greatest atrocity, to forward the purposes of the union. It is not in human nature to sit with its hands across, and see strangers introduced to work at reduced wages, and thus defeat all the purposes of the combination, without taking the short and simple way of knocking them on the head. The rapid growth of the atrocious practice of throwing vitriol in the manufacturing districts, proves how general the operation of these principles has become. It is truly observed in a late publication on this subject—

" If the working classes could be brought to combine without using violence towards those who do not enter into their views, the evil, how great soever, would be comparatively inconsiderable to what is now presented ; but, unfortunately, this never can be the case. Among the thousands and tens of thousands who are combined together to gain these common objects, there always have been, and always will be, found some reckless and worthless characters who will not scruple to exert violence, or even embrue their hands in the blood of such of their fellow-citizens as, by holding out, threaten to defeat the object of their combination. To the end of time such worthless characters will be found in all large bodies of mankind ; they may be calculated upon as a given quantity to the last days of the world ; and therefore, violence, intimidation, and bloodshed may be permanently expected to attend such combinations. The trades' unions, therefore, however plausible in theory, become, in practice, the mere association of violence and tyranny, over industry and peace ; they are the engine by which the most lawless and reckless of society

are enabled securely to exercise a grinding oppression over the more quiet and inoffensive. They subvert the whole objects of society, defeat the chief ends of the social union, and expose the poor to a tyranny the more galling and dangerous, that it is exercised by men of their own rank in society, and supported by the physical strength of vast masses in the state." *

But suppose that this were not to be the result, and that by a simultaneous strike of several hundred thousand men, over the whole country, the *present* object of obtaining a deduction of two hours a-day from the period of work is gained — What will be the result ?—Will wages remain at their present level, low as it is, under such a reduction ? Unquestionably not. They will, and must fall, just in proportion to the diminution in the produce of looms; and the condition of the workman will be more miserable than ever. By no human contrivance—by no intimidation or violence, or " inert conspiracy," can capitalists and masters be compelled to pay wages, which are a loss to themselves, or abridge materially the present slender rate of profits :—rather than do so, capital will take wings to itself, and emigrate to other and more tranquil lands; and the peopled houses of Britain will be filled with starving millions, deprived by their own suicidal hands of the means of subsistence.

The frantic anarchical course which the workmen are now pursuing, therefore, is as little calculated to afford the many effectual relief, as the blind and infatuated support of the democratic faction in towns has been; while it threatens to produce results more immediately ruinous and destructive than even the Reform Bill, that stupendous monument of general infatuation, is in the course of effecting. The one is a burning delirium, which will at once prostrate the patriot; the other a low fever, which will gradually, but certainly, exhaust his strength.

An extensive struggle has lately broke out in the west of Scot-

---

* Thoughts on the Reformed Ministry and the Reformed Parliament.—P. 37. Stillies, Edinburgh. 1834.

land, in consequence of a resolution of the masters to employ no calico-printers who were members of the Trades' Unions, and bringing down new hands to supply the place of those who refused to abandon these pernicious associations. The result has been just what might have been anticipated. Where the military were in sufficient force to protect the new workmen from the violence of the associated trades, the masters have proved victorious, and the fresh hands are going on; where they were not, the associated operatives succeeded in expelling them. Twelve delinquents, apprehended by the Glasgow police, were liberated by the mob: eight unhappy prisoners are securely lodged within the walls of Stirling Castle. The west of Scotland is approaching the condition of Ireland: the authority of law exists, where soldiers stand, or the guns of fortresses protect the prisoners. Where the defence of the industrious is left to themselves, they are compelled to yield to the unionists.—Such are the fruits of Whig Government! We insert with pleasure the following just observations of the *Glasgow Herald* on this subject :—*

"Nothing can equal the infatuation of the operative printers in the whole of this business: they had comparatively light work and comparatively high wages; but these very circumstances, along with the notion of more skill being required in their profession, led them to consider themselves superior to the ordinary run of workmen, and their vanity thus exposed them to become easy tools in the hands of the revolutionists. Elated with the brilliant figure which they had made in reform processions, they flattered themselves that they were the pets of Government, and would get their own way in every thing, even when they attempted to enact the part of tyrants over their fellow-labourers. While they affected the spirit of independence, they basely submitted to live on contributions from others; and those of them who were married had the injustice and inhumanity to deprive their families of more than a half of their usual rate of subsistence. While they were proudly lording it over others to whom they denied the freedom both of judging and of acting, a large portion of them-

selves were abject slaves, trembling under that very intimidation which they were labouring to inflict on others—at least such is the defence that is resorted to by those who have abandoned the Unions.

"Those Trades' Unions, which now cause so much confusion and alarm in the country, originated in the former Political Unions, which were organized under the direction of itinerant orators and agitators, of which apostles of mischief in this part of the country the chief was Mr Joseph Hume, M.P. No merit would have attached to his successful exertions to abolish the laws against combinations, which had existed in England since the time of Edward I., unless they had been followed by practical results, and those results we now see before us."

Is, then, the cause of industry and production utterly hopeless? Have the monied classes, the traders, the shop-keepers, succeeded, by the insidious spread of democratical principles, in for ever dividing the productive classes, who are the source of all their wealth, but, from want of equal cunning, have been the unhappy victims of their artifice? Are the working classes for ever to follow the red flag of democracy to their own perdition, instead of the old banner of England, under which all classes once throve and were prosperous? Will mankind ever be governed by words, and worship the demon who flatters their passions, regardless of the bread which is vanishing out of their mouths, the furniture which is melting away from their dwellings, the clothes which are slipping from their backs? Such is the force of public delusion, such the astonishing manner in which the productive classes have been arrayed against each other by the arts of the democratic or consuming faction, that we much fear their ascendency will continue, that the situation of the whole industrious classes, both in town and country, under their democratic leaders, will daily become worse, until at length the cup of misery is full, and military despotism closes the scene.

But one thing is perfectly clear, that if this deplorable result does take place, it will not be because the means of extrication are utterly lost

---

to the nation. By a cordial union with, and support of, the Conservative body; by a junction of the strength of the agricultural and manufacturing producers, they may yet shake off the monstrous load of shopkeepers, money-lenders, and traders who have risen into such fatal preeminence on their distresses. The classes who constitute the ten millions will be too strong, if united in a constitutional struggle, for the five; the producers of four hundred millions a-year of produce must, in the end, if they will only act together, overcome those who produce one. The Reform Bill, indeed, has quadrupled the political power of the urban and monied party, and reduced to less than a half the forces of industry; the manufacturing operatives have to thank themselves for having given this monstrous addition to the forces of their adversaries, and weakened so alarmingly the strength of their friends. Still the case is not utterly hopeless; their own acts are likely to relieve them; the extremity of suffering, which they have brought upon themselves, may perhaps prove the means of dispelling the universal delusions by which they have been blinded.

But let us not be misunderstood ; it is by constitutional means, and constitutional means alone, that the battle must be fought ; *the Conservatives never can, and never will, become Radicals ; the Operatives must become Conservatives.* We do not say Conservatives, in the false and odious sense in which the falsehood of the urban consumers uses it,—that is, as the supporters of unjust or corrupt power, such as the Democrats falsely assert governed the country before the Reform Bill,—we say Conservatives in the sense in which, and in which alone, we have ever supported it; as the defenders of all the great interests in the State, and especially of the vast bodies of agricultural and manufacturing producers, from whose labours four-fifths of the national income flows ; by whose hands all classes are fed and clothed, and lodged. We say Conservatives, not as the enemies of the real and just interests of the consumers and monied men, but of that unjust and oppressive advantage which they have gained by the town-directed legislation of the last fifteen

years, and which has brought on the nation the unspeakable calamities of free trade, contracted currency, Democratic Government, and the threatened change in the Corn Laws. We say Conservatives, as the steady friends of the Church, the shield of the poor against infidel attack and city corruption; as the supporters of the national faith against the combined attacks of Radical violence and public suffering, and as thoroughly convinced that it is only by doing justice, and protecting equally all interests, and most of all the Funds, the great Savings' Bank of the poor, that the national salvation can be accomplished. We say Conservatives, not as deluded by the idea so lamentably prevalent of late years, that it is by destroying the interests, either of rural or urban producers, by the free and unrequited admission of foreign produce, that the great surplus revenue of the nation, the fountain of prosperity to all classes, can be augmented ; but by such protecting measures as will secure to our operatives, whether in town or country, a due return for the fruits of their toil, and cease to grind down the British labourers for the benefit of the city Democrats, or the advantage of foreign states.

The views we have now sketched out, explain that gradual, but evidently increasing approximation of the Conservatives and the industrious classes, at which the Whigs so loudly exclaim as a monstrous union of Tories and Radicals. This outcry comes with peculiar consistency and good grace from the correspondents of political unions, from those who bowed to deputations headed by tailors, from the advocates of the brickbat and the bludgeon, and the Journals who, by the open threat of Radical violence, overturned the constitution. The approximation proceeds from no political coalition, from no insidious or designing ambition. It is the result of the experience of common injury; of the instinct which leads men, of whatever opposite opinions, on most subjects, to unite against those by whom they have both suffered wrong. But it must be a very different coalition from that which history will for ever execrate; be attended by no such dereliction of public duty as that of their opponents. What the servile ministerial Press, the Receivers of mandates from Lord Brougham and Holland House, call an union of Tories and Radicals, must be founded on very different principles from that atrocious combination of monied ambition and Radical delusion which has produced, and is producing, such fatal consequences. It must be founded on an abandonment of all anarchical designs, and all demonstrations of violence by the latter, and of all monied delusions by the former; a return by our rulers to the principles of just remuneration to productive industry, whether in town or country, and by our people to the subordination and loyalty of former times; a recurrence, in short, to the true principles and practice of the constitution, before the disastrous days of monied ambition, cheap labour, free trade, and Democratic, that is city ascendency. Whether by these or any other methods, it is possible to get the better of the Reform Bill, and the decisive superiority it has given to consumers over producers in the legislature, is perhaps doubtful; but this much at least seems certain, that in no other way is so fair a prospect even opened of shunning perdition, or avoiding that gradual but unceasing degradation of the working classes, and the Conservatives who depend on their labour, which has been constantly increasing since the deporable era when the Nation was surrendered to the guidance of its democratic deceivers.

COMBINATIONS.

It was lately well remarked in the *Sun*, that the Trades' Unions were undermining the very foundations of the social structure, and that unless they can be disarmed, it must sink into ruins. Were we asked, says the excellent author of " Character, Object, and Effects of Trades' Unions," to give a definition of a Trades' Union, we should say, that it was " a Society whose constitution is the worst of democracies, whose power is based on outrage, whose practice is tyranny, and whose end is self-destruction." How have such societies—in an age distinguished above all other ages—in spite of the strong and steady march of intellect, crushing all ignorance and all wickedness under foot—overspread the kingdom—not slowly springing up, as it might seem, from the seed—but as if an Upas-Tree had been planted, at its full growth, in every town and city, distilling poison, starvation, and death? The education of the people has been conducted by the people's press. Useful knowledge has been administered to them, and greedily swallowed, with condiments of the Entertaining; and thus have their minds been filled with power and pleasure far beyond the wisdom and happiness of their ancestors, and their champions have proudly and loudly exclaimed, in the light and liberty of the emancipated spirit, Lo! " a peculiar people, zealous of good works!" Yet, in the midst of all this illumination, the same millions, mole or bat-blind, as if they were working their way under ground, or flitting through the twilight, while pride and folly were declaring, that Britons were now walking erect, for the first time, like freemen, in the blaze of a new-risen day!

To explain such a contradiction in the nature of things and of man, would baffle a more searching philanthropy than ours; but no such contradiction exists—for much of their boasted virtue is a dream, and the people are wickeder than they know—their conscience is in the dark—and their intellect, so far from having been invigorated by what they have been taught, has been weakened—and lost its hold on many of those feelings which supported it of old, and reconciled the children of labour to their condition by the peace and beauty they brought with them to bless the poor man's lot. But we shall not be unjust to the character of the working orders. Heavy distress has come upon them—much of it not brought by themselves on their own heads; and there has been " grinding of the faces of the poor." Their rulers—Tories and Whigs—have often failed in their duties to the people—and much of the guilt that caused that distress lies at the door of many misgovernments. Nor have the rich, as Christian men, always done their duty to the poor, but have often, in the pride of wealth, been grossly neglectful of their duty; nor have the higher orders acted as if they felt for the lower those sympathies which nature prompts, but which too often are palsied and benumbed in the breasts of the great, by that very rank which, in noble natures, keeps them freshly a-flow; for surely 'tis of the very nature of gentle blood to inspire benevolence, and how so well can they in whose veins it flows prove its purity, than by shewing that by their very birth they are beneficent?

Upon an enquiry into the manifold causes of the present wide distress and disturbance, fearfully reacting on each other, we shall not now enter; but we shall continue as heretofore to touch frequently upon them, while discussing to the best of our talent, and we boldly say with good intention, the political, social, and domestic condition of the people of our beloved land. Labour has now declared war against capital —*plusquam civilia bella* are raging— and to whichever side is given the victory, disastrous must be the other's defeat—not to themselves alone, but to their conquerors too—so that in either event the whole country must suffer by the prolongation of a contest, which, if not terminated amicably, can be terminated but in blood. Heaven forbid the latter! Peace once proclaimed, then must law ratify it by its wisdom, and by its majesty preserve it from violation. Legislation is a more difficult science now than ever; but let us hope that a Reformed Parliament may be Conservative, and that the representatives of the people, chosen by the people, will consult, affectionately, firmly, and fearlessly, for the people's good. By many awful considerations are they called on so to do; for they have themselves—too many of them at least—helped all they could—and that too in part from the most selfish motives—the motives of a base ambition—to exasperate in the breasts of the people that restless and turbulent discontent which, not occasionally, and during bad seasons, as it once was, but at all times, now rankles there, and within these few years, all too many, has been fed and inflamed by the promulgation of the most pernicious principles by lay-preachers, who, while they have said they abhorred anarchy or misrule, denounced the throne and the altar, and hope eventually to overthrow them in a still more radical revolution than the state has lately undergone, till not one stone is left on another, and the very names become obsolete in the English language of priest, noble, and king.

The time is not so far by-gone as that it may not be remembered by people not yet old, when the relation between master and servant was strengthened by feelings of mutual kindness — and was in very truth literally an attachment. It was not so only in private households; but much of the same spirit belonged to the same relation throughout the whole system of affairs—making employers of labour labourers' friends—and preserving their common interests by mutual good-will and interchange of amicable affection. Then, that spirit, it was believed, so far from being injured by the care of law, was preserved by it—not by fear, which is a bad guardian—but by submission, which is often the very best. Law undertook—as far as law ever can — to protect the rights of labour by preventing labour from committing wrongs; in the opinion of men not deficient in wisdom and generosity, a law against Combinations of workmen to interfere with wages, might so be constructed as not to be unjust;

and judging from experience, they believed it was salutary—from the gradually enlightening experience of a length of years. We know better than not to say that at the same time men of the highest wisdom and humanity looked with suspicion or disfavour on all such enactments —and among them the illustrious and immortal author of the Wealth of Nations. But that Adam Smith would have counselled their repeal at the crisis of affairs when their repeal was passed, we see no reason to believe; far less that, supposing he would have done so, he would have dreamt for a moment of recommending to be substituted in their place the wretchedly impotent law against assaults by workmen on one another so frequent *in strikes*, which the wisdom of the repealers foolishly supposed would suffice to curb the violence and keep the rage of the "multiform beast" within the bounds of justice. It is with respect to the spirit of the arguments by which the repeal of all combination laws was effected, that we desire now to make some observations; for we have every year seen stronger and stronger reasons for believing, that to those arguments, spread with the spirit in which they were conceived and uttered, over all the kingdom by a powerful press, must be mainly attributed the present state of the popular mind, allowed on all hands to be most formidable—full of peril, not to our national prosperity only, but our national existence, and therefore on all hands condemned as wicked, by all, at least, who are unwilling to believe the people—the whole labouring people of Britain—to be simply fools. Fools would they be who should call them so—but miserably misguided they must have been—and the question is, by whom? We answer,—leaving the base crew of their enemies out of sight,—by many who, we shall admit, were, after a fashion, their well-wishers; by not a few who, beguiled by their own enthusiasm into most dangerous doctrines, were nevertheless their honest, sincere, and ardent friends. Among the number of the former we mention, as one of the most eminent, Mr M'Culloch; and among the number of the latter, the most distinguished by far, Dr Chalmers—who has ever zealously sought to promote the temporal and eternal interests of his fellow-men in all conditions, from the throne to the hovel. We cannot introduce our remarks better, than by a clear statement of their subject, from the admirable Charge lately delivered to the Grand Jury at Exeter on the case of the Unionists, whose trial, we observe, after the Grand Jury had found a true bill, was removed by a *certiorari* to the Court of King's Bench.

" From a very early period of history, as far back as the reign of Edward I., the laws against combination had commenced, and had continued down in nearly an unbroken series to the reign of Geo. IV. It appeared that from a very early period the law on these combinations was educed from the circumstances of the times. Our ancestors found it necessary to interfere—and interfere they did with a strong hand —to put down all combinations of citizens and handicraftsmen, who, so far back as the reign of that king, had been in the habit of combining to raise the rate of wages above the fair market value; to restrict the hours of labour, and to impose restrictions upon the masters who employed them. He was not competent, nor had he any wish, to enter into the political economy of the question. He would not enquire as to the policy or impolicy of the law. He thought that it was the business of those who filled either the judicial situation, or that of the Grand Jury, not to enter into considerations whether the law was wise or unwise, merciful or cruel—but to see what it really was, and then merely to consider themselves as the persons bound to administer it. Our Statute-book, as he had said, formerly contained a great number of laws on the subject of combination which came down to the reign of Geo. IV., when at length it was thought wise to reconsider the whole subject; and in the fifth year of that reign a statute passed of so comprehensive a nature, that it repealed nearly the whole of the laws on the subject of combination. They were repealed by a statute which was made on the ground that all interference was impolitic and mischievous; and in plain terms it was made no longer an of-

fence for artisans or mechanics of any description to enter into any consultation for the obtaining of an advance of wages, for lessening or altering the duration of the time of working, decreasing the quantity of work to be done in a given time, inducing others to quit the work of their masters, or to return it to him, or to regulate the mode of carrying on any business or manufacture, so that persons entering into any combination of this sort were no longer held liable to any penalty whatever, either by the statute or common law of the land. This statute for repealing the whole of the previous acts, was made for the purpose of leaving the whole principle of contract between the master and workmen entirely free ; it was passed in 1824. But the effects of it were found to be such that in the following year a state of things had occurred which, it was thought, made it imperative to reconsider the whole subject, and a very intelligent and influential member of parliament (Mr Huskisson), who had taken a very active part in effecting the repeal of the combination laws, once more introduced the subject to the legislature for their reconsideration. Accordingly, in the following year, the 6th George IV., a modified law, was passed, which repealed the statute of the preceding year, and laid down the law as it at present stands. This act, after imposing certain punishments on certain acts done by reason, or for the purpose, of interfering either with the rate of wages or the hours of labour, made this declaration on the subject :—that the act should not extend to subject any persons to punishment who should meet together for the sole purpose of determining the rate of wages or the hours of labour which they should work in any manufacture, trade, or business. This was the existing law upon the subject. The principle upon which it was grounded was this, that there should be perfect freedom on both sides—on the part of the master as well as the workman—that as the master could employ any workman he pleased, so the latter should be at liberty to get the best price he could for his labour, just as he would if he had any other commodity to dispose of. It went even farther than this, to shew that it would be lawful for two or more, or any number of persons, so to meet and consult together as to what price such persons so met together would sell their labour for, and what period of time they would work. This was the present law upon the subject, and the question was, whether what were called conspiracies, or combinations of a secret description, where the parties were bound together by oaths, meeting in private, and levying subscriptions, being bound by solemn and unauthorized engagements—whether under this law such meetings could be considered legal ? If illegal, then such combination would assume the character of a conspiracy."

We shall not expose the miserable attempts at reasoning which may be found in the reports of the debates in Parliament on the motion for the repeal of the old Combination Laws—nor shew them up in the ludicrous light in which they reappeared, when the new enactments consequent on their repeal were themselves repealed within one year's experience of their utter impotence, and a second set enacted as worthy of all contempt. But, as we said, we shall confine ourselves to two publications, widely circulated in 1826, and highly applauded—Mr M'Culloch's "Essay on the Circumstances which determine the rate of Wages and the condition of the Labouring Classes," reprinted, with additions, from several of his other works, in which it had appeared in various shapes and sizes and prices —then sold for the first time at two shillings, or one—and circulated by the friends of the people widely over all the manufacturing districts, as an epitome of all that was " wisest, virtuousest, discreetest, best;" and two chapters on Combinations in the third volume of Dr Chalmers's Civic Economy—a volume which, by its bulk and weight, could not have had either a rapid or wide circulation, but which was almost reprinted, piecemeal, in hundreds of publications that went among the poor, and was likewise cried up to the skies as a revelation of saving truth on the secular concerns and temporal interests of the million.

The consequences of the Repeal of the Combination Laws, so far from having been such as the supporters of that measure anticipated, had within the year been diametrically the reverse ; and to account for the flagrant enormities perpetrated by too many of the Combinations that sprung up on the repeal, they were forced to form a somewhat unsatisfactory theory, which would have done more credit to their wisdom and foresight, had they suggested it at the time of the repeal, or before it, in order to warn the nation of the first disastrous consequences likely to result from carrying the measure into effect. They endeavoured to attribute all those enormities to the sudden feeling of freedom from the tyranny of galling and unjust restraints. The Combination Laws had long been supposed by workmen to weigh heavily upon them—to subject them to the will of their masters—to keep down forcibly and unjustly the poor man's earnings throughout all trades —to make them, in short, slaves— and their employers tyrants. On being—argued Dr Chalmers—suddenly emancipated from unjust control, giddy with the intoxication of freedom, and thereby prevented from calmly consulting their own judgment and experience, they not only grossly exaggerated to themselves the evils which the former state of things had so long inflicted on them, but as grossly mistook the means of curing the real evils they might have endured. And thence all the guilty excesses of which combined workmen were guilty all over the country on the repeal; excesses never again to be committed, after that great teacher of Political Economy, Time, shall have taught them the folly of attempting to alter by force or intimidation that order of things founded in the very constitution of society.

Now, whatever truth there may be in this — and there is truth—why, it may be asked, were such effects, lamentable and disastrous indeed, not foreseen and predicted by the advocates for the repeal ? Not only were they not foreseen, and n' t predicted, by the advocates for the repeal, but all those persons who did foresee, and did predict them, ourselves among the number, and, on the certainty of

such effects flowing from a repeal
of the existing laws, opposed that
measure, were scouted as timid and
prejudiced adherents to a system of
slavery and restriction. Goodwill towards the masters, unanimity and moderation among the workmen themselves, order, regularity, and industry in all trades, and, above all, gratitude to their rulers and legislators,
were the effects, and the sole effects,
that any enlightened thinker was to
expect from the repeal : Not a word
of riots, and robberies, and assaults,
and homicides, and murders. Every
thing was to go smoothly, and all
the different interests of capitalists,
labourers, and consumers, to adjust
themselves without any violent outbreakings, by means of a great law
constantly operating for the good
of the whole.

As far, therefore, as regarded the
immediate consequences of the repeal of the Combination Laws, the
supporters of the measure were
in the wrong, and the opposers of
the measure were in the right. Had
the theory proposed to account for
the evils that followed the repeal been
proposed to prepare the public mind
for them before the measure was past,
more credit would certainly have
been due to the sagacity of its pro-
pounders. Their blindness, therefore,
or ignorance or error, ought greatly
to have detracted from the weight
of their authority on the whole question ; and put us on our guard against
yielding too entire and unqualified
assent to any of their other reasonings
built upon a reference to active principles in the human mind, which, in
this case, they appear either not to
have understood, or, from undue
zeal in support of a favourite measure, to have given a very false account of its probable operation.

" The effervescence which has
followed on that repeal," said Dr
Chalmers, " is the natural, and, we
believe, the temporary effect of the
anterior state of things. There was
nothing more likely than that the
people, when put in possession of a
power that they felt to be altogether
new, would take a delight in the
exercise of it, and break forth into
misplaced and most extravagant ma-
nifestations. But if the conduct of
one party have been extravagant, the
alarm of the other party we conceive

to have been equally extravagant."
Here we cannot help thinking, with all
respect for Dr Chalmers, that he
ought to have used more definite
language in speaking of such a subject. Effervescence—is not exactly
the word that may best express the
desperate and murderous character
of many of the proceedings of the
combined workmen all over England
—and many parts of Ireland. In
another part of his disquisition, Dr
Chalmers calls things by their right
names—because it was necessary to
do so to make good his masterly
argument in favour of the enactment
of the severest laws against actual
outrages of the workmen against each
other. But here he is anxious to
account for the immediate effects of
the repeal—and therefore uncon-
sciously has adopted such terms as
may render his notion the more
plausible. The same strong objection ought to be made to the expression, " if the conduct of the one
party have been extravagant." Extravagance is a somewhat too mild
word for days, weeks, and months,
and years' continued and systematic
outrage and violence, not unfrequently accompanied with bloodshed and
murder. Nor can we think, however
mistaken they might be in some things,
" that the other party were equally
extravagant," seeing that their extravagance consisted in an alarm for the
safety, property, and person, excited
by the crimes of combinations, that,
whatever might be the causes of the
delusion under which they committed them, proved by their words
and their deeds that they were determined to respect neither property
nor person, in their wanton and
violent efforts to disturb the order
and shake the structure of the commercial world.

Dr Chalmers makes use of a sin-
gularly unhappy illustration of the
theory by which he would account
for the " effervescence and extravagance" of the workmen in their combinations. " The repeal," says he,
" of the Combination Laws in England, has been attended with consequences which strongly remind us
of the consequences that ensued,
after the Revolution, from the repeal
of the game laws in France. The
whole population, thrown agog by
their new privilege, poured forth

upon the country, and variously accoutred, made war, in grotesque and unpractised style, upon the fowls of the air and the beasts of the field. In a few months, however, the extravagance subsided, and the people returned to their old quiescent habits and natural occupations. We feel assured, that, in like manner, this delirium of a newly awakened faculty among our British workmen will speedily pass away. They will at length become wise and temperate in the use of it." The two cases had no earthly connexion; and how has the Doctor's prophecy been verified by events? *Circumspice!*

Mr M'Culloch, in his Essay on Wages, says, that "Those who were fully aware of the practical operation and real effect of the late act, and of the feelings it had generated in the minds of the workmen, must have been prepared for most of what has lately occurred. The violence it did to the right feelings of the labouring classes, and the oppression to which it sometimes gave rise, led them to ascribe to it infinitely more powerful influence than it really possessed." Here, too, we should have expected some more definite proof, that previously to the repeal of the Combination Laws, the workmen throughout Great Britain and Ireland groaned under them—either under real evils which the law produced, or imaginary evils which it was supposed by them to produce. It is perfectly true that the former law could not be popular among the workmen—but where is the proof that it was, and had long been so execrated by them—so utterly detested—and, that it had in many cases been made the instrument of great oppression? Nothing short of utter detestation of any law, founded on real and gross grievances, will serve the purposes of this apologetical hypothesis. Now, it is granted, not only in the above passage but throughout the Essay, that the power given by the Combination Law to masters to depress wages had always been a bugbear—although in the above passage it is also somewhat invidiously as well as inconsistently said, that sometimes that power had been most oppressive. It does not therefore seem, on the whole, satisfactorily made out, that the many

enormities perpetrated by the members of the various combinations were to be attributed entirely either to "effervescence or extravagance," or to delight in exercising a new faculty, or sudden escape from a degrading and galling thraldom. To ascribe such enormities, either wholly or in chief part, to such a cause, even if that cause had existed in all the force ascribed to it, would not have been philosophical; but still less so was it to ascribe them to a cause taken for granted—and taken for granted too, not only without evidence, but in the face of all evidence.

For while we are far from saying that the Combination Laws were not in some respects objectionable, and, like most other laws, occasionally mingling injury with benefit, this is certain, and allowed on all hands to be certain, that they had not operated to sink below the proper point the wages of the labourers. The history of the country, and the experience of every one, replied in the negative. In good times, many of the working men of manufacturing and trading places could earn as much in five of the working-days of the week, as would both support their families, and enable them to spend the sixth perhaps in idleness and dissipation, although we are far from saying that they generally did so. If in bad times wages were too low, this was in general evidently owing to the inability of the masters to pay more, and not to the Combination Laws. Wages had, upon the whole, advanced, and the working classes at the time were enjoying a greater share of the necessaries and comforts of life than had been enjoyed by those of former generations. Now, although all this may not have prevented workmen from actually believing that they suffered some grievance from the Combination Laws, we think that, allowing them to have that degree of intelligence which is commonly and rightly attributed to them, they could not possibly have regarded those laws with such bitterness of hatred, and detestation, and anger, as to account for the crimes subsequent to the repeal, on the ground which Dr Chalmers, Mr M'Culloch, and many others then took. Injuries and grievances must be real, galling, grinding, oppressive, and of long establishment, before they can account for such effects following a repeal by which they were suddenly removed or redressed. The argument was a weak one, and pushed to an absurd extent; and we cannot help thinking that some of those who then used it so strenuously, felt, from the sophistical shape in which they occasionally put it, that its strength was not so great as in their zeal they wished it to be thought. Had they felt that it was conclusive and unanswerable, they would have used plainer words, and despised the feeble and suspicious aid of so many delicate circumlocutions.

We mention *those facts*, that they may be set against those vague and indefinite expressions—effervescence—extravagance—delight in the exercise of a new faculty, and so forth; not that they are to be considered as arguments conclusive against the repeal. Those excesses were thus written about by writers, who had the credit, with many, of having treated the subject most liberally, most philosophically, and most like Political Economists. Let those excesses then be, without exaggeration, stated; let them be attributed to their right causes; and then, if such experience could indeed be kept out of sight, and all the feelings repressed, to which it naturally and properly gave rise, —let the question be decided by abstract reasoning, and such principles as the science of Political Economy does in its present state supply.

All the world will agree with Mr M'Culloch's dictum, " that wages, like every thing else, should be always left to be regulated by the *fair and free competition* [attend to these words —*fair and free*] of the parties in the market, and ought never to be controlled by the interference of the Legislature." All the world will agree with Adam Smith, from whom that dictum is adopted—" The property," says Adam Smith, in a passage quoted by Mr M'Culloch for the hundredth time—" which every man has in his own labour, as it is the original foundation of all other property, so it is the most sacred and inviolable. The patrimony of the poor man lies in the strength and dexterity of his hands; and to hinder him from employing this strength

and dexterity in what manner he thinks proper, *without injury* to his neighbours, is a plain violation of this most sacred property." Now, although it is well known to all who have read the Wealth of Nations, that Dr Smith regarded Combination Laws with an inimical eye, it is equally well known to them, that this passage, constantly quoted as it has been, on this argument, has no reference whatever to the Combination Laws — but to Corporation Laws. It is the law of apprenticeship that he is reasoning against; and he goes on to say, " that it is a manifest encroachment upon the just liberty both of the workman and of those who might be disposed to employ him. As it hinders the one from working at what he thinks proper —so it hinders the others from employing whom they may think proper. To judge whether he is fit to be employed, may surely be trusted to the discretion of the employers, whose interest it so much concerns. The affected anxiety of the lawgiver, lest they should employ an improper person, is evidently as partial as it is oppressive."

It is, therefore, neither doing justice to the subject under discussion, nor to the person himself who may be discussing it, nor to his reader, nor to the illustrious author of the Wealth of Nations, to take a sentence from one of that great man's arguments on one subject, and transfer it, without saying so, to another —in many—indeed in all essential respects—different.

Thus taking their ground upon the authority of Smith—that is to say, upon the authority of an aphorism applied by him to the decision of a different question—some of the most eager, and, perhaps, not the least unprejudiced of the reasoners against the principle of the Combination Laws, —taking their ground, we say, on the admission that workmen should be allowed to dispose of their labour in any way they please, and that there should be no laws of apprenticeship —asked how that could be, so long as workmen were prevented from concerting with each other the terms on which they were to sell it, and so long as there were laws against Combinations? Adam Smith's observation applies to the one case, without any exception or qualification. For whatever other arguments may be advanced in defence of the laws of apprenticeship, or of corporate bodies — and there are many — still, certainly they do, in some sense, interfere with the property which every . has in his own labour, and prevent, under certain circumstances, its employment. But Adam Smith would not have used the same argument against the Combination Laws. He *has not* used the same argument; and for this manifest reason, that the combinations among workmen do as often interfere with the property which every man has in his own labour, as the laws against them.

"To shew," continued Mr M'Culloch, adopting the disjunctive form of reasoning, " that laws against combination of workmen are unnecessary, it has been stated, that the wages of any set of workmen who enter into a combination for the purpose of raising them, must be either, 1st, below the natural and proper rate of wages in the particular branch of industry to which they belong; or, 2d, that they must be coincident with that rate, or above it; and that in either case alike, such laws are of no avail.

" In the first place, if wages have been depressed below their natural level, it is affirmed that the claim of the workmen is fair and reasonable; and it would obviously be unjust and oppressive to prevent them from adopting any measures, not injurious to the just rights of others, which they might think best fitted to render the claim effectual. But a voluntary combination among workmen is certainly in no respect injurious to any of the rights of their masters."

Now, two remarks may be made on this passage; and the first is, that if there be any truth in Economical Science, it is true, that there are causes in continual operation, tending to equalize wages in all employments, and to keep wages from remaining permanently, or for any considerable time, below the natural level. How, then, can it be said that the claim of the workman for an advance of wages is fair and reasonable, since the depression or elevation of wages is no more in the power of the employers than of the employed, but

must depend upon circumstances affecting the trade of the country? Have the masters the fixing of the rate of wages in their own hands? Certainly not. And, should wages therefore for a time be very low—that is, so low as to reduce the labourer to distress—does it follow that they can, without injury and injustice to the employers of labour, be raised by combination? If the labourer thinks that his wages are too low, he can go into any other employment; but will he find wages higher there? He will not. Much stress is laid in the above paragraph on the words, " not injurious to the just rights of others," and on the word, " voluntary." But are all combinations, that call themselves and pretend to be voluntary, really so? Much intimidation—much compulsion—much deception—many arts and artifices, have ever been employed in most combinations—over many of their members; and although every body must agree with M'Culloch, when he says " that it is a contradiction and an absurdity to pretend that masters have any right or title whatever to the services of free workmen, in the event of the latter not choosing to accept the price offered them for their labour," yet there is no contradiction or absurdity in telling those free workmen to carry their labour to another market—each man being left free to judge and act for himself, which he is perhaps more likely to be when left to himself, than when he has become a member of a combination, and inspired with the *esprit de corps.*

" No master ever willingly consents to raise wages," says Mr M'-Culloch, " and the claim of either one or of a few individuals for an advance of wages, is likely to be disregarded, so long as their fellows continue to work at the old rates. It is only when the whole, or the greater part of the workmen belonging to a particular master, or department of industry, combine together, that it becomes the immediate interest of the master to comply with their demands."

This pernicious assertion, we maintain, is in direct contradiction to every established principle of Political Economy. And Mr M'Culloch himself overthrows his own reasoning in the very next paragraph. For he says truly, " that the competition on the part of the masters will always raise wages that have been unduly depressed, and that it is from not adverting to this fact, that the influence of the Combination Laws, in depressing wages, has been so very greatly exaggerated. If the wages paid to the labourers engaged in any particular employment, are improperly reduced, the capitalists who carry it on must obviously gain the whole amount of this reduction, over and above the common and ordinary rate of profit obtained by the capitalists engaged in other businesses. But a discrepancy of this kind could not possibly continue. Additional capital would immediately begin to be attracted to the department where wages were low and profits high, and its owners would be obliged, in order to obtain labourers, to offer them higher wages. It is certain, therefore, that whenever wages are unduly reduced in any branch of industry, they will be raised to their proper level, without any effort on the part of the workmen, by the mere competition of the capitalists. Looking, therefore, to the whole of the employments carried on in the country, we do not believe that the Combination Laws had the slightest effect on the average and usual rate of profits. In some very confined businesses, it is not improbable that they may have kept wages at a lower rate than they would otherwise have sunk to ; but if so, then, for that very reason, they must have tended equally to elevate them in others."

All this is perfectly sound doctrine—and by many had it been preached long before M'Culloch's day,—but we do not think that Mr M'Culloch deduces from it the soundest conclusions. According to his own views here, and they are the views of all good Economists, one does not see why workmen should combine to produce that effect which, without their combination, will flow from causes already at work ! He says, " that their combination may raise their wages *sooner*"—but if so, they will be doing injury to others—they will manifestly be interfering with the operation of those general principles, which it is the great object of all the advocates

of Free Trade to preserve unviolated,—because, in themselves, they do necessarily guard the interests of the workmen in all different employments.

But Mr M'Culloch should have stated distinctly what he meant by wages being " depressed below the natural and proper rate"—" improperly reduced "—" unduly depressed "—for these are the terms he uses—without any farther explanation. No doubt, if all the masters in any one trade were to combine to reduce the wages of their workmen, in order to raise unduly—*i. e.* above the rate of profits in other trades— their own profits, any counter combination to resist it could not be considered unjust : but such a case does not seem to have been in the writer's contemplation ; neither is it conceivable that any one master could ever hope to succeed in such an attempt. If the trade itself were depressed, then both profits and wages having fallen, the master would carry his capital elsewhere, and the workmen would do the same with their labour.

It is admitted, that the *object* of the second class of combinations, those which take place when the wages of the combining workmen are already equal to, or above their natural and proper rate, is *improper and unreasonable ;* but it is denied that this impropriety and unreasonableness furnish any ground for their prohibition by law. For, supposing that this mass of workmen should occasionally combine together, still it appears " *improbable in the last degree,*" that their combinations should ever enable them to obtain from their masters more than a due share of the produce of their labour. That the masters would resist a demand for any greater portion is certain ; and the slightest glance at the relative condition of the parties must satisfy every one that they cannot fail, in all ordinary cases, to succeed in defeating it. The workmen always suffer more from a strike than the masters. It is, indeed, true, as Dr Smith has observed, "that in the long run they are as necessary to their masters, as their masters are to them ; but this necessity is plainly far from being so immediate. The stock and credit of the master is, in almost every instance, infinitely greater than the stock and credit of his labourer; and he is therefore able to maintain himself for a much longer time without their labour, than they can maintain themselves without his wages. In all old settled and fully peopled countries, wages are seldom or never so high as to enable labourers to accumulate any considerable stock; and the moment their scanty funds are exhausted, there is necessarily an end of the combination, and instead of dictating terms, they must accept those that are offered to them."

Now, granting, for the present, all this reasoning to be correct, (but that when thus generally put it is incorrect—nay, wholly false —events, of which none can be ignorant, have now indisputably proved) to what does it amount? That in a pernicious and unjust struggle for higher wages, the workmen will ultimately be defeated by the masters. It is granted that their object was improper and unreasonable; and it is shewn that in their attempts to attain it by combination they will be impoverished, baffled, and forced, perhaps, at last, to accept terms that are too severe. Now, might it not be better for all parties, particularly the workmen themselves, to prevent, by law, all such improper, unreasonable, unavailing, and ruinous combinations?

We cannot, therefore, agree with this very dogmatical writer, that, when workmen enter into a combination to enforce an unreasonable demand, or to raise wages that are already up to the common level, " they must lose, and can gain nothing, by entering into an employment to which they have not been bred; while it is equally evident that a small extra sum will be sufficient to entice a large supply of other labourers to the business they have left. All the great departments of industry have so many closely allied branches, that a workman who is instructed in any of them, can, without much training, readily, and without difficulty, apply himself to the others; and thus the workmen who had entered into the combination, would not only fail of their object, and be obliged to return to their work, but, owing to the influx of other labourers into their business during the period of the strike, they would be compelled to accept a lower rate of wages than they had previously enjoyed."

Throughout all this passage it is assumed, by far too generally, that there is such a close connexion between trades, that men can turn effectively from one to the other at a few days' notice, or with a few days' preparation. It may be so with a few of the clumsier trades; but, with nine of ten, the very opposite is the truth. Nor, in the case of a general strike, is it, except rarely, in the power of the master to employ hands from another trade. Indeed, Mr M'Culloch himself was well aware of that; and the knowledge of the fact led him into a most ludicrous blunder in logic. For he says, that, in the case of a strike, the workmen who enter into a new employment must necessarily lose; and yet he maintains, that, without loss to the employer or the consumer, their place may be supplied by workmen to whom this business is equally new. So that, to make out the argument, it is assumed, that workmen can turn themselves without loss to a new trade, and also that they cannot. "The Duke of Hamilton, and the proprietor of the Calder Iron Works, have, by acting on that principle, effectually suppressed a combination among their colliers, by bringing other labourers into their mines; and though they may perhaps lose a little in the first instance by the change, there can be no doubt that it will, in the end, be as advantageous to them, as it is sure to be ruinous to the miners who are turned out of employment."

This is but an indifferent argument against Combination Laws. In the case of collieries, that seems to be possible which in most, certainly in many, manufactories is impossible; but it is scarcely conceivable that it can be advantageous to the owners of extensive coal-pits to work them with new hands—that is, workmen who never had been in a shaft during their lives. And what security is there against these workmen combining too, when they have learnt all the facile mysteries of the trade? Meanwhile, the consumers of coals have been suffering from the combination, and the miners themselves, it is allowed, are ruined. Now if the question simply were, Which party suffered most by combination, when resisted? Perhaps the answer is given, The combiners, who are all ruined. But this is not the question. The question is—Would it not have been better to have had a law, of which the operation would have been to hinder the miners from bringing ruin on themselves by themselves?

Mr M'Culloch therefore concludes, " For these reasons, we think it impossible that any one who seriously considers the subject can resist coming to the conclusion, that a combination for an improper object, or to raise wages above the proper level, must cure itself—that it must necessarily and surely bring its own destruction along with it." Now, the short and simple answer to that is—that in numerous instances the evil did not cure itself—and that when it does, it is only by the substitution of one evil for another—the "chastisement"—that is, the ruin and beggary of the infatuated workmen who have combined. That they may have deserved to be ruined and beggared may be very true; but the discussion is not ethical, but economical, and we are enquiring into the nature and extent of evils which, when there are no Combination Laws to control them, ignorant men may bring upon themselves, and which, by combination laws, many persons are strongly inclined to think might have been prevented.

Mr M'Culloch then goes on to say, that " a strike must, under all ordinary circumstances, be a subject of the most serious concern to workmen; and the privations to which it unavoidably exposes them form a strong presumption, that they are honestly impressed with a conviction that the advance of wages claimed by them is moderate and reasonable, and that the strike has been forced upon them by the improper resistance of their masters. Even in those instances in which wages are notoriously depressed, workmen will, in general, if they consult their own interests, be shy about striking, and will resort to it only as a last resource."

This passage contains many direct contradictions—both to Mr M'Culloch's own doctrines, and to no-torious facts. He has himself allowed that it is only by competition of masters that wages can be raised—and he has also admitted that workmen are unfortunately ignorant of the principles of Political Economy, and ought to be instructed in the elements of that science. Then how inconsistent to expect from men ignorant of their interest that they should nevertheless judiciously consult it! "If they consult their own interest!" Did the colliers at the Calder Iron Works consult their own interest —when they combined to raise wages already high, and by combining, brought chastisement upon themselves—and got the evil to cure itself by reducing them all to ruin? Did the Bradford wool-combers consult their own interest, when they stood out so long, first in insolence of funds, and finally in starvation of poverty, against their masters, and when on the sound of the machinery within the deserted mills, they broke up their combination, and afraid lest their services might be wholly dispensed with, accepted, with sullen gratitude, the wages they had spurned, and continued to work in fear lest the multitude of wheels should reduce their wages to a pittance? People have a strong passion, from nature, to consult their own interest; but they often do not know how to set about it —and it is poor philosophy to think of settling a question in Political Economy by a common-place moral maxim, indifferently understood, and worse applied.

A man of Mr M'Culloch's talents and knowledge would scarcely have written in this way, but from some strong prepossession in favour of that side of the question which he adopted, blinding his better judgment—for he admits the existence of many formidable and pernicious combinations. But then he adds, with that extraordinary inconsistency that runs throughout his whole Essay, " that though we lament the bad use they have made of this newly-acquired freedom, yet when the universal ignorance of the working classes with respect to the circumstances which determine the rate of wages are taken into account, we do not think there is much reason for wonder at their conduct!" Now, it is this very ignorance against which the Combi-

nation Laws were a safeguard; and
while it exists—what better, what
other safeguard has society against
the recurrence of such evils? Would
it not have been wiser to wait till
that ignorance was enlightened or
dispelled? And what reason have
we *to* believe that that period will
soon arrive? The artisans of England are not an uneducated set of
men. On the contrary, it is the creed
of almost all the eminent writers of
the day, that they are better informed
by far than the agricultural labourers.
Still they do not know, it too often
appears, their own interest, and it
would be presumption in any writer
to expect that, after all that has been
written on the principles regulating
the rate of wages since the days of
Adam Smith, and after all the lessons
of experience which have been read
to them, that his lucubrations, however excellent, should very soon direct their understandings to such a
clear and steady perception of the
abstract truths of the science as shall
stand in the room of law, and at
once teach and induce them to square
their conduct, under all temptation,
to the rule of justice and right reason.

Mr M'Culloch then asks how Government can interfere in any question respecting the rate of wages that
may arise between master and workman? "Shall Government," he asks,
"apply for information to the masters
or to the workmen?" He says they
may as well apply to the workmen,
for "that their opinion is just as deserving of attention as the other;" and
he says so, immediately after having
told us that the workmen are in a
state of total and universal ignorance
with respect to the circumstances
that determine the rate of wages!

It was remarked some years ago,
in a paper on this very subject, that
"whatever may be the case with an
individual, a corporate body has no
rights except what the laws may
please to give it. Now the workmen
of a trade form themselves into an
actual corporation,—obtain the complete control of labour in that trade
—fix its price—prohibit all persons
from being employed who are obnoxious to them—render the capital
of their former employers useless—
subject the|poor to severe privations"
—and finally, bring on themselves, as
it is on all hands allowed, frequent

ruin. It could not be said that the
colliers at the Iron Calder Works—
the shipwrights of London—and the
seamen of Sunderland had a right
to act as they did act ; but it is
about such conduct as theirs that the
question is—and it is not to be settled by any general maxim about the
right of property, which, in itself a
truism, may, in its application, be
a falsehood. "A criminal act can
never be generated by the mere multiplication of acts that are perfectly
innocent," says Mr M'Culloch —
meaning thereby to shew, that if one
man may, without blame, decline
working at wages he thinks unsatisfactory, a hundred may combine to
do the same. But this is not sound
Philosophy. For there are many actions that change their very nature,
under varying accompanying circumstances—and which, when performed by one person, are blameless,
or even praiseworthy—become, when
performed in concert, very much the
reverse. Thus it may be very proper
for the most pious man to take an
evening walk after divine service, on
a Sabbath, for the purposes of relaxa-
tion or meditation. But were he to
collect together all his friends and
acquaintances in the parish for the
same purpose, the cavalcade would
be indecorous, and contrary to the observance of the sacred day. It would
be so—even if the whole party
marched along the high-road with
due regularity and subordination—
but how much would the spirit of
each man be necessarily by the very
aggregation of numbers changed, so
that, without any overt act, the whole
party would be violating the spirit
of the Sabbath. But is it not more
than probable—that, although each
individual came, or thought he came,
to meditate or enjoy the calm of
the day of rest, the entire tone of his
feelings would be altered—and that
the conduct—that is, the act of the
whole—would be the very opposite
of the conduct or act of any one individual who had been taking his evening walk by himself, or with his wife
and children. A workman, of himself leaving his employer and seeking higher wages elsewhere, is not
performing the same act, as when in
league or combination with five
hundred others. The aim and object
of the combination is different—the

means which it employs to effect its object are different—the spirit in which it acts is different—and Mr M'Culloch's maxim or apophthegm falls to the ground.

In our opinion, Mr M'Culloch has grossly exaggerated the bad effect of the Combination Laws on the spirit of the workmen towards their employers—and of the employers towards their workmen. "They taught them," he says, "to believe that there was one measure of justice for the rich, and another for the poor. They consequently set the interests and the feelings of those two great classes in direct and hostile opposition to each other; and did more to engender hatred between the different orders of society—to render the masters despotic and capricious, and the workmen idle and turbulent, than can be easily conceived or imagined by those who are not pretty intimately acquainted with the state of society in the manufacturing districts. Instead of putting down combinations, they had the effect of rendering them universal, and to give them a dangerous character. For the fair and open, though frequently foolish and extravagant proceedings of men honestly endeavouring to advance themselves in society, and to sell their labour at the highest price, the Combination Laws gave us nocturnal meetings, secret cabals, and oaths of privacy." The statement is in part by much too highly coloured. That the workmen occasionally were irritated by laws which they did not understand, and generally disliked, is certainly true; that their whole tempers, dispositions, and state of mind, were thus disturbed, agitated, incensed, and rendered fierce and savage, is what cannot be granted by any one intimately acquainted with the character of the working classes in Britain. It is all along admitted by Mr M'Culloch, that the Combination Laws were in truth harmless—or nearly harmless, in as far as the rise and fall of wages depended upon causes altogether out of the power either of workmen or their employers long to control. Now, ignorant of political economy as the working classes are, and long will be, is it not plain, that they never do suffer themselves, for a long se-

ries of years, and without any abatement of their feelings, to be exasperated by any law, that is not in itself both theoretically unjust, and practically pernicious? A law *must bear* upon them and their comforts, and pursuits, and pleasures, before we can admit that its influence on the whole temper and character can be such as Mr M'Culloch has described. There are few such laws in this country, but perhaps the Game Laws were of that kind; and they produced such effects. Many—in our opinion, most of the nocturnal meetings alluded to—the oaths of privacy—and secret conjurations, among the idle, the profligate, and the disaffected—were meetings of a very different character—for different objects, and for the concert of very different means. They were meetings of a political character—such meetings as will often take place, whether there be Combination Laws or not, in such a country as ours, where, from the very nature of our prosperity. there must be severe fluctuations in the condition of the people—where, from the very nature of that people, licentious as well as free, there never will be wanting dark spirits to aggravate distress by disaffection—and where, from the nature of our civil polity, incendiaries and demagogues are long suffered to plan their nefarious machinations against the peace of the poor, rather than that Government should, in its anxiety to guard the social blessings we enjoy, do in any danger aught to violate that liberty which is our safeguard while we are good citizens, and a shield even between the agitators of the public peace, and the infliction of punishment on political crime.

It is true, that unjust and pernicious legislation produces the very crimes it cruelly and inexorably punishes. But the Combination Laws, however objectionable, cannot be spoken of by any judicious person, as partaking of that character. The enormities alluded to must have proceeded from causes altogether unconnected with Combination Laws. Sober, honest, industrious workmen do not become drunken, idle, unprincipled, and profligate, because they are exasperated against their masters, by laws leaning too much in favour of those masters. Such persons may be dissatisfied, and may act, under the impulse of occasional irritation, more violently than otherwise they would have done—but the evils we talk of were not the sins and crimes of such classes of workmen, but they were chiefly the work of the thoroughly bad, whom the opportunities of the times brought forth into warfare, secret and savage, against the interests and welfare of those whom they pretended to befriend.

But, is any man entitled to say, from his acquaintance with the character and conduct of the working classes, that before the repeal of the Combination Laws, they were possessed with this sullen or ferocious spirit towards their employers? Quite the reverse.

Dr Chalmers, in his Civic Economy, argues, that masters have little or nothing to apprehend from any combinations among workmen. He speaks of a system of prevention, namely, "to engage their labourers for a service of months, instead of weeks or days, and then to put forth a legitimate strength to compel their fulfilment of the stipulated period. To make the security more effectual, they could hire their workmen in separate classes at all separate periods, so that, at the worst, it could only be a partial, and never a universal strike at any one time." This suggestion is not original; neither could the plan proposed be carried into effect without great difficulty and inconvenience, and frequent dissatisfaction on the part either of master or workmen, when, owing to the alternations in trade, the one or the other might be paying or receiving more or less than the state of the trade would, but for the long bargain, have of itself caused. The plan would be a bad one, and could only be resorted to to prevent the greater evils of combination. But better surely to prevent an evil by law, than to attempt it by circuitous, clumsy, and, we must say, impracticable modes of hiring and paying labourers.

But the Doctor maintains, that besides this system of prevention, "such is the plenitude of the master's means for the counteraction of his associated workmen, that he can afterwards find compensation for any losses which he may have sustained by the suspension of his works. Masters and manufacturers can lay an assessment on the wages of the readmitted workmen, or, which is the same thing, can take them in again upon reduced wages, till they have received, by the difference, a complete indemnification for all that they have suffered by the interruption of the manufacture." Nothing more easy than to make such an assertion with all possible seriousness and gravity. But is it not surprising that Dr Chalmers did not suspect that this indemnification was not of such easy accomplishment, when he himself adds, in the very next sentence, that "this has often been held out as a threat, although we are not aware of any instance in which it has been put into execution!"

But Dr Chalmers is determined that masters shall not suffer by any imaginable combinations, and advances the somewhat startling doctrine, "that in the mere working of such a transaction, as a strike among workmen—there does naturally and at length cast up a most liberal compensation, I will not say to each individual master, but certainly to the general body; so that their interest, viewed as a whole, does not suffer by it. The master, in truth, is only the ostensible, or at most the temporary sufferer by this conspiracy of his workmen; and if there be any sufferer at all in the long run, it is not he, but the customer. He loses profit for a season; but it is all made up to him by the eventual rise of profit that ensues on the production of his commodity being suspended. This is the well-known effect of a general strike among operatives; it relieves the overladen market of the glut under which it labours, and by the time that workmen at length give in, the manufacturer enters upon what to him is the most enriching of all harvests, the harvest of a brisk demand upon empty warehouses. These cessations are the very calms that not only precede, but ensure the gales of prosperity that come in between them."

Now, suppose this doctrine to be sound—it follows, that the loss which is generally and universally supposed to fall on the employers of workmen from a strike, *falls on the consumer.* What the better is society at large of that? The loss is incurred—and the main question is, not who bears it, but what is its amount? But Dr Chalmers has not shewn that the additional profits of the manufacturer, when the men return to work, will more than compensate for the loss he sustained by the non-employment of his capital during the strike. He has merely said that profits will rise, because there will be a brisk demand on empty warehouses—and because the cessation of the workmen from labour had relieved the overladen market of the glut under which it had laboured. But what right has Dr Chalmers to assume that the overladen market had laboured under a glut? It had done no such thing; for in most cases, and certainly in the cases to which he alludes, the strike had taken place when there was a great demand, and an inadequate supply, and therefore when the workmen were making high wages. The very reason why the workmen struck was their knowledge of that fact; the knowledge that their work was wanted—and therefore they would not give it except its price was considerably augmented. Had there been a glut in the market, the masters would not have complained of a strike among their workmen surely, but they would of themselves have diminished their number.

But it is altogether a mistake to think that the profits of the masters would be greater in consequence of the strike. The demand had not been supplied—but after the supply again answered the demand, the demand would not be greater because of its former disappointment of supply. I do not burn more coals in my family this month, because I had been obliged to burn fewer the month before. I do not wear two pair of shoes this month because I did not wear out one the month before. The consumers are not increased in number—and their wants are the same as before—therefore the demand cannot be greater—and the master's profits cannot be greater than before the strike. Therefore there is no compensation

provided for him for the loss sustained during the strike.

Dr Chalmers confines himself solely to what the combiners may suffer—and is of opinion with Mr M'Culloch, that great as that suffering may be, it is better that they should be taught by experience than fettered by law. " It is," he thinks, "altogether misplaced and unnecessary for Government to meddle with the steps of a process that will so surely terminate in the very result which it can be the only object of Government to effectuate." That is to say, that it is and ought to be indifferent to Government whether the people suffer frequent and severe distress, since things are so sure to come right again, or whether the natural course of trade and manufactures, agriculture and commerce, be undisturbed, and permitted to proceed by the direct laws by which the interests of all classes are regulated and guarded. So confident is Dr Chalmers in the soundness of all his doctrine on this subject—that he treats it almost in a style of jocularity—and talks of all the distress, misery, and vice and wickedness, that attended the combinations, as mere exercises and discipline, and schooling which it was advantageous to the community that the working classes should endure. " We are aware," says he, " of the spirit which is going forth in succession through the manufacturing districts of the land. But truly, we contemplate the progress of these outbreakings with no other feelings, and no other anticipations, than we should regard the progress of an ambulatory school, whose office it is to spread the lessons of a practical wisdom over the face of the country, and the peace and meekness of wisdom will be the inevitable result. In some places they have acquired the lesson, while in others they are only learning it. The country is still at school upon this subject, and it were a pity she was not permitted to finish her education." ! ! ! ! ! ! ! ! !

It is admitted by all, that every kind of violence used to force workmen into combinations is unlawful—and by the new act enacted after the repeal of the old law—it is punishable—as it is at common law. " The truth is," says Dr Chalmers, most eloquently, " the truth is, "that the workmen require the strongest protection from a still more odious and oppressive tyranny than that which they so often denominated the tyranny of their masters, which is apt to spring up among themselves. We can confidently appeal to the experience of many workmen, whether they ever felt so grievously thwarted and overborne out of their own free choice, as by the terrors of their own association, whose secret and mysterious power wielded a far more despotic sway over their imaginations than ever did the old law in the plenitude of all its enforcements. We venture to affirm that the dread of ruin to their families, and of injury to their persons, has been far more frequently inspired by their new despotism, within these few months, than has been done by the statutes against combinations among all the working classes put together for a whole century. An act for the further protection of workmen from this regime of terror, so far from even the most distant approach to a re-enactment of the Combination Laws, would in fact be tantamount to a grant of additional liberty; and notwithstanding all the clamour and jealousy of the obstinately disaffected among them, would be substantially felt as such by the body at large."

Nothing can be more justly and forcibly said than this; but if such conduct be so deserving of the severest inflictions of the law, so destructive of all freedom, all comfort, and consequently so destructive of the interests of society, what would Dr Chalmers, or any other enlightened man, say of the crime of driving others, against their will, into combinations by another kind of despotism as dreadful as this—and of which the quiet, the simple, the sober, the sensitive, the timid, the home-loving, and the respectable, are in general the victims? That kind of despotism the law, as it now stands, cannot punish or prevent; it works precisely the same evil that Dr Chalmers so indignantly denounces as a fit object of severest punishment. But the combinations are still called voluntary—and every man, forsooth, has a right to the disposal of his own property—his labour—and under the brutal power of such a tyranny he does dispose of it, often to his own ruin. The old Combination Law guarded workmen against this sort of evil, just as the new law for the protection of workmen affects to guard them against open and direct violence; and if the latter be worthy of Dr Chalmers' most eloquent panegyric, or rather, if in his panegyric he point out the necessity of imbuing the law with a still sterner and more unsparing spirit, on what principle must we withhold our approbation from the old law that had the same object in view, and guarded against both classes of the evil at once?

Not once during the whole of our argument, have we mentioned the Trades' Unions. They have refuted the speculations and assertions of Mr M'Culloch and Dr Chalmers, with other weapons than ours; and have made worse than ridiculous the predictions alike of lay and of clerical prophet. They have smashed all that pseudo-science which was sold to them at a penny a-pound, or given gratis; their "effervescence and extravagance," eight years and more after the recovery of their rights, of which the Combination Laws had deprived them, has got hotter and wilder, and more "grotesque;" the "ambulatory schools" are in more active motion than ever; the country is still attending them, even by night; and does Dr Chalmers continue to think that "it would be a pity she were not permitted to finish her education?" Some of the aptest scholars—and who had made the greatest proficiency—though not long ago simple clod-hoppers, and still given to the singing of psalms—have most tyrannically been hindered by a Whig Government from finishing their education in this country, and shipped for Botany Bay; though guiltless, says Mr Roebuck, who bounds over an impediment in the way of an argument, as his namesake would a paling in the season of love—though guiltless of either moral or legal offence. The punishment does, indeed, seem a sorry and savage substitution for that of the mild and merciful old Combination Law. But a fearful field lies before us—and we must contemplate it steadily to understand and describe it.

D2